A Guide to the I Ching

A
Guide to the I Ching

Third Edition, Revised and Enlarged

Carol K. Anthony

Anthony Publishing Company
Stow, Massachusetts 01775

Anthony Publishing Company
206 Gleasondale Road, Stow, Massachusetts 01775

Library of Congress Card Number 88-70776
ISBN-0-9603832-4-7

Printed in the United States of America
Cover design by Leslie A. Iverson

First edition published 1980. Second edition 1982.
Third edition 1988.

Time is not of the essence, time is the essence

Contents

viii

Preface to the Third Edition

It has now been over ten years since I began to assemble my collected notes into *A Guide to the I Ching*. A number of concepts have occurred to me since, which I have found helpful to understanding the counsel given by the *I Ching*, consequently I have thought it time to make these changes available to others.

The general format of the *Guide* remains the same, however, a *capsule* has been inserted at the beginning of each hexagram. Its purpose is to focus on the message most often indicated by the hexagram.

Also new to the *Guide* are appended essays on meditation, non-action, and on consulting the *I Ching*.

Another change is the new cover. I wish to express my thanks to Leslie Anthony Iverson for this excellent cover.

For this edition I have also had the benefit of Pierre Seronde's indispensable editorial help, for which I am most grateful.

Users of the first two editions will have noticed my frequent use of the sovereign "ourself." It may be helpful to explain that the word "self" has often been inadequate in speaking of the pluralistic parts of self defined by the *I Ching*. I have therefore used the sovereign "ourself" to mean the Superior Man (our essential self), and "ourselves" to mean the "inferiors," (bodily or emotional self) whether they are taken in combination with the "Inferior Man" (ego-self-image), or not. Seen in meditation the essential self listens to and observes the other parts of self. Sometimes it sits like a sovereign, listening to its ministers; sometimes it is like a Gandhi, walking among its people.

Readers of the previous editions of the *Guide* may have noticed that upon occasion I have quoted from the commentaries on the lines rather than from the lines themselves. I have done this only when the commentaries seemed more to the point of what the lines are trying to say. For example, in *Enthusiasm* (Hex. 16), the quote, *Boasting of aristocratic connections*, is from the Duke of Chou's commentary, rather than from King Wen's judgment, *Enthusiasm that expresses itself brings misfortune*. Many people, it appears, mistakenly think that the commentaries on the lines were written by Richard Wilhelm. However, Wilhelm's *Introduction* makes it clear that the judgments on the lines were written by King Wen, and that the commentaries on the lines were written by his son, the Duke of Chou, prior to 1150 B.C. It seems valid to quote from either one, if doing so adds clarity.

I have included in this edition the two main attitudes which seem to be central to the counsel given, in a variety of ways, in the various hexagrams. They are: (1) a total inner independence which has, as its basis, a dependence on the Higher Power, and (2) an unwavering suspension of disbelief. These two attitudes seem to be in perfect harmony with the Cosmos, and therefore are always productive of good.

The inner independence indicated is a rock-like steadiness of purpose and disengagement in the face of all challenges. The steadiness of purpose is to be purposeless. We soon learn that by maintaining this attitude we engage the power of the Creative; the Creative either leads us to a correct solution of our given problem, by which we carry out some action, or, as it more often occurs, to a solution of the problem without our active interference. At the heart of inner independence is our dependence on the help of the Creative, or Higher Power.

The suspension of disbelief becomes a humble acceptance of whatever is going on as part of the zig-zag workings of the Creative. These two attitudes combine in an unshakeable modesty which exemplifies *The Receptive*. While they appear to be passive attitudes, they are not. The secret is that they perfectly arouse the powers of the Creative to work out all things correctly.

The student of the *I Ching* develops these attitudes in the context of his relationship with the Sage, who teaches through it. The development of inner independence is a lengthy process requiring us to master a number of lessons experientially. It is as if a program of experiences has been set up with the purpose of challenging opinions, concepts, and beliefs we have hitherto taken for granted. Each of these experiences unsettles us for a time, until we gain the new insight intended. This challenging goes on, it seems, interminably. Sooner or later, however, we realize that true inner independence is based on acquiring the "Cosmic point of view" that we are developing through our studies with the Sage of the *I Ching*. Soon, we cannot imagine any other method of learning.

In time we gain the definite impression that to consult the *I Ching* is to have a conversation with the Higher Power. This marvellous book is not just an obscure oracle, in the ancient Greek or Roman sense. The Higher Power speaks through it plainly and definitively in reply to our inner questions of need.

The *I Ching* will respond in this manner, of course, only if our attitude is sincere. It speaks with a polite reserve to the merely curious, and unintelligibly to the skeptical. To benefit from its great ability to help, we are required only to suspend, at least momentarily, our disbelief.

Among the newer concepts I have discussed in this edition are: how to deal with 'crescendo of awfulness' situations; envy in others and in ourselves; our egos in the guise of the 'white knight in shining armor'; and the 'king-of-the-heap game.' In all these situations our inner independence is challenged, and the question arises, "How should we react?" The *I Ching* consultations make it clear that the traditional way in which we have reacted is incorrect. To progress we must take the risk of reacting in a new way. In doing so, we develop the self-understanding and strength that underlies inner independence and an open mind. Freed of barriers, pacts, and defenses, we learn to serve the good and true without coming to harm, and without losing our dignity. We learn that by being a best friend to ourself we are able to be a true friend to others.

Frequently the *I Ching* consultations teach us to correct what the *I Ching* regards as decadent thinking. This often entails accepting new limitations which, ironically, lead to a liberation of our true self. For example, we may think it our duty to like people. We find, however, that we are not obligated to like anyone. We should, however, avoid actively disliking them. We learn how to keep neutral. If a person has made mistakes, we try to see his mistakes in a just and moderate light. If he has violated our trust, we go on our way, leaving him to find his own way. We help him only if and when he becomes sensitive and receptive. We disperse alienation and work constantly at suspending our disbelief.

Throughout the *I Ching* we find the concept of working through the power of 'inner truth.' Inner truth refers both to what we know, on the inner level about others, and to what they know, on this level, about us. It also refers to the higher truth that exists in every situation, whether we see it or not. Once we perceive this higher truth, it is automatically communicated to others with no effort on our part.

The power of inner truth revolves around our perception of the events we observe. Often we note incorrect actions but dismiss them because we cannot see anything constructive to do about them. The problem with dismissing wrong actions is that we communicate a tacit endorsement of them to the perpetrators. The *I Ching* would have us be strict and disciplined to recognize wrong situations as wrong. However, we turn the matter over to the Cosmos to be corrected, and we disengage from it. Disengagement empowers the Creative to correct the problem. If we allow ourselves to become alienated, or if we intervene to correct the situation, our distrust isolates us from the help of the Creative. When our ego prescribes the remedy, or enforces solutions, what the *I Ching* calls 'lawsuits,' or 'wars' begin. These inner lawsuits and wars may continue between individuals during their entire lifetimes; they may continue between nations and peoples for generations.

The *I Ching* does not, as may be thought, lead us into a true passivity. We are, as it is put in *Contemplation* (Hex. 20) capable of correcting every wrong we see, simply by aligning our point of view with the higher truth. This requires that in every situation we correct and purify our inner attitude.

What, in short, is a correct inner attitude? It is to recognize our dependence on the Higher Power to grant us the correct perception, and to serve the Higher Power by keeping our thoughts humble and good.

It is the way of the *I Ching* to correct the world through correcting ourselves. Indeed, the more we experience the way of the *I Ching*, the more we realize that society cannot be regenerated through any other means.

Another concept related to inner independence is 'going on,' or as the British put it, to "carry on." In the 6th line of *After Completion* (Hex. 63), we are counselled not to look back with egotistical satisfaction at hazards conquered, but to keep steady on our path. The principle is also described in *Approach* (Hex. 19): we should not stop to luxuriate in good times, or despair during the bad times, but go on.

This does not mean that we rigidly focus on the future, so that within ourselves we look like the Leaning Tower of Pisa. Seen in meditation we are erect and still. "Going on" means to keep detaching and returning to the path, because life is a going on. We go with it, whether we make mistakes or succeed, greeting each change with humble acceptance. The goal is to retain our humility and constancy throughout our lifetime; thus we go on "to the very end" (see *Modesty*, Hex. 15), reacting to all constraints, accomodations, and sudden liberations with equinimity. As it is put in *Shock* (Hex. 51), although the shock and thunder reverberate a hundred miles around, the developed person does not allow one drop to spill from the sacrificial spoon. This is the high degree of character we are capable of attaining through following the way of the Sage. A humble, open-minded equinimity is the most powerfully creative attitude of all.

Carol K. Anthony

Preface to the First Edition

Since my own study of the *I Ching* has always been of the Wilhelm/Baynes translation published by the Princeton University Press, this guide is based on and meant to accompany that edition.*

The advantage of the Wilhelm/Baynes translation arises from Richard Wilhelm's great knowledge of the *I Ching*, and Cary F. Baynes's excellent translation into English. The *I Ching* has survived thousands of years because it is vital and alive. The Wilhelm/Baynes translation conveys this vitality and usefulness.

It is assumed that the reader will have familiarized himself with the manner in which the *I Ching* is to be used. This guidebook does not attempt to paraphrase the *I Ching*, but to give insight into its hexagrams and lines, to make it usable in self-development, and to solve important life problems.

I never anticipated writing this book. In fact, it was not "written," but "collected." Little by little the notes I kept over the years became a complete commentary on the *I Ching*'s 64 hexagrams and 384 lines. Because these notes were and are continuously helpful to me and my friends, I have compiled them into a book to make them available to others.

So many people have come forward to help make this book possible that its completion has never been a task, but I particularly want to thank Jeanne Seronde for her cover drawing, and Gwen Bell for invaluable advice relating to the publishing process. These and a number of other people are part of the creative thrust that has brought this book to you, the reader. That it may now help you mine the gold of the *I Ching* and of your own being is our greatest wish.

Carol K. Anthony

*The *I Ching* or *Book of Changes*. The Richard Wilhelm translation rendered into English by Cary F. Baynes. Bollingen Series XIX. Copyright 1950, 1967 by Princeton University Press. Copyright renewed 1977 by Princeton University Press.

Introduction

The purpose of this guidebook is to help the reader understand the *I Ching*. Very often we understand exactly what it says and know precisely to what it refers, but at other times we seem to be in a fog about it. Later, the fog clears and we understand. It is as if our gaze, at such times, is fixed in one direction and we are unable to turn it elsewhere. This writer found that taking notes of the way the hexagrams applied during moments of clarity helped to interpret them during moments of obscurity. Eventually, a complete collection of notes developed which broadened and deepened over the years. While inevitably they will undergo further enlargement, they are offered here as a basis for the reader to begin his own set. The advantage of this practice, and of this guidebook, lies in helping us free our inner gaze, enlarge our perspective, and always, return to the underlying principles of the hexagrams. In doing this, the hexagrams and situations to which they refer are brought into alignment, the fog clears, and we understand.

Blockages in our point of view occur for other reasons as well. At times we "over-read" the *I Ching*. For example, "crossing the great water" may be thought to mean we are actually going to cross water, or take a trip. While such an interpretation may occasionally be warranted, most of the time it refers to getting past a situation that is dangerous to our inner equilibrium. The guidebook helps us understand the analogous way in which the *I Ching* tends to speak.

It must be emphasized, at the outset, that this guidebook is meant to accompany the *I Ching*, not replace it. Its proper use is in reading the *I Ching*, then the corresponding sections of this guidebook. In the final understanding, we should not have lost sight of the *I Ching* images.

The Student and the Sage

In the *The Well* (Hex. 48), the *I Ching* likens itself to an old, but good well. It has an endless supply of clear, refreshing water, available to anyone and everyone who comes, who puts his rope down all the way, whose jug for holding the water is not broken by doubt or cynicism, and who is willing to drink its wisdom.

In *Contemplation* (Hex. 20), the Sage who speaks through the *I Ching* is likened to a guest who knows the secrets by which the kingdom may be made to work. If we treat this guest hospitably, we may avail ourself of his expertise.

In *Youthful Folly* (Hex. 4), the *I Ching* is described as a Sage of great wisdom, whose help in solving difficult life problems is invoked by a childlike openness of mind.

These and other hexagrams reveal that the *I Ching* is a medium between ourself and the hidden world that underlies our existence. We cannot ignore this hidden world. It is paired with our external existence the way positive and negative electrical impulses are paired in a completed electrical circuit. In going through life many of us lose contact with this hidden world. To renew ourselves we must journey through it to regain the innocence and purity of our original nature. The *I Ching* is our lantern, the Sage our guide through the hidden world. This guidance and help is available to all. No one is turned away. If we have difficulty in learning, we should persevere. In time we will be helped to overcome the problems which obstruct our progress.

To obtain the help of the Sage it is essential to throw the pennies or yarrow stalks. Only by this means can the Sage reply. Merely reading the *I Ching* will not develop an interpersonal relationship. Willingness to throw the pennies means that we have the humility and open mind necessary to establish this relationship.

Although the Sage identifies himself in the *I Ching* as the teacher in *Youthful Folly* (Hex. 4), the helpful friend in *The Well* (Hex. 48), the father in *The Family*(Hex, 37), the prince who seeks able helpers in *Oppression*(Hex. 47), and the guest in *Contemplation*(Hex. 20), he has no real identity. When we assign an identity, whether this be as human, male, female, as having a certain age, or whatever, we do so only to suit our own prejudice and sense of comfort. If this idea becomes an obstruction to our growth, in time the Sage will correct us. There is no harm in calling it "he" as long as we realize it is only for purposes of convenience.

The *I Ching*

Unlike a conventional book, the *I Ching* is part of a method used to consult our fate. Through throwing pennies or using yarrow stalks (see the *I Ching* for a description of the various methods), number combinations are used to form six-lined figures called hexagrams. These are then looked up in the *I Ching*. The hexagram obtained in this chance manner is the Sage's message to us.

Each throw of the pennies (or yarrow stalks) gives either a positive or negative line. The pennies are thrown six times to obtain all six lines. The hexagrams range from all positive, unbroken lines, to all negative, broken lines, in 64 possible combinations. Each hexagram we receive in this chance manner is capable of acting as a mirror to our current life situation.

The hexagrams reflect the path we follow and where it leads. If our attitudes are out of harmony with the great harmony of the Cosmos, the hexagrams reflect this. If we are in harmony, the counsel given will help us keep our inner balance. If forthcoming events may threaten our inner equilibrium, the hexagrams give us warning so that we will not lose the way. Every situation in which we are being carried away from our true direction contains the means of return. Thus, every hexagram is capable of indicating the way back from a wrong decision or action.

The philosophy unveiled in the *I Ching* is simple and consistent: if we relate correctly, keeping ourself in tune with the Cosmos, all things work out beneficially to all concerned. If we are out of harmony, we are out of relationship. Even our good luck is "snatched away."

Through studying the changing lines and developing ourselves accordingly, we are able to make our lives complete. The *I Ching*, therefore, is a lantern through the hidden world that underlies our everyday lives. In counseling us it does not take over our self-direction, it leaves us entirely on our own. It does not spell out right and wrong as a religion does; instead, it draws on our inner knowledge of what is good and reinforces this.

The effect of using the *I Ching* is nutritious, mentally, physically, and spiritually. Because the user is helped to understand the polarities of life and how things change, he is able to align himself with his own inner axis. He does this through correcting his destructive inner attitudes. This mental harmonizing, not surprisingly, helps release him from degenerative physical effects. Because this self-development brings him into accord with all that is regenerative, his everyday life is one of growth toward self-sufficiency and inner harmony. Moralizing, a negative principle, is never part of the process. Many times the *I Ching* will counsel, "Do what is right," or "Return to the path," but in each case the user must search his heart to determine what is right and find the path of return. If self-deception occurs, the *I Ching* will persist in indicating that he has not yet found the right path. This process is sometimes frustrating, but it is a principle of the *I Ching*'s teaching that if the user is to make progress, the work must be entirely his own, and undertaken at his own initiative. The rewards also are truly his own.

The student of the *I Ching* is held to it by no bonds other than his own desire to learn. In this respect he is drawn to it by his initial perception of how good it is to come into harmony with himself, hence, the Cosmos. From this time forward, to be out of harmony is to lack something important.

Use of the *I Ching*

Although there is no logic that supports throwing pennies or manipulating yarrow stalks, the procedure is useful in taking the choice of hexagrams out of the user's hands. The use of chance provides a meaningful sequence. That it works demonstrates that great and profound meanings often lie in small and seemingly insignificant things. This simplicity is in keeping with the virtue of modesty, so highly prized in the *I Ching*. There is a playful but mysterious aspect in consulting chance, yet one is aware in doing so that a higher power is involved. In this respect the *I Ching* is metaphysical.

The attitude of the user is aided by engaging in the activity of throwing coins, as it displaces excesses of pride. All that the Sage requires, to answer, is the humility of an open mind. Responding to this attitude, an open and free conversation may be had between our inner thoughts and its replies. However, a cross-examining, suspicious, hostile, proud, or arrogant attitude will be ignored.

The *I Ching* may be approached by a direct question, or simply be consulted with no question at all. A specific question is useful at times, but the answer may be unintelligible if we try to make it fit our question, for it may be focussing on some other, more important inner question in our mind. Or, the answer may hinge on our understanding something else first. Sometimes the *I Ching* will ignore questions to prepare us for difficult or impending situations. It is best, therefore, to consult it without specific questions, as its answers are directed to what we need to know, anyway.

The first hexagram we get in a study session is the subject to be discussed for that session. All hexagrams that follow will be about the same subject until the matter is fully understood. The *I Ching* rarely jumps from subject to subject. It teaches only one lesson at a time. Because of this, it is good to construct at least three hexagrams, to allow space for the subject to be developed. Three hexagrams, together with their changing hexagrams, make up a basic conversation for the beginning student. Advanced students more familiar with the text will find that six hexagrams, with their changes, are even more instructive.

The beginning student's main problems are those related to language. The Chinese language is pictorial and suggestive. There are many possible ways of looking at the ideograms. In contrast, the one-dimensional nature of western languages leaves little room for suggestion. In reading the *I Ching*, the original many-faceted quality of the ideograms must be put back. The commentaries in this guidebook serve this purpose, enlarging the possible ways in which the images may be interpreted. As such, they are meant to aid, not become the final interpretation. The final interpretation is something the Sage works out between himself and the student. The student finds the meaning inside himself, whereby it becomes the source of enlightenment and growth.

1.

Ch'ien / The Creative

Ch'ien ☰
Ch'ien ☰

(The Creative is at work; change is in motion in a dynamic, creative way. This hexagram is also about attaining the Cosmic viewpoint.)

Ch'ien represents the etherial, heaven, initiating principle called *yang*, as the natural opposite of the material, earth, nurturing principle called *yin*. It represents the male principle in its cosmological sense, as purely male attributes occur in nature. It is identified with the sun, the light-giving force, which acts on the dark, light-absorbing earth force. The yang force expands, the yin force recedes. As in electrical energy, yang is positive, yin is negative. As an initiator, the father of the family is identified with Ch'ien, while the mother is identified with *K'un*.

Ch'ien, as the heaven power, is identified with the Ruler, or Sage. The Sage rules through the power of insight, and what the *I Ching* refers to as "inner truth." Because his point of view is cosmic in proportion, beyond the narrow dualities of love/hate, like/dislike, and comfort/discomfort, he has no need to produce results through leverage or force. As the Cosmic Father he seeks the best for all. Because of his dispassionate interest in the development and completion of our highest potential, we find him strict in his principles, but also mild, kind, and devoted.

In the *I Ching* cosmology the human being stands poised between heaven and earth, with a foot in either, so to speak. We often draw this hexagram when we begin to think that external affairs are the only reality. We forget that everything in the external world is

1

activated by and dependent on the higher reality (the Heaven Principle). The image of having a foot in either world means that we cannot disregard the Heaven Principle; it is present and central to every question.

Every individual possesses both higher and lower natures. It is our destiny and personal *Tao* to cultivate and bring "to completion" our heaven potential (called the "Superior Man" throughout the *I Ching*). This heaven potential exists as a celestial image, or blueprint, stored in the mind of the Diety. Rejection of this destiny is not only contrary to our fundamental drives; following the leadership of our "Inferior Man" creates a hostile fate which can be reversed only by returning to a humble acceptance of our destiny to develop ourselves.

When an individual develops his heaven nature, he shines like the sun. Such a person keeps conscious of, and clings to, what is good and great within himself. He is unwilling to sacrifice his sincerity, his sense of truth, his kindness, or his sense of what is humane and just, to other considerations. Although he has achieved strength of character, he remembers the difficulty he had in correcting himself; therefore, he is able to remain tolerant of those who have not yet developed themselves. He is alert, ever searching to discover the inner truth of each situation, and to act from this understanding. He avoids losing his inner independence and detachment by resisting the clamoring of his childish heart. He constantly seeks to be responsive to the quiet but inwardly audible will of heaven. Because he is reticent, he creates a respect for reticence; because he is tolerant, he creates tolerance; through his sincerity he activates respect and love for truth in others. Like the sun, he shines on everyone with equanimity, awakening a small bit of the higher life within them.

Ch'ien also represents the creative idea (Cosmic image) before it is transformed into reality. Everything that now exists, first existed as a Cosmic image. Accordingly, Ch'ien also represents the hidden, creative potential inherent in any situation. By creative potential is meant the path which, if taken, will further everyone and everything in that situation. This creative potential is the particularly appropriate answer to the problem at hand. There is one particularly appropriate answer, and that can be found only by being receptive to it (we allow it to emerge through maintaining an open mind). Other answers may come close to serving all needs, but they require adjustments on adjustments before the problem can securely, if ever, be resolved.

One of the most significant meanings of 'I' in *"I Ching"* means 'the easy.' It also means that the easiest way to achieve success is to invoke the help of the Creative, by which the particularly appropriate answer emerges. (This answer often emerges as if it were the surprise dénouement in the last act of a drama.) When, on the other hand, we strive to achieve success through our intellects (through the brilliance of planning and wit), or when we strive to force success (through leverage), just to satisfy an emotional demand to create a more comfortable situation, we become forced endlessly to correct the jumbled effects produced by our imperfect thinking. In addition, we must endure the often poisonous fallout which results from having interfered with the correct resolution designed by the Higher Power, a resolution that would have evolved had we not interfered. It is the way of the Creative, however, to be able to use our mistakes creatively once we recognize them, and return to a correct attitude.

Furthering through perseverance. Furthering refers to the inherently beneficial nature of the Creative which nourishes and protects all beings. Because the furthering process involves completing stages of development, time is the vehicle by which the power of the Creative works. Just as the seed sprouts and the plant emerges, the Creative takes the Cosmic image and gives it form. By such gradual means the light of understanding dawns (the Cosmic image emerges), permitting us to respond correctly to situations. Only in this slow, organic way does everything become as it should be. Because time is the means, perseverance is necessary.

For the furthering potential to become actual, the Creative must be activated by the Receptive. Just as male energy is activated by the presence of female energy, Ch'ien is activated by K'un. Through our perseverance in receptivity, we arouse the power of the Creative and draw it into action.

Perseverance means to wait in an attitude of docility and acceptance, free of hope and doubt, with an alert and open mind. It also means that the ego, or childish heart, must be subdued, or kept at bay. This means that we resist the demonic insistence of fear, the egotistical demands of vanity, and the interjections of our great pretender, the intellect. If need be, we ascetically deprive our body of its powers of instinct and emotional thrust.

It is the nature of the Creative to be ironic, to make the unlikely work, and to bring success 'one day late.' We may be required to

3

wait passively until failure to act seems totally unreasonable (at least to our ego). This seeming obstinacy by Fate (the Creative) occurs because the Creative will not respond to the presumptions and demands of our Inferior Man (ego), or to a begrudging or indolent surrender. So long as we hold to the timetables set by our hopes and fears, we will be obstructed. So long as we listen to the voice of doubt within, which urges us to take matters in hand, and causes us to try to force comfortable conclusions to our problems, we continue to compete with the Creative. If, however, we humbly cling to the Creative for help, and accept non-action as an integral part of the creative process, then our attitude will be harmonious and sincere, and we will achieve the correct result. The way of the Creative is the way of the Master Playwright who keeps everything in suspense, even in a state of misunderstanding, until the last minute. When our acceptance becomes truly humble, when we recognize that we need the help of the Higher Power, and when we ask for that help, the dénouement comes, and with it, enlightenment and success from the highest source. The answer is so correct and appropriate that in no way could we have apprehended it merely by intellect, nor could we have achieved its sublime results through a consciously designed solution.

When we understand the way the Creative and the Receptive interact within ourselves, we understand the way the Cosmos works, and why the judgment of this hexagram says, *The Creative works sublime success, furthering through perseverance.*

First Line: *Hidden dragon. Do not act.* There are hidden elements in our situation, which within the limits of our current understanding, we are unable to perceive. To act now would be like walking in the blackest night past a perilous place without a light. We should wait until the hidden element becomes visible, and until we reach a clear understanding of the situation. By waiting in a state of non-action, the perilous time will be safely bypassed.

Second Line: *Dragon appearing in the field. It furthers one to see the great man.* The "great man" is one who surrenders to the will of the Higher Power. He obeys the command of the Sage and trusts his counsel to prove itself; he resists his ego and encourages his inferiors to follow the aspirations of the higher self.

We "see the great man" when we place ourselves above the

dualities of love and hate, hope and fear. In developing the Cosmic view, we gain the strength needed to discipline our inferiors. In this way we establish the right direction and influence others without conscious effort. When we influence others through a correct attitude it is said, the "dragon appears in the field"; we are still in training, however, and until this way of relating becomes thoroughly established, we will lose the correct attitude many times.

Third Line: *All day long the superior man is creatively active. At nightfall his mind is still beset with cares. Danger. No blame.* Creative action, in *I Ching* terms, is spontaneous action that emanates from an unstructured attitude. Here plotting and planning begin, so that spontaneity is lost. The ever-ambitious ego is quick to propose how it may make speedier progress. We should be alert, therefore, to moments when we suddenly see the role we are to play, or when we enthusiastically think, "So this is the path of action!" Such thoughts are Trojan Horses. We should remain unstructured and assume no role, but allow events to proceed forward or backward as they will, without losing our composure.

The commentary says that "ambition destroys integrity." Ambition is at work when we say what another person wants to hear, or if we fail to say what comes to us as essential because we are afraid we might lose our influence. In such ways our integrity is sacrificed to ambition. If we cater to people when we ought to be reserved with them, we sacrifice our principles. The way of the Creative is to win others' hearts through following the truth within ourselves. We respond simply and naturally to each situation, keeping a humble and open mind. Then what we say or do penetrates to the essence of the matter and draws everyone into agreement. We can safely allow truth to show us the way to success.

On giving up ambition we achieve freedom of action; this does not mean, however, that we acquire the freedom to display power, or to say or do whatever we please. Freedom of action is never meant to be an invitation to license.

Fourth Line: *Wavering flight over the depths. No blame.* There are two meanings to this line. The first is similar to having taken off in flight over the ocean; halfway across we wonder whether we should have started. Now is not the time to wonder or change direction. Our will to go forward, despite any difficulties we might anticipate, must hold firm. We must avoid dwelling on the difficul-

5

ties, and keep our thoughts clear and alert.

The second meaning has to do with inner pacts we have made at some past time. These pacts, by which we have predetermined what we will do, or not do, hinder our inner freedom to act spontaneously and innocently as each moment requires. We are not meant to memorize a path, then slavishly follow it. To follow the way of the Creative we need to be aware of the areas of inner burnout which may suddenly cause us to reject what is happening. In part, this line may be telling us to inspect our thoughts, and to de-program any set ideas we may have of "how things should proceed," or "what the situation is."

To keep our mind open, we resist deciding whether a situation is good or bad. Such decisions are based on hidden doubts about the power of the Creative to correct wrongs; they prevent us from perceiving the hidden doorways of opportunity which contain the correct means to achieve change or make progress.

Fifth Line: *Flying dragon in the heavens. It furthers one to see the great man.* The influence of the Creative is being felt: the correct image comes to mind and we understand. Because we are in a state of clarity and inner correctness, our influence spreads outward without any conscious intention to everyone.

Sixth Line: *Arrogant dragon will have cause to repent.* It is arrogant to ignore warnings against taking action, and to press ahead. It is arrogant to engage self-confidently in conflicts, or to dwell on people's behavior, or to tell them what they are doing wrong, and otherwise interfere in their affairs. The Creative is activated only by persevering in humility, and by our devotion to discovering the inner truth of each situation, and to holding steadfastly to it. If we fail to observe the limits that define creative action, we act in contradiction to the correct interworkings of yang and yin, and so energize hostile forces to defeat our purpose. Only *mildness in action, joined to strength of decision, brings good fortune,* because this is the way of the Creative.

We need to be aware that the element in us we see as the 'white knight in shining armor fighting the black knight,' is only our puritanical and obstinate Inferior Man (ego-self-image). In the guise of doing the right thing our Inferior Man metamorphoses into yet another image by which it usurps control of our personality. This happens particularly after we have made progress and the pressures of the situation begin to ease, and we fail to keep our Inferior Man under surveillance.

The hostile forces we engage through arrogance are not evil. Nature (the great Tao of yin and yang) acts in a balanced, harmonious, complementary way. The moment we act in opposition to the way nature works, through becoming unbalanced within ourselves, we activate these forces to bring us back into balance. Indeed, evil is arrogantly to act in opposition to the way of nature, thereby to be the willful cause of imbalance. The event we often see as hostile is nature's way of restoring balance. Wrong moves which seem insignificant to us might create a trajectory of imbalance, and so become an evil force that contradicts the way of nature; the forces of the Creative and the Receptive become activated to stop this trajectory by whatever means is necessary.

2.

K' un / The Receptive

$$\frac{\text{K'un}}{\text{K'un}} \quad \equiv\!\equiv$$

(Bear with everything as the earth bears with all that lives on it.)

In this hexagram the trigram *K'un*, being doubled, represents the essence of the material, earth, nurturing principle, just as *Ch'ien,* when doubled, represents the essence of the Creative principle.

K'un represents the female in its cosmological sense, as purely female attributes occur in nature. As the receptive, absorbing, resilient, dark, and nurturing earth power, it is the opposite of Ch'ien as the radiant, outpouring light source, the sun. By allowing itself to be acted on by the light power of the sun, the receptive power of the earth gives birth, nurtures, and "brings to completion" the life principle generated when the two come to meet each other halfway. (See *Coming to Meet*, Hex. 44.)

Furthering through the perseverance of a mare. A good mare lets herself be guided. She endures the burdens put on her, and bears with people and things. Shown the way to go she proceeds without hesitation, alert and ready to be checked in accordance with her master's will. This image specifies a form of receptivity to the Higher Power (the Sage, or one's higher self) that is beyond grudging compliance. It specifies a willing spirit to follow the good.

The superior man who has breadth of character carries the outer world. This means that we do not allow ourself to be perturbed by what happens. When people are unfaithful, indifferent, or insensitive, we keep detached from watching, wanting, and expecting; we let the world go without being harsh, vindictive, activated by fear, or collapsed in self-pity. We do not allow ourself to become rigid through defensive pacts to act or react in a particular way. Nor do we, because of injured pride, or from allowing ourself to be worn down, decide that other people are "impossible." We neither fix others in our mind as adversaries, nor lock them in a mental prison, nor mentally execute them. We keep our thoughts pure, our heads clear, our hearts open Through keeping open-minded we give others space and time to correct themselves.

A part of our receptivity is to let things happen by allowing ourself to be guided by the moment. We keep attuned to the 'openings,' times of light when people are receptive, and to the 'closings,' times of darkness when they begin to misunderstand and close themselves off. With the openings we advance, with the closings we retreat. In retreating we are detached and free. We proceed on our way, allowing others to depart. Indeed, receiving this hexagram is a challenge to perfect one's receptivity, humility, and patience.

First Line: *Hoarfrost underfoot.* Hoarfrost refers to doubting the way events are proceeding. When we doubt the life process we begin to strive to divert the stream of events toward something more to our liking. We should cease resisting the flow of events and return to the path of humble acceptance and dependence on the Unknown. Doubt is the hoarfrost that precedes the ice of giving up.

Hoarfrost also refers to falling back on traditional defenses such as fear, doubt, anger, envy, desire, negation, hedging, or alienation. We cling to such defenses because we still harbor distrust that following the true and the good will bring about harmony and justice. We must aggressively rid ourself of the demonic inferiors who clamor to rule through slandering the truth, and through the self-flattery that "no one is going to help us but ourselves, therefore we must take forceful action!" Such thoughts may not be as conscious as this, but exist merely in seed form as an unquiet feeling, as if a bad mood might be coming on. Such moods are the hoarfrost which precedes ice. (In *Enthusiasm*, Hex.16, Line 2, we are counseled to "know the seeds" and withdraw in time.)

Through contemplation we begin to see that our spoiled inferiors are interested only in promoting self-comfort. When we listen to, or even consider their complaints and proposals, others mistrust us because they intuitively sense that we are harboring selfish thoughts. When we selflessly follow the good for its own sake, their distrust gradually melts away. If we wish to have a good effect on others we should closely monitor and control our inmost thoughts.

Second Line: *Straight, square, great. Without purpose, yet nothing remains unfurthered.* Just as in geometry straight lines can be

9

joined to form rectangles, and rectangular planes can be joined to form cubes, so it is that in each situation there exists the raw ingredients which can be used to give shape to the creative idea; nothing need be added, nothing taken away. Through remaining open, we perceive the appropriate responses, and what we do fulfills the requirements of being straight (straightforward), square, and great (perseveringly open-minded, never exceeding a just and moderate view of people's mistakes and misdeeds). Such is the essence of the action we can take that is in harmony with the Cosmos. Our actions need to be in harmony with the way nature works—completely natural and within the context of the circumstances. Without forethought, and from innocence we say or do what justice and moderation require. Reticence and modesty protect us from going too far, and from losing our detachment, whereby our ego becomes involved in striving.

We can rely on the beneficial action of the Creative to complete what we initiate. Things go wrong only when we seek to do too much, and to do everything by ourselves, advancing when we ought to retreat, and vice versa. We must allow others the space they need to perceive and react to the truth. Only then can we make solid progress in solving our problems and in correcting our relationships.

Third Line: *Hidden lines. One is able to remain persevering. If by chance you are in the service of a king, seek not works, but bring to completion.* We should not be concerned with whether someone will like or dislike what we say, or whether they will credit us for our achievements, but whether what we say or do is sincere, modest, and essential. Vanity—concern with how others see us—interferes with our following what is essential and correct by forcing on us selfish considerations. For example, in making a speech we may be concerned with what our audience wants to hear rather than with the essentials of our topic. If we are modest and sincere, and if we stick to the essentials of the subject (what will most help people to understand), what we say will be of use. In serving a higher master it is important to serve to the best of our ability, without thought of how it reflects on us, or whether or not we receive recognition. We attend only to our sincerity and humility.

This line also has to do either potentially or actually with losing our reticence. Reticence is an essential ingredient of receptivity and modesty. We lose our reticence when we get caught up in the egotistical enthusiasm of having an influence. We relish being recognized as "having the truth" and forget to give others the space they need to perceive things for themselves. In making this mistake we soon find ourselves isolated, and our influence undermined. Then our pride is injured from having put forth effort only to achieve nothing. We should retreat from feelings such as wounded vanity, which would have us consign others and their problems to the rubbish heap.

In making these mistakes we need to realize that they are mistakes everyone makes. It serves no purpose to wallow in self-chastisement. It is enough simply to return to the path of humility and acceptance. This frees us from blame.

If we can be content to achieve our work from a background position by holding to the power of truth, then we will give people the space they need to discover the truth for themselves.

This line also has to do with times when an eclipse develops in our influence with others (see *Abundance*, Hex. 55). When this happens we should not be offended or shaken, but accept it as part of the learning (or teaching) process. Just as the Sage allows the student to go out into life to put what he has learned to the test of experience (see *Youthful Folly*, Hex. 4, Line 1), we must allow others to err, and even to jeopardize all they have learned; this is essential if they are to develop a true perspective. Misunderstanding is invariably tied to understanding. Learning inevitably involves making mistakes and retreating from them, therefore, we must trust others to learn by themselves, otherwise our distrust traps them in error. If we think we must personally intervene, then our vanity is involved. As the line counsels, "seek not works"—to be seen as the prime mover, or as infallibly possessing the truth.

Fourth line: *A tied-up sack. No blame, no praise.* Our actions have aroused the dark force in another either through our mistakes (as in the previous line), or through being misunderstood through no fault of our own. Being isolated and misunderstood is to be in a *tied-up sack.* The false dragon (the unreasoning and compulsive element driven by fear) is engaged. We should avoid challenging this force by a frontal assault on the problem, which would only cause hatred and retaliation. We also need to avoid the appearance of capitulation. We simply need to maintain reserve. Our inner attitude should

11

be neutral, harboring neither negative nor positive emotions.

Fifth Line: *A yellow lower garment brings supreme good fortune.* The commentary to this line mentions "inconspicuous decoration." This symbolizes virtue which does not show. (We follow and do good without thought of whether others will notice.) The color yellow symbolizes both discretion and what is reliable and genuine. This means that we relate to people only when they are receptive to us, and withdraw when they are not. Sometimes responding in this way causes people to misunderstand us, and judge us as impossible to understand. If our virtue is not put on to be seen, we will not concern ourselves with their reactions. In time they will acquire a respect (perhaps only grudgingly at first) for our way of life. Our steadfastness gradually makes them aware of the truth through what the *I Ching* calls "gentle penetration." To be willing to work in a background position is to be a true assistant to the Sage, who also does his work invisibly, through the ferment of the situation.

Sixth Line: *Dragons fight in the meadow. Their blood is black and yellow.* When we listen to inner fears and doubts, the stress of inner conflict weakens our will to persevere in receptivity and acceptance. When we no longer depend on the Unknown, we are pressed to act. This is a dangerous and destructive path to follow.

3.

Chûn / Difficulty at the Beginning

K'an
———
Chên

(If we persevere, things will work out.)

This hexagram is composed of *K' an* (rain) and *Chên* (thunder), two of the most active trigrams. Their interaction describes the "teeming chaotic profusion" which creates multiple possibilities at the beginning of new situations, so that we do not know which way to go. We must not allow ourselves to be intimidated by the storm—the flux and ambiguity of such times—so that we jump to the conclusion that Fate is against us, and that we are left to resolve the situation without any help. Restless action interferes with the creative process unfolding. If we can persevere in non-action and disengagement, the Creative will resolve everything correctly.

Often we receive this hexagram when we have allowed the stress of the situation to prevent us from gaining a true perspective. Feeling unable to wait for the perspective to become clear, we virtually jump to any solution which offers itself, or we fall back into old ways of doing things and abandon the slow, step-by-step way of the Sage to 'go with the flow' and allow the correct way to show itself. A true perspective is possible only when we disperse the pressures which urge us to act, and when we relinquish seeing the situation as a problem requiring intervention. It is also important to ask help of the Higher Power to gain the insight that makes progress possible.

During the difficult times at the beginning we need to realize that everything that happens has good purposes which will be understood later. We are at the dynamic moment in which an inner-world change is beginning to precipitate into an outer-world change; whether the change is carried to completion depends on our not interfering, and on our seeking guidance from the Sage of the *I Ching*, and following it.

First Line: *Hesitation and hindrance. It furthers one to remain persevering. It furthers one to appoint helpers.* When we are confronted with difficulties at the beginning of situations, we should resist giving up. We may be on the correct path, or only slightly off it. Help comes through being careful not to force matters. Frequently, help comes as a relieving insight.

Second Line: *The maiden is chaste. Ten years—then she pledges herself.* The "turn of affairs" mentioned in the commentary refers to an idea that presents itself as a solution to the difficulty. This, however, is the wrong solution. Although we look forward enthusiastically to relief from the situation, taking action based on this idea would commit us to embarrassing obligations. We should remain "chaste," or uncommitted, and avoid trying to free the stuck Wheel of Fate through contrived solutions.

Third Line: *Whoever hunts deer without the forester [the Sage] only loses his way in the forest. The superior man...prefers to desist. To go on brings humiliation.* This line means that the difficulties of our situation are such that we cannot overcome them without the aid of the Higher Power, whose help we may obtain only if we cultivate a humble and open mind.

We receive this line when we wish to be out of a situation to the extent that we consider taking action. We are advised to wait until a "real influence" shows itself. This means we wait until we attain the help of the Creative to understand what we must do. In the meantime we need to remain in the situation, free of resistance. It is as if we are participants in Act I (or even Act II) of the drama, and it is not yet time for the dénouement of Act III.

Fourth Line: *Horse and wagon part. Strive for union. To go brings good fortune. Everything acts to further.* In our enthusiasm to solve the matter, we thrust it aside; we cease trusting the Unknown, and take comfort in comprehensive solutions, or we give up altogether. It is our duty to pick the burden back up and carry on, however humiliating this might be. This means we submit to being guided, without knowing any answers in advance; we allow the correct way to show itself as if we were watching oncoming moving picture frames. In trusting the Unknown to show the way, we return to the correct path.

This line may either refer to our relationship with another person, or to our relationship with the Sage. If we have departed from the way of the Sage through mistrust, then we need only ask for help to "hitch up" our wagon again. If we have given up on others, then we need to realize that the difficulties which push us toward feeling that the task is hopeless are only part of the general difficulties that occur during new beginnings.

When the "Wheel of Fate" gets stuck in the mud, to revolve in its own vicious circle, a hopeless attitude holds it in that pattern. Only when we stop doubting the power of truth and the power of the Creative can the Wheel of Fate become unstuck and start rolling forward in real progress. So long as our ego insists on visible progress, so long as we condition our effort at doing what is right by saying to God, in effect, "I will work only if I can see that you are doing your part," the Cosmos cannot come to our aid.

We cannot make demands on the Higher Power. Only when we unconditionally follow the truth and do what is correct can things work out. Certainly, giving up insures failure. We must allow that people can, and will, find the way if we will allow them to discover it by themselves.

Fifth Line: *Difficulties in blessing. A little perseverance brings good fortune. Great perseverance brings misfortune.* Here, the dark force prevails and everything one does meets with suspicion. We must remain firmly centered within. This brings about the confidence necessary to succeed. To regain objectivity, we should persevere quietly, allowing ourself to be led out of the danger of doubt.

Sometimes this line is related to the fifth line of *Peace* (Hex. 11). Both lines refer to the need to be patient with people who feel a sense of inferiority; envy and feelings of inferiority create tension. What helps most is to be steady, independent, and detached.

Sixth Line: *Horse and wagon part. Bloody tears flow.* Desire and fear prevail. The child within us rules. Despairing that the Sage will ever come to our aid, or that things can work out, we give up our path. *One should not persist in this.*

4.

Mêng / Youthful Folly

$$\frac{\text{Kên}}{\text{K'an}} \quad \begin{array}{c}\equiv\!\equiv\\[-2pt]\equiv\!\equiv\end{array}$$

(A new lesson; you are learning something you never knew before.)

It is not I who seek the young fool; The young fool seeks me. This hexagram explains the relationship between the Sage who speaks through the *I Ching*, and the follower who consults it.

The Sage will speak through the oracle and come to our aid only if we have a correct attitude, that is, we have willingly suspended our disbelief and distrust of the Unknown. If we are skeptical, indifferent, cynical, hostile, or cross-examining, the answers will be unintelligible, as the Sage remains in retirement. To the extent we hedge in suspending our disbelief, we block the Sage's help, for it is against his principles to respond to anything less than the humility of an open mind. Because he is firmly committed to what is good, he will not throw himself away by seeking our approval, nor will he attempt, by persuasion, to overcome our predetermined views of how the Cosmos works, of what is good and bad, or of the nature of God, or Fate, however erroneous those views might be.

In approaching the Sage we should take care to rid ourself of predetermined ideas which prevent learning. We may be afraid that his reply might upset our defenses, or that we will be unable to face the truth about some situation. In the folly of spiritual youth we fail to realize that learning the truth always lightens our load by lifting away the oppressive burdens of fear and doubt.

To study with the Sage of the *I Ching* is to be permitted to see life from the Cosmic viewpoint. At the conclusion of each lesson we gain a Cosmic insight. Whether we consult the *I Ching* daily or occasionally, its answers concern the next step in our understanding. Each new lesson entails a new beginning, with its characteristic difficulties. The problem put before us for solving during each lesson generally provides the circumstance by which the lesson may be worked out. The lesson is concluded when we understand the problem from the Cosmic viewpoint. On gaining this insight, the problem either is resolved, or else progresses one more step towards its ultimate solution.

If we consult the *I Ching* daily, then each lesson may be concluded in as short a time as a week; if we consult it once a year, each lesson may require a much longer time to master. Such lessons, of course, do not take place only through the *I Ching*. The Sage is life's invisible teacher, and our daily life's experiences are our classroom. Such lessons may be learned without consulting the *I Ching*, however, the *I Ching* provides a lantern by which we may safely cross the plain of pitfalls that exists in the domain of spiritual progress. Without its help, the learning process may require that we fall into them time and again.

Receiving *Youthful Folly* as a second hexagram is to say, "You are not expected to know Cosmic lessons in advance. The matter at hand is simply youthful ignorance." Folly, therefore, means lack of spiritual knowledge, and, "you are learning something new." Sometimes, the hexagram calls us to put things in perspective: to err is natural; if we have erred, then our error was a "deep place" blocking the path; recognizing the error fills in the deep place. With the danger past we can forget our errors and go on with our learning.

Another meaning of *Youthful Folly* has to do with others' folly. Just as it is necessary to have an open mind to bring the Sage out of retirement, it is necessary to approach others with an open mind to bring out the hidden "great man" within them. If they remain unreceptive or unresponsive, then we adopt the Sage's point of view: we let them go; we do not contend with them, or try to convince them. We let them go, even to danger and difficulty, for it is only when they are exposed to the hazards and consequences of their folly that they will learn the Cosmic lessons. We also allow them to return, for letting them go does not mean we give them up as hopeless, which, in *I Ching* terms is to "execute" them. In letting go we do not indulge in anger; instead, we disperse our emotional reactions and "cut our inner strings," to become neutral in attitude. Disengagement means that we no longer watch, with our inner eye, what others do or fail to do; disengagement is a form of trust that empowers their superior nature. Giving people space is a form of universal love that enables them to come back, in time, to their true selves. This is how the Sage teaches us, and is the way we are meant to teach others.

Sometimes this hexagram reminds us of our tendency, on facing

17

dangerous obstacles (here pictured as a chasm into which the youth stares), to think there is no way to overcome them. The hexagram says that the correct way out of (or around) difficulties is found through perseverance: we hold to what we already know to be correct, and remain receptive to the Higher Power so that further insight may be received. The Sage does not give us comprehensive answers, but keeps unfolding before us each single step to be taken; it is only our ego that wants comprehensive answers and instantaneous results, because of its fears, and for its selfish purposes.

First Line: *The fetters should be removed. To go on in this way brings humiliation.* It is one thing to learn about life by being told, but finally we must apply our learning. This often happens by direct and sometimes unpleasant experience, but what we learn makes us stronger and the lesson becomes committed, not just to intellect, but to the heart as inner truth.

Second Line: *To bear with fools in kindliness brings good fortune. The son is capable of taking charge of the household.* This image refers to the son's taking the father's place only when he has learned to govern from inner truth. Knowing the difficulty of correcting his own weaknesses, he is capable of viewing others' mistakes and weaknesses, especially those who have not developed themselves, with chivalry. It is important to be modest and kind, not proud and vindictive. Until we have achieved such modesty and kindness in the face of challenges, we are not capable of drawing others to the correct path by our example.

Bearing with fools in kindliness can also mean bearing with things our inferiors hate; thus, bear with streaks of bad luck, "bad situations," and whatever comes, however inappropriate it may be. It is true modesty not to be deterred by bad chance. As in playing tennis, we should immediately forget the bad shots, the mistakes, and concentrate on readiness for the next shots through keeping disengaged from inner dialogues. Even labeling the shots as bad or good has a negative effect, upsetting our equilibrium. In the elevated Cosmic view, everything, good and bad, is really as it needs to be for our self-development.

Third Line: *Take not a maiden who...loses possession of herself. Nothing furthers.* This line refers to a servile approach to learning.

18

If we tell people what ought to be done, then they will follow the form rather than the content of things; they will concentrate their attention on conforming to appearances rather than on what is correct and essential. We must let people go into error until they have exhausted the enthusiasm that led them astray. Only when they really need help will they seek instruction in a childlike and unassuming manner. This is also true of the way we learn: the Sage would not have us be servilely good, but learn the joy of following what is good for its own sake. Similarly, we should not want people to learn servilely, or require more of them than what is correct, because of our pride, or because of our desire to be vindicated.

Fourth Line: *Entangled folly brings humiliation.* This line often refers to the egotistical assumption that we can guide our way through life purely by the power of intellect. This arrogant self-confidence isolates us from the help we need from the inner world, and guarantees that we will not be open-minded enough to understand such help, were it offered. The Sage lets us go our way until we acquire the humility needed to end the vicious circle of no progress.

Fifth Line: *Childlike folly brings good fortune.* When we acquire a childlike openness of mind we will certainly be helped to understand the secrets of the inner world, through which the Sage alone can guide us.

In teaching others we need only cling to the power of truth to show itself. Instead of striving to make ourself understood, we should innocently follow the truth of things, without worrying what others will think.

Sixth Line: *In punishing folly it does not further one to commit transgressions. The only thing that furthers is to prevent transgressions.* Fate punishes us when we disregard Cosmic laws, yet it does so dispassionately, and only as necessity requires, and to the degree required to break down obstinacy in our attitude.

The line also implies that anyone who obstinately follows a dead-end road meets with disappointment. Only that which is founded on correct principles can ultimately succeed. Unpleasant events serve to jar our minds, telling us we are on the wrong path.

We should keep these principles in mind when we deal with obstinate indifference in others. We involuntarily and automatically punish others when we recognize their faults and transgressions. This involuntary punishment registers in their psyches. When we dwell on them as problems we punish them excessively. We cease punishing when we come to a just and moderate view of their transgressions. Punishment does not mean 'execution,' by which we give up on people and cast them off as impossible; nor does it mean that we commit them to more than a temporary imprisonment in our mind. As *The Image* in *The Wanderer* (Hex. 56) says, "the superior man is clear-minded and cautious in imposing penalties" and "protracts no lawsuits" (going too far incurs a rebound); and, "penalties and lawsuits....should be quickly passing matters, and must not be dragged out indefinitely." Correct punishment is to seek the help of the Sage (Creative), to whom we then turn over the entire matter. It is "entangled folly" to think it is entirely our responsibility to right matters by punishing. We must acquire help by retreating and disengaging, and by leaving the work of correction to the Sage, otherwise, we ourselves transgress.

Note, this line, as well as the fourth line, may refer to transgressing by becoming lax in our tolerance of evil. We give an inch, so the spoiled one takes a mile. To a certain extent, therefore, the transgression is our fault; when we punish, we ought to remember that part of the fault is ours.

5.

Hsü / Waiting (Nourishment)

K'an

(Waiting in the correct attitude empowers the Creative.)

The image of this hexagram is that of steam—the breath of the Creative—rising up to heaven to form clouds. Before rain can come, clouds must form. So it is with progress generated by the Creative: progress results from accumulative stages of development. Steam that accumulates into clouds symbolizes the creative energy generated when we attain a correct 'waiting attitude.' Progress results when we perseveringly maintain this creative attitude. In a correct waiting attitude we avoid the doubt and impatience which dissipate energy; we also avoid indolence— engaging in diversions and dissipations which cause us to lose sight of our work and contact with our inner voice. We cultivate attributes which accumulate energy, such as modesty. We patiently cooperate with time as the vehicle of change, realizing that when the time comes to act, the Creative will indicate the correct way to respond.

A correct waiting attitude is modest, unassuming, and independent. By clinging to a modest viewpoint we avoid comparing ourselves with others and thus are able to keep doubt dispersed; this helps us to remain free of the hopes and desires which destroy inner independence. The more we maintain inner independence and the more we keep attuned to the essential needs of the moment, the stronger and more profound the power of the Creative becomes.

The superior man eats and drinks, is joyous and of good cheer. If we perseveringly maintain a cheerful and detached attitude, while holding to our principles, the force of inner truth (see *Inner Truth,* Hex. 61) will be able to work on the entire situation. The force of inner truth penetrates gradually, influencing everything that needs to be influenced. Rushing another's development, or trying impatiently to force changes, only causes reversals. At best we achieve surface reforms, but the changes do not endure, for they are not based on inner assent. Steadfast waiting leads to slow but perma-

21

nent changes in which we accomplish what is correct for everyone concerned.

We often receive this hexagram when our waiting attitude becomes incorrect, so that progress halts. Perhaps we (our ego, or inferiors) doubt that through waiting in non-action, or allowing ourselves to be led by the Sage, we will achieve anything. Perhaps we suspect that in the end we will only be cheated of happiness. Such doubts arouse fears, causing our inferiors to become impatient, demanding that we speed things along, "or else" get rid of the problem.

All effort is fueled by subtle invasions of doubt put forward by our Inferior Man (ego-self-image). Effort always indicates a loss of inner independence. Such doubts (and our loss of inner independence) are always perceived intuitively by those we wish to influence, and arouse their distrust. Effort implies that we doubt their ability to find their own way; it also implies that we doubt the truths we supposedly follow. It implies that we distrust the hidden power of the Creative. We still cling to the idea that making progress depends on external effort. The ego ever seeks a straight line to success and distrusts the slow progress achieved through following nature's zig-zag way. The creature of our fear, the Inferior Man (ego) seeks to dominate and manage affairs; in so doing it encroaches on others' space and interferes in their self-direction.

Each changing line of this hexagram indicates potential defects of attitude we need to avoid while waiting. We are meant to search out negative influences and resolutely deal with them. For example, doubt influences us so long as we listen to its arguments. Doubt is not quiescent, but actively destructive. Even though we may seem powerless against its negative pressure, and find that we are unable to rid ourself of it, we can, through holding firm, overcome its power. There exists what seems to be a three-minute rule: if we can withstand ego pressures for only three minutes, the assault of the negative force will collapse. The force of doubt is impotent in the face of true resoluteness and firmly clinging to what is good. Like standing in a surf, the first wave is strong and powerful, but the second follows at half its strength; the third is a mere hint of a wave. These waves are renewed only if we reconsider the thoughts which originally caused them.

First Line: *Waiting in the meadow. It furthers one to abide in what endures. No blame.* This line warns that a challenge is impending. The correct response is to prepare, not by anxious anticipation, but by keeping still within. We refuse to listen to our clamoring inferiors and their arguments. We need to be ready, yet not weaken ourself with dread. Whether we are preparing for a battle, a speech, a tennis match, or for meeting someone under adversative conditions, we should not rigidly pre-structure what we will do or say, or allow ourself to consider the good or bad which may result; to do so feeds our inferiors' fears. We need only hold firmly to what is good, essential, and correct, for this is what endures; beyond that, we should keep our minds open and alert, ready for anything that comes.

Second Line: *Waiting on the sand....The end brings good fortune.* Sand provides an uncertain place to wait, and waiting on sand means we wait in an attitude of doubt and uncertainty, afraid to rely on the Unknown to pull us through the impending challenge. Because we doubt, it is not time to act; we should retreat, keep still within, and allow events to take whatever course they will. We act only as each thing presents itself, without predetermining what we will do or say. Inner doubt invites attack, therefore we should avoid being drawn in by exchanges, or pressured into adopting courses of action. Until we discover and rid ourself of what it is we fear, we should resolutely decide not to listen to any inner arguments.

Third Line: *Waiting in mud brings about the arrival of the enemy.* Mud represents a careless, self-indulgent attitude; careless presumption is an imbalance which invites a Cosmic correction in the form of challenge and shock. We never have the luxury to abandon a firm, resolute, and correct attitude. We must ever remain careful, alert, and persevering.

Waiting in mud symbolizes waiting in fear and doubt. We doubt that even though we follow our path perseveringly, anything will be accomplished. "We won't succeed," says the inner voice of despair; "This will take forever!" says the nagging voice of frustrated desire. If such fears are not resisted, the actions we take will damage the overall situation. "Waiting in mud" symbolizes sincerity in listening to dangerous ideas offered by our Inferior Man in the form of desire, envy, passion, self-comfort, self-assertion, anger, alienation, pride, doubt, hate, and petty likes and dislikes. If we steadfastly refuse to listen to these elements, then we deny nourishment

to the Inferior Man. In denying him nourishment, he withers up and
blows away, like the Wicked Witch of the West.

Mud also symbolizes times of indecision when we are tempted to
give in to an unfavorable pattern of action.

Fourth Line: W*aiting in blood. Get out of the pit.* Here we
contemplate taking a stand to force results with the uncompromis-
ing hardness that comes of giving up on people, and of mentally
killing them in our hearts. In *I Ching* terms, this is to execute them,
hence the image of blood.

Blood also symbolizes having come to a negative assessment of
people.

We wait in blood when we suspect, with inner bitterness, that Fate
has set out to ruin us; thus, it refers to a resistant or vindictive mood,
either toward others, toward Fate, or toward our job. We should
retreat from such moods and allow Fate to take its course. Other
forms of blood involve harboring an "either they do this or else"
attitude, or a "do anything to change the situation" mood. On
discovering such sharks in our inner attitude, it is wise to return to
the path of humility, and to cease challenging Fate which, like the
tiger of the 10th hexagram, can bite.

Fifth Line: *Waiting at meat and drink. Perseverance brings god
fortune.* Although moments of respite occur in the midst of difficulties, we should not assume that our problems are resolved; we
should be aware that we have only reached the eye of the hurricane,
and that we would do well to prepare for new challenges. By
keeping our attitude disciplined and correct we avoid spoiling the
progress gained, and remain prepared for any new challenges to our
inner balance.

Sixth Line: *One falls into the pit. Three uninvited guests arrive.
Honor them, and in the end there will be good fortune.* Although we
have waited correctly, it seems we have not accomplished anything.
Progress, however, often involves retrograde movements. Before
we can make a new beginning we must bring old, decadent ways of
relating to an end. Waiting correctly is part of this necessarily slow,
regenerative process. If we keep an open mind, we will see that
"Even happy turns of fortune often come in a form that at first seems
strange to us."

6.

Sung / Conflict

Ch'ien	☰
K'an	☵

(Stop asking "Why?")

Wondering why things are the way they are, or what to do about them, is in conflict with the Creative, for in trying to find comprehensive answers, or in seeking the security of knowing, we distrust that the Creative will show the way, and will unravel the ambiguity of the situation at just the right time.

The heaven trigram, *Ch'ien*, which represents peace, order, inner balance, and independence, is being undermined by *K'an*, the trigram of active, white water. This symbolizes conflict. The hexagram concerns both self-conflict, as when we ask, "Why is life this way?" and adversative situations in which we argue. However, self-conflict is the ultimate cause of all other forms of conflict.

Self-conflict arises when we view God, the Sage, Fate (the scheme of things), other people, or ourselves negatively, as an adversary. Such conflicts form because we misunderstand the way the Cosmos works, and our part in the scheme of things. Ideas which are contrary to our true natures and to our inner sense of truth always create inner conflict. While we may successfully suppress our inner sense of truth, a subliminal inner argument continues.

Receiving this hexagram confirms that we are in a state of self-conflict. By its nature self-conflict is a vortex created by our ego in which we seek to be released from the pressures created by doubt and fear. In this pursuit we seek answers that will satisfy our emotional cravings; all reasons serve that end. While such reasons may seem reasonable, they are not the creations of an objective mind; since they do not solve problems, holes in our thinking keep appearing, therefore we experience continuing rounds of argument. Caught in this vortex we would be unable to recognize or understand the correct answer even if it were presented to us; therefore the hexagram counsels us to withdraw from all questions, disengage from looking at what disturbs us, and leave everything unresolved.

25

This is to "halt halfway." We "go through to the end" when we adopt a solution just to end the ambiguity, or to be released from its disagreeable pressure. Such action is certain to bring misfortune. We need to gain a true perspective. This is possible once we emotionally disengage from the problem.

We view others as adversaries when we give up on them; we view ourselves as an adversary when we mistakenly assume that we have to accomplish everything all by ourselves. Sometimes we mistakenly think that we are meant to approve of others' insensitivity or wrong acts, a misunderstanding which gives rise to inner conflict. While we are not meant to approve wrong situations, neither are we meant to become alienated. Alienation is yet another emotional involvement which clouds all issues.

Caught in the vortex of self-conflict, we are unable to see that the Sage and Fate work together to bring things to completion. The Sage leads and guides while Fate determines the way events twist and turn. Fate presents us with adversity either when we are on the wrong path, or when adversity provides the only contrast by which we may be taught important lessons.

Other types of conflict revolve around crossroads situations. Deadlocked about which road to take, we continually mull the question over. We need to cease inner conflict and disengage from the problem; then the solution will come of itself, at the right time. If we have already made a decision and passed through the crossroads, we should avoid looking back to see if we have made the wrong move. Instead, we should go forward; if we have made a mistake, our sincerity in trying to relate correctly will either correct the situation, or neutralize its bad effects.

Sometimes we receive this hexagram as preparation for a situation which might give rise to conflict. We should prepare, not by pre-structuring our response, but by being alert to the clues provided by events which indicate the appropriate response. We should respond only to the essentials of the situation and carefully avoid being drawn into conflict. If we get off course, we should retreat; if we find ourselves participating in conflict, we should quickly withdraw.

In all situations it is necessary to act only as truth and necessity require, even though doing this sometimes entails being isolated from others. We are never required by Fate to be loyal to what is wrong so that we carry through acts which cause self-conflict. Even if it seems difficult to do what is right we should remember that heaven helps those who cling to the life raft of inner truth.

Halting halfway also refers to situations in which we have gone too far. For example, after having withdrawn as necessity has required, we condemn those who have erred. We avoid conflict when we refrain from making sweeping judgments about the situation, such as deciding that our withdrawal is "forever." It is important to leave the future up to the Higher Power.

In all his transactions the superior man carefully considers the beginning. Conflict with others can generally be avoided at the beginning if we carefully determine fair and just terms. In business relationships the written contract serves this purpose, but contracts are reliable only if they correspond with what everyone, in his heart, would consider to be just.

As just contracts prove helpful in business relationships, thus do they also in marriage. To put that relationship on a firm footing one must take the time to allow an understanding of fair and just principles to develop. However, before we can successfully marry another, we must first marry ourself, for being true to ourself is the only basis for loyalty to others. Marrying oneself does not mean we rigidly hold to dogma or to belief systems; it means that it is our responsibility to be true to our inner feelings, and to our personal experiences of truth. We do not allow ourself to be impelled by logic, persuasion, leverage, or seduction, but by insight which comes to us on its own terms. The person who has married himself is unwilling to do things which cause a loss of his inner balance and integrity. He cannot forswear to anyone else his relationship with the Higher Power, or compromise his dignity or integrity merely to respond to another's selfish demands and expectations. Others need to realize in advance that we are committed to such personal integrity, in order to avoid misunderstandings. This is not something we may tell them, but is something they will understand if we are firm and unwavering in following our values. Once we have gained another's respect because of our love of the good, we will have no reason to lose his loyalty.

If either now or in the past we have promised to participate in an act which is fundamentally wrong, or which is detrimental to our spiritual growth, the contract or promise does not require honoring. If we are inwardly firm in adhering to this principle, we will not need to force the issue; some way out of the situation will show itself. In dealing with the situation we must be firm, but not personally offensive, as the fifth line of *Modesty* (Hex. 15) counsels.

If we are neither firm in our values nor just in our requirements, all understandings, agreements, and contracts will eventually be undermined, for people sense our laxity. Where we are lax we will be tested; where we fail to uphold our principles, we will lose others' trust.

It is a little like training a horse. If we never let him eat along the trail, the horse will not develop the annoying habit of suddenly stopping at his favorite spot of grass. Allowing him to do so just once creates the problem for the next several times we pass that spot. If we seek to be free of conflict, we must be consistent in maintaining a correct attitude.

First Line: *If one does not perpetuate the affair....In the end good fortune comes.* The easiest time to retreat from conflict is at the beginning, when we first allow ourselves to become involved in trying to change the situation. If we cannot withdraw or disengage, then we need to examine our attitude for egotism.

Second Line: *One cannot engage in conflict....The people of his town, three hundred households, remain free of guilt.* The ego looks at externals, weighs, measures, calculates, estimates, and concludes, in an effort to get around the way things work as if its major business were to resist Fate. We should retreat from such conflict, keeping inwardly still until verbal rationalizing ends and clarity can be restored. The Superior Man sees in his situation the creative ingredients needed to solve the problems he encounters, and he works with these ingredients to produce a beneficial effect for all. If he can see no way to have a beneficial effect, he retreats and waits until the situation changes.

Third Line: *To nourish oneself on ancient virtue induces perseverance. Danger. If you are in the service of a king, seek not works.* Ancient virtue calls for perseverance—accomplishing things from a background (often invisible) position. This is difficult because our Inferior Man (ego-self-image) always seeks acknowledgment for what has been achieved; lacking this recognition it resists, and in an "or else" mood, pressures us to give up.

We seek prestige—to be known for our work—when we self-confidently expostulate to establish ourselves as knowledgeable, or argue to prove we are right, as in "Didn't I tell you so?" and when we seek to be the center of influence, in the hopes of accomplishing something dramatic. Such assertiveness comes from our ego—the white knight in shining armor which strives aggressively to save the situation. Ancient virtue would have us modestly take the low road of patient perseverance and reticence, rather than the high road of brilliance. We should not brandish the light but allow it to shine through us, as if we were not there. Danger also comes from the fear, or conviction, that others are irrevocably committed to doing wrong, or that they are incapable of perceiving the truth, and of realizing their mistakes. This fear causes us to intervene. As this line assures us, we need not fear; we cannot lose what we have already created through our good example. Meanwhile, we need to depose the white knight—our masquerading Inferior Man.

Sometimes, on realizing that we must achieve results from an entirely invisible position outside the scene, or from the side-line, our ego interjects that we cannot possibly win from this position. It is true, nevertheless, that great things are achieved in this way, just as in the dark of the womb all things are brought into being. When we can trust the creative process, and wait in the appropriate attitude, the growth process continues and birth occurs.

Fourth Line: *One cannot engage in conflict. One turns back and submits to fate, changes one's attitude, and finds peace in perseverance. Good fortune.* Inner conflict motivates us to strive to influence, and to try to serve as a fulcrum for action; we do this because our inner attitude is infected with ambition to make swift progress. We would skip the slow, step-by-step way of the Sage if doing so would put us closer to our goal. Thus, desire motivates us to sacrifice the correct way to make progress. Desire occurs when we doubt the creative process. Doubting, we say, "the creative process does not serve my ends." In doubting and desiring, we lose the inner independence which empowers truth. To avoid this kind of conflict, we need to become path-oriented and patient, rather than goal-oriented and impatient. In our desire we forget that the step at hand—that of patient waiting, is the only step which leads our goal. Waiting patiently is the important work of the moment. Peace comes from accepting that only slow progress endures.

Fifth Line: *To contend before him brings supreme good fortune.* We may safely turn the matter over to the Sage and to Fate. In this way the conflict will be resolved in the correct way.

Sixth Line: *Even if by chance a leather belt is bestowed on one, by the end of a morning it will have been snatched away three times.* We insist on mulling the issue over and over, thus we become more and more embroiled in self-conflict and doubt. The issue is not to be resolved in this way. We can argue all we like with Fate, but nothing will be changed.

7.

Shih / The Army

$$\frac{\text{K'un}}{\text{K'an}} \quad \begin{array}{c} ==\ ==\ ==\ ==\ ==\ == \end{array}$$

(Prepare for a 'war'—a test about to take place.)

The army needs perseverance and a strong man. We receive this hexagram when we are about to be challenged by a trying situation or 'war,' whether the trial be an objective problem, self-conflict, or a situation which threatens our emotional independence. Regardless of its nature, the challenge involves firmly subjugating our childish heart (ego).

To achieve our goals by way of the Creative requires waiting in the correct attitude. A correct attitude is one of inner independence and alertness. We maintain a steady heart, regardless of the length of time required to achieve changes. Such inner steadiness accumulates great creative power; this power can be maintained only by strict inner discipline, and by holding steadfastly to our principles. The heart that wavers betrays us, as when we vacillate about having taken the *I Ching* path, or when, in punishing others by withdrawing, we do so with a sense of vindication. In such thoughts we abuse power, we achieve no progress, and we create more obstacles. The secret of all progress lies in controlling our inner selves, symbolized here by the image of bringing order to the army.

The "Army" refers to achieving the correct relationship between the superior and inferior elements of our personality. Our personality (the army) requires a leader (the Superior Man) who has a strong and persevering attitude, for strength is required during situations in which the undisciplined and spoiled child within us attempts to enforce its will. When the spoiled child rules, it is as if the sergeant has convinced the privates that he knows best how to run the army. Because he lacks an overall perspective, he brings defeat to the army during times of war. Having usurped the place of the leader, the sergeant becomes the "Inferior Man"; the troops are the "inferiors." When the inferiors are led by the Superior Man (one's higher nature) the army advances and retreats as the situation requires. Because he uses correct means, the good is served and the personality remains strong and superior.

The Superior Man prepares the troops (inferiors) for upcoming battles by explaining to them the need for discipline under fire; they must act only if and when he commands. He informs them that the battle will be lost if the emotions hold sway.

The inferiors seem to be a simple-minded body intelligence. Body cells inform us of their needs; we are subliminally aware of these nonverbal feelings, but they also emerge verbally as inner voices; if we ignore them they become insistent and vocal, saying, "I am hungry," or "I am tired." They also respond to information given them by the superior self, as when we reassure them that food is coming shortly, and they agree to be patient. Doctors and dentists frequently use such verbal techniques to acquire the willingness of the inferiors to endure pain and discomfort—something they will do if they are made aware that it is for their own good, and if they are made to realize that their discomfort is temporary and endurable.

War in this hexagram refers to long-time inner conflicts between ourselves and others which originally began as "lawsuits" (see *The Wanderer,* Hex. 56). A lawsuit which has been resolved by force results in a war. Although we may have won the case, as when we have taken our grievances to courts of law and have had the judgments resolved in our favor, the fact that we have resorted to such means creates a war which goes on and on, perhaps for years.

War also refers to individual battles in which we are challenged by people who doubt us, or who are envious of our independence. They test to see if our values are firm, or real. Some people have actively prowling egos; wherever they sense areas of weakness and uncertainty, they attack. It seems they want to disprove that truly unselfish good exists so that they may be excused from following the good in themselves.

Wars also occur between ourself and our Inferior Man. Our marauding ego puts forth doubts; sometimes these must be combatted; at other times we must retreat from them. In all war situations victory comes when we successfully detach from the situation. This is made possible by returning to the inner stillness symbolized by the serenity of the shining lake; in this state of mind clarity, inner strength, and emotional independence are restored.

In following the principles of the *I Ching,* all challenges must be won by modest means. Any overall wars are to be won through incremental gains which are painstakingly established.

After each battle we consolidate and protect our gains by retreating (recouping) to restore our inner independence and simplicity. This requires that we sacrifice any sense of power gained from victory. We never attempt wholesale changes, skip steps, or stop to luxuriate in our gains; we keep ourself guided steadily forward, aware of what has taken place, but not dwelling on it. We never allow our ego to seize anything from it.

First Line: *An army must set forth in proper order. If the order is not good, misfortune threatens.* "Obedience and coordination of the troops" means being determined to remain modest, to cling firmly to what is just, and to resist any pressure from our inferiors to plunge ahead and take action. Modesty means being conscientious to do what is right.

Obedience of the troops (inferiors) is easier to achieve if we remember that our inferiors respond well if we explain to them the need for discipline, much as a dentist explains the sensation of drilling before he begins. The Inferior Man, on the other hand, is always a traitor within the ranks and must be directly resisted. To bring the Inferior Man under control we need to search out and rid ourself of any demands based on fear, or on selfish or vain considerations. If this effort is unsuccessful, we should prepare to resist any new attempts by the ego to take command. Preparedness gives us strength to keep the ego under control.

Second Line: *In the midst of the army. Good Fortune.* This line acknowledges the heavy burdens that have been placed on our inferiors. It also counsels that it is the job of our superior self, as the leader of the army and its center, to encourage the troops (inferiors) to be patient and to endure the difficulties. One tells them, with sympathy, "I know it's difficult, but your obedience and loyalty are necessary for everything to work out to the best interests of all." This both reassures the inferiors and gains their willing assent to follow the correct path. Our superior self, in turn, serves what is high and good, and is obedient to the Sage. He adapts to the demands of the time, and allows himself to be led as the twists and turns of the battle demand; through 'going with the flow' (*wu wei*), by remaining opaque and unresisting, he finds guidance and is aided in his work. When we become rigid and fearful, the Inferior Man leads; he does not serve what is higher, he pursues only self-interest and comfort.

Third Line: *Perchance the army carries corpses in the wagon. Misfortune.* Wrong elements have usurped control, either in the external situation, or within ourself. Sometimes this line is a warning to be on guard against ego elements which try to force things their way, either by inner resistance, or by outright actions. We should not try to overcome the ego, but prevent it from usurping leadership through asserting itself as "I", as in "I can't stand this anymore!" By the simple trick of asserting that it is ourself, it gains mastery of our personality. If we deny it this identity by saying to it, "You are not me," it remains powerless. The self-image, with its claims of who it is, along with its petty likes and dislikes, becomes real only if we accept its demonic and parasitic assertion that it is "us." If this ego self-image takes control during a war, the war will produce "corpses." Whenever we strive, our ego is involved. Our true self does not need to contend or strive.

If our actions have already led to defeat, we should modestly accept the situation, not allowing hard elements such as anger or pride, to take over. If we disperse all such negatives, the bad effect of our mistakes will be dispelled.

When we do things incorrectly, a residue of remorse remains—here called corpses—which must be put to rest (in their graves). We need to forgive ourself and bury our mistakes, along with the injured pride, anger, and impatience that accompany them, which darken our inner light.

Fourth Line: *The army retreats. No blame.* On being confronted by the inferior element in others, or with a situation which arouses our emotions and pressures us to act, we should retreat. Retreat is a disciplined disengagement from all emotional response into neutrality and acceptance of the situation as it is. Disengagement must proceed step-by-step in a determined way, so that we do not change direction or allow ourself to become further involved. Thus, our army retreats.

Fifth Line: *There is game in the field. It furthers one to catch it. Without blame.* The evil element has come out into the open to attack (either in ourself or in others). We must punish this element by firmly withdrawing and steadfastly going on our way. Once the evil element has given way, we should let go of the matter and punish no more. To take up new issues or go further now would lead to defeat. In any case we should not hold to grievances for more than a short time. To do so means that we put the person concerned into a mental prison. As it is said in *The Wanderer* (Hex. 56), "penalties...should be quickly passing matters," and "prisons ought to be places where people are lodged only temporarily, as guests are. They must not become dwelling places."

Sixth Line: *The great prince issues commands, founds states, vests families with fiefs. Inferior people should not be employed.* The war has been won. If, however, we have used any means other than modesty to achieve success, we should avoid assuming such means to be correct. By such an assumption we institutionalize them. The path of reticence, wherein slow progress brings about enduring change, is best.

8.

Pi / Holding Together [Union]

$$\frac{\text{K'an}}{\text{K'un}} \quad \begin{array}{l} \equiv\!\equiv \\ \equiv\!\equiv \end{array}$$

(We hold all things together by holding to what is correct within ourselves. Our inner attitude determines everything.)

In this hexagram, *K'an*, the trigram of water, is placed over *K'un*, the trigram of earth; water and earth hold together because of their natural affinity. This affinity is symbolized by the strong, yang line in the place of the ruler, which holds all the weak lines together. Translated into a principle of human behavior, the firm fifth line represents inner independence. If one puts his integrity foremost in his hierarchy of values, so that he never sacrifices it to fear, or compromises it to desire, then he is capable of drawing out others' higher natures, and of uniting with them in a common moral accord.

Holding together with others begins when we hold together within ourselves morally and spiritually. By marrying our inner sense of truth, we follow a way of responding to situations which is called one's *Tao*—the way that is in harmony with our essential self and with the Cosmos.

At first we do not recognize what accords with inner truth and we find it necessary to sincerely ask the Higher Power for help. The phrase, "to see the great man" often found in the *I Ching*, means that we must search for the answers within ourself, thereby awaken and learn to follow the great man (or woman) within. The discipline of discovering what is true and of being true to ourself at all times is our work.

To help us find inner truth, the *I Ching* is given us as a guide. (The *I Ching* is not a religion, but a guide to discover the hidden, inner truths of life, and to help us reflect these truths to others.) Our search becomes a spiritual journey which leads to moral and spiritual integration. Through the hard lessons of experience, through mis-understanding, and making mistakes, we discover the guidelines that are to be applied in the field of action. Through 'holding

36

together' with these guidelines, which constitute our inner sense of truth, we influence others without effort. Lacking them we are indecisive and unclear, and we invariably reflect our uncertainty to them.

This hexagram also affirms that it is a natural human drive to seek harmony with others. It confirms that anyone who develops his potential for greatness, consistency, and strength, automatically functions as a center for uniting people. Such a person is a rallying point; anyone can trust and follow him without betraying his higher nature, losing his dignity, or coming to harm. Only one such well-developed person is needed to hold together all those who surround him.

The hexagram questions the reader: *Do you possess sublimity, constancy, and perseverance?* This means, are we able to retain our inner independence and hold to our principles in the face of challenges and temptations? Are we able to remain firm when we would rather be soft, constant when we would rather quit, and steadfast in spite of pressures from the emotional baby within, which demonically insists that we force matters to a conclusion? Few people, on beginning their spiritual journeys, possess such capabilities. Although we are born with them, we lose them at an early age through acculturation. Only by being challenged, time and again, do we regain them.

This hexagram forewarns that the situation is here, or will soon arrive, which will challenge us to hold to our principles. If we allow ourself to be led aside by considerations that spring from fear, desire, pride, anger, or self-interest, we will be undermined. Weakness is intuitively perceived by others, causing distrust, for no one can rightly follow our ego, which is the source of these weaknesses. If we become aware that fear and doubt, and their attendant emotions, have their origin in our tendency to wonder, want, and worry, then we will avoid the seemingly harmless tendency to look aside (or ahead, or behind), which gives rise to wondering, wanting, and worrying. Our path lies in proceeding straight ahead innocently, holding to our inner independence in the face of all challenges, keeping ourselves alert, steady, and serene as the shining lake.

First Line: *Hold to him in truth and loyalty. This is without blame.* While friendliness may woo people, it does not hold them to us.

What holds them is our first loyalty to the truth. Sometimes this loyalty requires us to be reserved so that we are misunderstood as aloof, or indifferent. Often we must let others go through bad experiences. This may be the only way they will see that incorrect attitudes lead away from their goals. So long as we play lifeguard to those who swim near the sharks, they will feel safe. Letting them go does not mean we cast them off; we cling to the help the Cosmos can give. This help is always there for them too. All they need to do is ask for it.

Second Line: *Hold to him inwardly. Perseverance brings good fortune.* It is in keeping with our higher nature to preserve and guard our personality. We avoid throwing ourself away by associating with inferior elements, either in ourself, or in others. Everyone has a superior and an inferior nature. When we become comfortable or intimate with another person's selfish, childish self, we not only cultivate the tyrant in him, we diminish our self-esteem and undermine our dignity. If someone is determined to follow his inferior nature, we can only relate to him in a reserved way. When he returns to sincerity and humility, we may relax our reserve a bit and share our thoughts and feelings with him, but we must not allow ourself to become easy and comfortable. We must maintain our dignity, otherwise his respect will degenerate into insolence.

'Throwing ourself away' also refers to compromising our principles in the heat of the moment through losing our sense of limits. Instead of waiting to find the correct route past obstructions through becoming detached, we vent our anger and frustration and further complicate matters. Holding together inwardly means soothing our frustrated inferiors and encouraging them to be patient until the way past the difficulty shows itself.

'Hold to him inwardly' also means that we should never give up on others' superior potential. In withdrawing, or letting them go, we do not abandon them by dismissing them as hopeless. We hold open the possibility that they will grow and understand, just as after years of making mistakes, our higher nature has been awakened and we are learning and growing. We must not arrogantly decide the future, or forget that the Sage has ways of teaching, and that truth has a power quite in itself to overturn what is wrong, and to defeat what is decadent. Through such reminders we retreat from wrong uses of power and return to simplicity and humility...the way of the Sage.

Third Line: *You hold together with the wrong people.* Receiving this line means we are off the path, or that we are approaching a situation in which we will be tempted to revert to an incorrect attitude.

"Wrong people" often refers to wrong elements in our attitude, as when we abandon a firm attitude for one that is indulgent.

We also receive this hexagram when we dwell on what is wrong with life (the scheme of things), with ourselves, or with others. Holding to what is wrong in others imprisons them in our negativism and "protracts lawsuits," as it is put in *The Wanderer* (Hex. 56). We hold with our inferiors and allow them to lead when we harbor incorrect ideas, participate in wrong relationships, or indulge emotions such as pride, anger, or desire. When we allow our inferiors to lead, we lose the help of the Creative (Sage).

Fourth Line: *Hold to him outwardly also. Perseverance brings good fortune.* We have been applying *I Ching* principles only to close personal relationships. We are meant, as students of the Sage, to apply them to all situations. We need only take the risk to see how effectively they work.

Fifth Line: *Manifestation of holding together....Good fortune.* The fence or enclosure pictured in this line symbolizes the moral limits that apply to relationships. The beaters who drive the deer up on three sides symbolize both the events provided by Fate, and our efforts to establish moral limits. If someone who has become aware of our limits chooses not to respect them, we must allow him to go his way, because in every case he must adhere to them voluntarily, through his insight. We draw people into a correct relationship only by our inner strength and consistency. When they perceive that we are firm in our values, they will cease testing, or trying to manipulate and dominate us; then they will become sincere. We cannot presume, however, that they will remain sincere; we must always accept that they can only stay through free will.

The image of the hunter's killing only the animals which voluntarily expose themselves also refers to the way people sometimes confide their errors to us. We must relate only to the problem thus exposed and not take it as an excuse to discuss other errors we may have perceived. This accords with slow progress and kingly conduct. We do not "slaughter all."

Sixth Line: *He finds no head for holding together. Misfortune.* If we begin a move without firmness, caution, and resoluteness, our position will constantly be undermined. Almost every difficult beginning in which we have cautiously felt our way, ends in success. It is the too-easy, self-confident beginnings that generate problems. Such situations can be resolved, but each tangled strand must be painstakingly untangled.

Having "no head" refers to our not having established a relationship on correct principles. If we carelessly dismiss someone's insensitive behavior just to get on with things, we pave the way for future difficulties. That which holds things together is a firmly established hierarchy of values. In the process of establishing relationships we may not skip steps; we must wait until the conditions for unity are made possible by others' sensitivity and openness, and by their choosing independently to follow the good.

Receiving this line indicates that either we have already forged ahead on our own without waiting to be led, or we are tempted to do so. The resulting danger can be surmounted if we correct our attitude.

This line also refers to times when, after having gone through a crossroads, we keep wondering whether we took the right road. It is not important whether we have taken the right road, but whether we have been sincere in seeking to do the right thing. Even the wrong road will bring no misfortune if we remain sincere, for then an opportunity to correct the mistake will avail itself. It is important to go forward and leave the crossroads behind, otherwise we have "no head" (no eyes, or cognition) for going forward, being preoccupied with looking backward.

Still another meaning lies in our not being able to see the possibility of the great man in another person. By deciding he is hopeless, we also discount the ability of the Sage to awaken his higher nature (as the Sage has awakened ours); we also discount the power of truth to accomplish its customary miracles, and we deprive the person we deem hopeless of the space he needs to discover himself—a space we grant him when we remain open-minded. In all these ways we discount the all-important, all-powerful "head" of the matter, and so insure failure.

Finally, there are limits to what we can accomplish at any given time in striving for unity. Beyond these limits we must let people go and turn to our own path. Ironically, to hold with others, we must also remain detached from them. Sometimes it is necessary to leave them behind. Love externally expressed, is oftentimes not love at all. True unity is achieved through love as patience and tolerance, and as determination on our part to relate to them correctly. Before we can love another, we must become firmly devoted to the sanctity of our inner being, for until we follow good within ourself, we cannot draw it out in others. When each person's will is independently directed toward good within himself, unity is the natural, inevitable result. By drawing out these potentials in others through our example, we create a movement toward the great and the good and thus bring about peace and justice.

9.

Hsiao Ch'u / The Taming Power of the Small

$$\frac{\text{Sun}}{\text{Ch'ien}}$$

(One more step in the process of correcting the situation has been completed.)

The central image of this hexagram is that of the strong element (all the *yang* lines) being "temporarily held in leash" by the weak line in the fourth place (the place of the minister). The minister, by nature of his position, lacks the authority (the complete confidence of others) and the strength to subdue the strong elements once and for all, yet he may, by "firm determination within, and gentleness and adaptability," continue to have a restraining influence.

In practical terms this hexagram indicates that our influence is limited by the circumstances. Other people are beginning to understand our firmness of character and respect our way of life, but not enough to permanently correct their way of relating to us. We have made progress only to the point that the other person's insolence is restrained; therefore, we should not presume all problems are resolved. Until relations are firmly and fundamentally corrected, we need to remain reserved and cautious, retaining a sense of careful responsibility to do what is right. The temptation always exists to abandon self-discipline. Particularly after small victories, our inferiors ask, "Now may I relax?" and "Must I still pay attention, be circumspect, responsible?" and, "When am I going to be able to enjoy myself?"

We should also avoid ambition to make progress. (Ambition, at its beginning, exists only as an ill-defined, discontented mood.) Not only is a final victory impossible now, but ambition would exert a negative pressure. The presence of ambition indicates that we do not yet trust the path of non-action, or the power of clinging to the truth to change the situation. This doubt, which is subconsciously perceived by others, inhibits our having a good effect. We need to rest content with the small gains achieved. Modestly accepting the slow way in which nature works gives others the space they need to discover where their path lies, and their self-interest in following it.

First Line: *Return to the way. Good fortune.* We become negatively involved in the problem when we adopt an either/or attitude to force a change in our fate. This also happens when we relapse into negation and alienation through impatience, because there is no visible progress. Impatience, which springs from desire and doubt, indicates our ego's attempt to dominate the situation, an effort which is doomed to failure. We should conscientiously return to the path of humility and acceptance, and to dispersing alienation and negation.

Second Line: *He allows himself to be drawn into returning. Good fortune.* We may have begun to waver (doubt) about what we inwardly know to be true, so that we are tempted to abandon the correct way to make progress. Sometimes it is as if we threaten the Sage, saying that if we are not helped to achieve our goals, we will discard his guidance. Such a threat inevitably comes to nothing, and in making it we merely jeopardize our personality and engage our pride. In spite of feeling humiliated, we should allow ourself to be drawn back from this thinking, and return to the path of perseverance. We often receive this line and the preceding line just prior to the situation which will draw out such feelings in us; this preparation helps to give us the strength we need to keep from being dominated by our emotions.

Third Line: *The spokes burst out of the wagon wheel. Man and wife roll their eyes.* This image symbolizes that our inner attitude has collapsed into alienation and impatience, and therefore has lost its integrity and usefulness. Our situation falls apart when we abandon patient waiting, or when we bring controversial matters up rather than allowing them to arise spontaneously. We rush things when we become afraid that the right time may not occur soon enough. Under the influence of fear, negation, and desire we are unable to attain the objectivity we need to find the right solution. Without the right solution, things turn out badly and we have regrets.

Pressing forward forcibly means that we try, under the influence of negative and alienated feelings, to force progress by threatening to drop our task to rescue the others. This ploy by our ego does not work. We cannot steal happiness by challenging Fate.

Fate does not respond to threats.

Pressing forward forcibly also refers to times when we try to assert our 'inner worth' by taking a stand based on our inner sense of truth. In making this effort our ego has intercepted our sense of truth in an attempt to rule forcibly rather than to allow people to perceive the truth for themselves. The Superior Man simply relies on his sense of inner truth to convey inner messages. If the injustice is such that he knows a correction is needed, he relies on the Cosmos to provide the correction. Because he is free of doubt, he activates the power of Truth to rectify the problem.

Power lies with the weak. True power, in dealing with the obstinate power of the ego, or for that matter, with Fate, is in letting go, not in trying to make points, or engaging in arguments, or in striving to overcome the situation. True power lies in reticence, tranquillity, and detachment.

Fourth Line: *If you are sincere, blood vanishes and fear gives way. No blame.* Three interpretations are given. First, although we may not like some of the lines we get in the *I Ching*, they are given sincerely, in the spirit of helpfulness. Despite the danger that we may despise him for it, the Sage offers this advice.

Second, we are in a responsible position, giving example of the way of the Sage to others. We must do what is correct, disengaging from the challenges laid down by other people's egos, and letting them go, even though our actions will be misunderstood. In the end, because we are true to our principles, we achieve the correct effect. To live correctly is to "mediate" the message of our leader to others.

Third, if we are sincere in our path, we will not resort to wrong means. In retreating from wrong means, "blood vanishes." This means that the threat of disruption and long-lasting bitterness is avoided. Blood refers to words and acts which emotionally wound, as when we brandish the white light of truth as a sword. We need to realize that truth is never a harsh, cutting white light, but the yellow light of moderation. When our understanding departs from modesty and moderation, it departs from truth. Saying too much in a state of emotional heat resembles the effect of an atom blast—the fallout is poisonous and contaminates the relationship for a long time thereafter. Then, instead of dealing with the person, we can only deal with the fallout.

Fifth Line: *If you are sincere and loyally attached, you are rich in your neighbor.* The Sage is trustworthy; being wholly directed to what is true and good, he cannot respond to what is unworthy in us. When we are sincere in trying to do what is right he shares his great wealth with us in the form of a friendly presence, reinforcing us in times of trouble, and giving us a sense of protection and well-being that is sorely missed when we stray from our path.

When we are sincerely attached (married) to our principles, we bring out the best in other people. This inner truth has the power (by itself) to do the work of correcting all situations. All the communications are inner ones, emanating from the strength of accepting things exactly as they are, and from being utterly at peace within oneself (being happy in one's inner marriage).

"Loyally attached" also means being wedded to conscientiously seeking the correct way, and not turning this responsibility over to others. We must do our own work and not look to others to do it for us. If we have labored hard all our lives to save money, we are not then meant to abandon ship by lightly turning it over to someone else to manage, just because we are tired of responsibility. Loyally attached means that we remain careful with the responsibilities entrusted to us.

To share our wealth instead of hoarding it means to remember how we have been helped. If we regard ourself as better than another, the gained wealth is "hoarded," and modesty lost. To be rich yet remain modest is to be devoted; only then are we rich in our neighbors, who do not feel overshadowed. When we are taught by the Sage, we must become more modest and conscientious, not less. Shall we overshadow the Sage, who is invisible? Shall we obscure the Sage with our wrong actions?

Sixth Line: *The rain comes, there is rest. This is due to the lasting effect of character....If the superior man persists, misfortune comes.* Victory has been won by persevering in a firm, correct attitude. However, it is a partial victory, not one founded on the slowly penetrating light of inner truth, or on a thorough understanding that secures us from reversals. If we can retain our modesty and humility, sacrificing any sense of power we may feel, our gains will be consolidated.

10.

Li / Treading (Conduct)

$$\frac{\text{Ch'ien}}{\text{Tui}}$$ ☰☱

(On attempting to force progress.)

Treading upon the tail of the tiger. Becoming involved when we ought to remain innocent, is to challenge Fate, or "tread upon the tiger's tail."

The tiger symbolizes Fate. So long as we are sincere, conscientious, simple, and innocent in our conduct, the tiger does not bite. However, if we self-confidently and obstinately follow the wrong path, as we do when we try to create opportunities to influence rather than allowing them to evolve, we get bitten. We challenge Fate when we step over the thin line (however gingerly) to tell another what is wrong with him (or with his position, or conduct). We must be wary of supposing that because we have a more correct position we have such rights.

Difficult situations are caused by faulty attitudes and traditions that have accumulated over time. It is our fate to resolve these difficulties by correcting our mistakes. To try to change the situation by wrestling with it, by blindly resisting it, or by rejecting it, is to challenge Fate as a "blind and lame man." We must become resigned to slow, patient self-development to reverse the trends which have become established. To try to overcome them all at once is foolhardy; the situation will improve only to the extent that we improve ourselves in an enduring manner.

The superior man discriminates between high and low. This means that we accept the discipline and patience required to correct our poor relationships with others. Rather than listen to the self-pitying, whining, impatient voices of our inferiors, which look to external circumstances for guidelines to act, we need to concentrate on finding the egotisms and errors which have led to our difficulties.

The difficulties in question are referred to elsewhere in the *I Ching* as "lawsuits." Lawsuits are continuing inner conflicts with others which result from having adopted hard, vindictive, or impatient attitudes. Lawsuits always occur when we give people up as hopeless. We initiate an inner quarrel in which we say, "You don't exist," to which they reply, "Yes, I do, and I will prove it to you." Sometimes the argument is, "You are hopeless," to which they reply, "I will pay you back for your arrogant assessment of me." Lawsuits are evident in any actions which involve people's forcing us to be conscious of them (or *vice versa*). These lawsuits occur because we do not truly let people go. Instead, we supervise their behavior or attitudes. We seek to punish them for having trespassed on our values, injured our pride, or wounded our vanity. When we truly let people go, healing begins, and the lawsuit dies down. A creative relationship then becomes possible.

When we allow ourselves to fall into negation and alienation, we "leave the wagon behind." The wagon symbolizes our fate to rescue those to whom we are bound by inner ties. Negative attitudes resist that fate. If we ignore the higher, essential meaning and purpose of life by rejecting our duty to discipline ourselves, we will not find true happiness. Fate's mandate that we can find happiness only by following the correct path cannot be circumvented.

First Line: *Simple conduct. Progress without blame.* We make progress so long as we remain detached and free of selfish considerations, but we should be on guard against wanting to regain lost comforts. Such wanting gives rise to restlessness and ambition to force progress, or to conclude matters. We should remain content with slow progress, and not allow the desire to make progress, or the desire to end the situation, to influence our attitude. The correct attitude is always a humble acceptance of the situation as it is; we relinquish any anger, uneasiness, or disappointment we may feel about the length of time required to accomplish things.

Second Line: *Treading a smooth, level course. Perseverance ...brings good fortune.* We should stay free of inner conflicts, such as questioning "Why is this my fate?" and "What should I do?" We should avoid the danger of challenging Fate by frontal assaults, and by quarreling with the way things are. To circumspectly remain disengaged is to "tread a smooth, level course."

Third Line: *One eyed...lame....The tiger bites the man. Misfortune.* When we self-confidently think we can overcome Fate by aggressive effort, we are sure to experience a rebuff. To plunge ahead is to meet with failure. Even though we are in the right, we should not assume a strong position. It is necessary to control blind ambition, and not employ powerful means. Instead, we should rely on the beneficial action of nature to correct things. The more correct our position, the more modest we must become.

Fourth Line: *He treads on the tail of the tiger. Caution and circumspection ultimately lead to good fortune.* The "dangerous enterprise" is to think we must interfere to avert disaster or unwanted consequences. To interfere is to plunge ahead willfully. The encroachment of our ego is best combatted by going forward with our studies, trusting that further enlightenment will help us overcome the danger that comes of doubting the correct attitude.

Fifth Line: *Resolute conduct. Perseverance with awareness of danger.* This means to be neither too hard nor too soft. Resoluteness must not become entangled with anger, feelings of retribution, or hardness, so that we lose our modesty. Danger is incurred when we self-righteously think what people "ought to do." Such thinking is an interference in their spiritual space. Not only do they sense our feelings of superiority, our supervisory attitude prevents them from doing what is right of their own volition. This is because it is against a person's inner dignity to respond servilely to other people's demands. Our duty is to truly let people find their own way to doing what is right.

While avoiding self-righteousness we need to remain firm about what is correct and associate only with people's better selves. To pander to their desires and demands is to throw ourselves away. To overlook evil put before us is magnanimously to play God. While we may not tell people what they can or cannot do, it is our duty to make clear the limits of what we are willing or unwilling to join in doing. Until others are correct in relating to us, we should remain reserved in our inner attitude.

Sixth Line: *Look to your conduct and weigh the favorable signs. When everything is fulfilled, supreme good fortune comes.* When we have correctly persevered through the challenge of the time we can be assured of good fortune.

This line frequently refers to getting out of danger, especially the danger of doubt, ambition, restlessness, or immodesty—dangers which result from worrying, wanting, or allowing ourself to be directed by pride. Driven by these emotions we recklessly strive to get out of difficulties, only to make them worse, and more dangerous to our inner balance. To regain inner balance it is necessary to come to a humble acceptance of the situation as it is. The acceptance needed is unconditional, like that required of Katherine in Shakespeare's *The Taming of the Shrew*. Here, Fate is the taming factor. When we accept that we must engage the helpful energies of the Higher Power, we are led out of our problems.

11.

T'ai / Peace

$$\frac{\text{K'un}}{\text{Ch'ien}} \quad \equiv\equiv \atop \overline{}$$

(Through relating correctly we have achieved peace; maintaining peace, however, requires that we remain firm in inner discipline.)

Compared with other hexagrams, this hexagram is perfectly balanced. The heaven and earth forces are in equilibrium. This symbolizes a person who has correctly balanced the heaven and earth qualities within himself so that he is in harmony with the Universe.

The heaven force in the lower trigram symbolizes our having made our inner attitude correct: we are persevering in our principles and are self-contained; whether events proceed here or there, we do not lose our inner equilibrium. The earth force in the upper trigram symbolizes that we have attained an open-minded receptivity toward events in the outer world; we have ceased to erect defensive barriers, or to try to manipulate events, either by adopting what we think to be appropriate attitudes, or by doing specific things. Such a balanced, neutral attitude reduces tensions and resolves problems in our relationships with others.

We need to remain aware, however, that times of peace invite us to forget that good luck arises from having balanced our attitude; furthermore, it is dependent on our remaining balanced. In relaxing from tensions we easily lose our inner independence. For example, we lose our independence both when we seek ways to preserve the good times, and when, through lassitude, we forget to uphold our principles. Being more relaxed, we may forget our responsibility to rescue those to whom we have inner connections, or we may become self-oriented and overconfident. Therefore, the hexagram reminds us to remain conscientious and persevering.

Perhaps the greatest danger posed by having attained peace in the external situation is that we tend to work at our spiritual development only when we are under the pressure of adversity. We presume that since we are in harmony with the Cosmos, there is nothing we

50

need to learn. It is important to continue with our learning, and to remain aware of our dependence on the Higher Power.

As a second hexagram, *Peace* implies that peace will result, or has resulted, from making the changes called for in the first hexagram's lines; it also cautions us to remember the dangers and to persevere.

First Line: *When ribbon grass is pulled up, the sod comes with it....Undertakings bring good fortune.* When people are open to each other they are "connected by their roots," hence good influences are possible. Openness is the prerequisite to having an influence.

Similarly, although we are connected by the roots to the Sage, this connection becomes obstructed when we doubt we will get the help we need. When we withdraw from a negative assessment of affairs and return to a humble acceptance, the obstruction evaporates. The image of pulling up interconnected roots suggests that by dealing with the root of the problem—our inner attitude—we remove existing obstructions to the peace and progress we seek.

Second Line: *Bearing with the uncultured in gentleness, fording the river with resolution, not neglecting what is distant, not regarding one's companions. Thus one may manage to walk in the middle.* During times of peace we are tempted to be hard on those who make mistakes, or to be alienated through having to deal with their troublesome egos. It is in keeping with modesty not to form a mental faction against them, but to bear with them, and to bear with the situation.

Fording the river with resolution. When we are in a peaceful mood and situations arise that require withdrawal and going on alone, we should not neglect to do so; this is to follow our path and "not neglect what is distant."

Not regarding one's companions. This means that we do not condition what we do by what others do, but keep to our path. We must not watch with our inner eye what they do .

To walk in the middle means that we serve as an intermediary between the Sage and others through remaining careful and conscientious. Especially during peaceful times we must avoid being sidetracked by indolence, or weakened by indulgence in small vanities and flatteries. Sometimes we indulge in small, seemingly harmless attitudes because we presume that peace, having been attained, will maintain itself. We must remember, however, that Fate will not be presumed upon.

One of the dangers of peaceful times is our tendency to become dependent on things remaining free of tension. Such a dependency entails a loss of inner independence; in striving to keep the *status quo* our responses become conditioned; we are no longer able to respond spontaneously from innocence. Such a dependency invites others to challenge us.

A similar danger sometimes occurs when people present themselves as interested, caring, and sensitive. Although manipulative and unworthy, the intention is often to keep things pleasant. At other times it is manipulative flattery designed to lure us into carelessly exposing ourselves. There is almost always a leader put out, with a hook on it, which engages our ego. Then, once we expose ourselves we are greeted with a contrived indifference or an insolent attack. Such tactics, part of the king-of-the-heap game, are meant to unbalance us so that those who initiate the game can gain the upper hand. We should avoid being seduced by flattery so that we become involved in these games. At the same time we should remain open-minded and patient with those who play them.

Third Line: *No plain not followed by a slope....He who remains persevering in danger is without blame.* During peaceful times we tend to assume that good times will continue indefinitely. By this assumption we begin an emotional dependence on people, God, Fate, and events, that they should all stay the same. We become unwilling to allow the situation to change; then when problems recur, we are unprepared; being unprepared, we waver and fall back into hoping and doubting. This disintegration of personality can be avoided if we do not allow ourselves to depend emotionally on people, or events. We can better keep our independence if we remember that each event is part of the zig-zag path by which the Creative resolves problems. By expecting the unexpected, and by always being prepared for tensions to resume, we avoid making plans based on things "always going well," or "always going badly."

Fourth Line: *He flutters down, not boasting of his wealth, together with his neighbor, guileless and sincere.* Receiving this line often refers to receiving the help of the Sage to acquire insight into the correct way to approach a problem.

It may also be a simple confirmation that our guileless, sincere way of relating has had creative results.

At other times this line counsels us to allow our contacts with others to be guileless and sincere. This means we refrain from any temptation to contrive or manipulate what we want to happen.

The line also counsels us against "boasting of wealth." We boast of wealth if we try to impress people with our wisdom, wit, or charm, or if, in any way, we try to impose our point of view. We should make every effort to remain sincere, simple, and serene.

Fifth Line: *The sovereign I gives his daughter in marriage. This brings blessing and supreme good fortune. A truly modest union.* This line means that it is the Sage ("sovereign I") who decides when the time is right for things to work out, and when the conditions for unity will become possible. Until then we must wait.

This line also presents us with the analogy of a marriage between two people of unequal status. The princess must adapt to being married to someone beneath her rank. This means that when we must deal with someone, who for lack of self-development, or for other reasons, is not on our level of understanding, we should not unthinkingly add to his natural feelings of inferiority. The princess is pictured as placing herself beneath her husband. This does not mean that she is lesser, but that she avoids a competing or dominating attitude; thus she prevents envy from spoiling their relationship. In situations of close personal contact, the person with the stronger character must become more modest, sacrificing his sense of self, power, and authority; in this way he dissolves tension and striving. This creates "a truly modest union" which "brings happiness and blessings."

Sixth Line: *The wall falls back into the moat. Use no army now.* It is time to dismantle the defenses and strategies which comprise our resistance to Fate. We must disperse all effort and striving. In humbly submitting to and accepting the situation as it is, without resentment or resistance, we will gain the help of the Higher Power to correct the situation.

12.

P'i / Standstill (Stagnation)

$$\frac{\text{Ch'ien}}{\text{K'un}}$$

(No progress.)

This hexagram refers to dealing with difficult and obdurate situations in which there appears to be no progress. The hexagram instructs us in how to relate to such times of darkness and difficulty.

When we perceive that there is no progress in our general situation, tension and inner conflict arise. The remedy is to disengage from looking at the situation. We abandon neither our principles nor our goals. When we have re-established inner calm, the clarity needed to put things into perspective becomes possible. Until then, nothing can be done.

The entire thrust of the hexagram is to adjust one's attitude, since adapting in the correct way can cause the situation to change. If standstill has its roots in our defective ideas, following the counsel given in the hexagram will counteract the bad effects of those ideas.

The "time of standstill" refers to the time prior to becoming a student of the *I Ching*, and to all the ideas we had at that time about the way things work. Receiving the hexagram is meant to make us re-examine ideas and values we have taken for granted as correct. We are meant to realize that the "Wheel of Fate" is stuck in the mud and that progress is stalled because we still cling to ideas the *I Ching* regards as decadent.

Receiving this hexagram also refers to times when we are stopped at a crossroads, wondering which direction or attitude will lead to progress. It is important not to linger in the crossroads of self-conflict, or to search for the precisely correct attitude, for the solution is not to be found in this way. In all striving the ego attempts to find some way to make things work in order to stay in control. It is better to detach from looking at the situation and go on our way, taking care not to engage either in hope, or hopelessness. If we can accept that we are meant to patiently persevere, then, by itself, Fate will indicate the way.

54

First Line: *When ribbon grass is pulled up, the sod comes with it....Perseverance brings good fortune and success.* The root of the problem is pulled up (resolved) when we disengage from looking at, and from trying to influence, the negative situation. The effect of disengagement is to deprive either our own or someone else's ego of anything to strive against. With the basis (root) of the problem removed, the problem ceases to exist, thus the analogy, "in pulling up the grass, the sod comes with it." This is also the path of least resistance.

The ego derives its energy from perceiving itself as being seen or heard, feared or loved, hated or envied, or whatever is required to give it a sense of power and importance. When those to whom a person is attached no longer give the ego recognition, or otherwise feed it, it loses its power and gives way. For a time the ego seeks this recognition from substitutes, but this effort yields no real satisfaction; ultimately the person is driven to grow and change.

Second Line: *They bear and endure...good fortune for inferior people.* This means to bear and endure inferior aspects of human character, either in ourself or in others. On witnessing the manifestation of people's inferior nature, our inferiors (our childish self, with its inner voices) become discouraged by the course of events and complain. They cease to trust the power of inner truth, and disengagement. They review old wounds and areas of inner burnout to support their view that non-action does not work, even though they have never practiced creative non-action before. Through their self-flattery (comparing our condition to others who seem better off) they call us to pursue self-interest, and insist that we "do something," such as correct our ambivalent attitude about the situation we have decided is bad. Our inferiors argue that the problems are insuperable and demand respite from them, if by no other means than to cast them off as "hopeless." However, the Superior Man (superior self) does not allow himself to be influenced; he perseveres in the face of such danger and clings to his goal to rescue the others. Seeing his firmness and courage, the inferiors once more take heart and begin to cling to what is correct. This change ends self-conflict and striving. Under the leadership of our Superior Man, alienation and hardness are avoided, and one ceases looking at other people's negative behavior with one's inner eye.

Third Line: *They bear shame.* This line often means that because we have related to a problem in the correct way, someone who has misunderstood or wronged us is beginning to have regrets, although this is not apparent externally. Ideas he has allowed to "seize power" prove inadequate and he is ready to cast them off.

Bearing with others who are returning to the path means that we are tolerant and open-minded. We do not, however, interfere to make their return easy. Their work must be their own. We are patient, but we retain our firmness, and our willingness to go on alone if circumstances require it. Especially we should avoid a soft, comfortable, careless relationship, in which we halt in our forward direction or wait for others to catch up. We should always maintain the integrity and independence of our path. Through watching others' progress, or lack of it, we overstep our bounds and lose our inner independence.

"They bear shame" also refers to times when we have allowed our inferiors (childish self), through not resisting pride and anger, to attain power, only to find that this has had a bad effect. Seeing these bad effects, our inferiors feel ashamed. We have allowed our inferiors to fasten their attention on the disagreeable situation, and to demand that, in addition to making correct changes, those who have offended us humble themselves to our ego. People cannot respond to any form of ego-demand, for to do so would compromise their spiritual integrity. Any time our ego becomes involved, those we want to change are prevented from improving and changing. When we release people from our mental prison, when we hold our minds open, and cease watching them with our inner eye, we give them the space they need to correct themselves.

Fourth Line: *He who acts at the command of the highest remains without blame.* Our fate works as a mathematical certainty. When we are correct and balanced, everything in the Cosmos comes to our aid. In playing with dice there are times when every roll seems magical and we win, time and again. When we are inwardly correct progress occurs in this way, but if we are not in harmony with ourself, every move leads from obstruction to obstruction. Only inner growth leads to progress which springs again and again from itself.

By receiving this line we are meant to examine whether our attitude leads to progress, or whether it remains caught in the standstill of convention. A correctly balanced attitude is firm and independent, neither presumptuously bending, as if we were gods, exercising the power of beneficence (called "magnificence" in *Preponderance of the Small*, Hex. 62), nor too hard.

When we focus on keeping our inner attitude innocent, pure, and alert, we allow the Sage to be the Master Playwright. Having the correct attitude, we are called into action by events. We advance with the light (when people are open to us) and retreat with the dark (when their sensitivity declines). Remaining free of ambition, we serve the true and the good.

Fifth Line: *He ties it to a clump of mulberry shoots.* If we have produced a change for the better through attaining humility and conscientiousness, we may secure progress only by holding to these attitudes perseveringly. Thus, we must continue to examine ourself and to correct our mistakes.

Tying things to mulberry shoots means we cling to that which is firmly rooted and strong (the true and the good); we cling to the Higher Power, and we retain the attitude that whatever happens will lead us in the correct direction. This perfect acceptance of events as devices of the Creative, and reliance on the power of the true and the good, defeats the negative effects of hope and fear, and guarantees success.

Sixth Line: *The standstill comes to an end. First standstill, then good fortune.* Through the creative effort indicated in the previous five lines of this hexagram, we have the ability to change Fate and bring about better conditions in the world.

The creative effort required is that of consistently keeping our inner attitude correct. The thoughts that spring from a pure heart and mind, like Cupid's golden arrows, automatically hit their mark in the hearts of others, influencing them for the good without their being aware of it. Thus, the simple sorrow and embarrassment that is generated on seeing others' misdeeds is transmitted with the great power of inner truth. Trying to produce such effects by consciously willed thoughts, however, is a misuse of power that has unfavorable results. Only an innocent mind and a pure heart are capable of responding to evil in a wholly beneficial way.

13.

T'ung Jên / Fellowship with Men

$$\frac{\text{Ch'ien}}{\text{Li}}$$

(True fellowship is founded on fellowship with the Sage.
Exclude the Sage and there can be no true or lasting
fellowship.)

Fire flaming up to heaven provides the image of friends gathered in
fellowship, as around a camp fire, or hearth. The achievement of
peace and harmony among one's fellows is the natural drive of the
human heart. This hexagram points to gentleness and refinement of
spirit, and the sense of humanity known in Confucianism as *jên*.

Fellowship with men in the open. Success. This means that only
openness in fellowship succeeds. The phrase "in the open" specifies
that which makes true fellowship possible. This idea is reiterated
and elaborated in the first line by the statement that "the basic
principles of any kind of union must be equally accessible to all
concerned. Secret agreements bring misfortune." One is reminded
of treaties and contracts in which the fears, doubts, and expectations
of each party are brought into the open. If all parties seek to deal with
these issues sincerely, an agreement based on just principles and
mutual trust can be established successfully. Harboring secret reservations, or hedging for selfish purposes, ruins all possibility of
creating fair and just agreements. In making agreements with others
we should take care that no secret reservations exist in either party's
attitude; such reservations usually surface if we are attentive; when
they do, we should postpone or abandon the agreement until the
wrong attitudes are corrected.

Fellowship in the clan refers to hidden reservations and elements
of factionalism by which a person seeks to protect his interests (or
those of his group) at others' expense. We often receive this line
when we resist following the way of the Sage because of such
mistrust.

The third line, *He hides weapons in the thicket,* illustrates a type
of hidden reservation or element of factionalism. One of the parties

holds back a "weapon" because he distrusts the situation. For example, he calls a meeting on an innocent pretext, knowing that he intends to ambush the others with accusations and claims.

The commentary to the hexagram focuses on the idea that enduring unity, whether it be between ourself and God, between husband and wife, or between those further removed, must be based on concerns that are universal. This refers to a point of view which anyone, through reflecting on what is fair, would agree to be just and correct. Petty likes and dislikes, and judgments based on trivial considerations, are put aside in favor of the essentials of the matter.

We often receive this hexagram when some adjustment or change in attitude is needed. Either we need to review the basic principles of 'fellowship with men,' so that we make sure that what we require of others is correct, or we need to search out hidden reservations in our attitude which isolate us from the Sage. Typical of such reservations are plans of what we will do in case the *I Ching*'s counsel doesn't suit us, or of what we will do if the changes we desire fail to materialize within the time frame we think reasonable.

Secret reservations of attitude are regarded as factionalism. In learning about the various forms of factionalism we soon realize that by correcting our relationship with the Sage, we correct all our relationships. Indeed, our relationship with the Sage is the model for all human relationships.

Consulting the *I Ching* frivolously, just to see what it says, is a factionalism in which we form a partnership with our ego which excludes the Sage. This isolates us from the help the Sage can give, because he cannot relate to such arrogance. Factionalism exists when we agree, in our hearts, to go along with something that is incorrect, and when we sacrifice the higher good to obtain a lesser benefit. Factionalism occurs when we receive aid from the Sage without accepting any responsibility to set a good example. Factionalism exists when we use the *I Ching* as a tool to gain selfish ends. Many beginning students of the *I Ching* harbor an inner demand that the Sage prove himself before they will relinquish distrust. They stand back with a "show me" attitude. The Sage, in such circumstances, remains reserved. While the Sage does not require that we believe he exists, he cannot, with dignity, cater to an arrogant distrust. In the face of such defects of attitude the beginning student often finds that his relationship with the Sage varies. When he is sincere and open-minded, he understands the hexagrams and is nourished by them. When he distrusts, the Sage becomes remote and the *I Ching* lines incomprehensible. He also finds that so long as he clings to his secret distrust, he remains locked in the vicious circle of no progress.

Following the principles of fellowship does not mean that we are obligated to like people when our inner feelings are to the contrary; nor does it mean that we must regard people as credible before they have made us aware of their credibility. In business we are not obligated to extend credit or trust before customers have given evidence of their creditability and trustworthiness. Just as the Sage 'comes to meet' us only halfway, in response to our sincerity and conscientiousness (see *Coming to Meet*, Hex. 44), we should remain similarly reserved and reticent when others are not sincere and open to us. All 'coming to meet' (joining in fellowship) should be approached with care so that we avoid succumbing to the subtle flatteries and seductions implicit in social forms. Flatteries and seductions have power when we lose contact with our inner voice, and when our ego becomes involved through enjoying the comforts of self-deception.

Factionalism always results in negative reactions. When we hold secret reservations based on a general distrust of people, we not only awaken distrust in them, we insure that a satisfactory relationship cannot occur, simply because of the actively undermining power of doubt. We inadvertently do the trustworthy person an injustice, and mentally fix the untrustworthy person in his untrustworthy ways. Distrust traps the mistrusted one into unfavorable patterns of response.

We can have a creative effect on the untrustworthy person if we are willing, after acknowledging his defective attitude, to turn the matter over to the Cosmos, and return our attitude to neutral. Thereafter, we neither believe nor disbelieve him, but relate to him with caution and reserve until he changes his ways. We do not measure his progress; instead, we react to the momentary ways in which he reveals himself, keeping attuned to his eclipses of personality. We respond sincerely and openly when he is sincere and open; we retreat into non-participation when he regresses into suspicion, indifference, and insensitivity.

The only reservations of attitude we can justly have in any relationship are those which conform to natural and universal morality. We always reserve our dignity and self-respect, and do only what accords with our moral limits. If we have not been morally correct in the past and discover our error, we retreat and correct ourselves. No immoral agreement is binding, and all Cosmic law supports our retreat from doing wrong.

Other forms of factionalism occur when we attempt to attain unity with some by excluding others; when we tolerate misbehavior in some, but are harsh on others who transgress; when we indulge thoughts which make others feel inferior; when we assume rights over people or things—our children, mates, or animals. We do not have the right to abuse, degrade, or humiliate any thing. Among Western customs considered decadent by the Sage are those which give us the feeling that we are masters of the universe, and that the earth and its inhabitants were made solely for our use and benefit. Our rightful purpose is to serve the Higher Power in bringing order to the myriad things of creation. In this work we are responsible to the Higher Power for everything we do.

First Line: *Fellowship with men at the gate. No blame.* The foundation of enduring unity is openness. Receiving this line reminds us to inspect our attitude for unfair conditions which have not been stated; it also reminds us to be on guard against unstated feelings and expectations which others may have toward us. If one is careful at the beginning of fellowship, although the extra effort may seem petty and troublesome, the agreements and associations we make will prove more satisfactory than those we slip into carelessly and quickly. Easy relationships always contain hidden presumptions and expectations.

This line also refers to secret reservations of attitude we have in our relationships. Secret reservations occur when we put a time limit on accomplishing our goals; when we are tempted to abandon the path because it is more difficult than we expected; when, after realizing the time and effort required, we doubt the effort is worth it; when we doubt that the goal can or should be attained. All such thoughts threaten perseverance. Hiding behind a grandiose image, the ego feels superior as it weighs and judges the Sage's leadership. Such presumption is based on a secret agreement we have allowed to develop between ourself and our ego; this factionalism rules out an open, sincere fellowship with the Sage.

Another secret reservation occurs when we wait in ambush to press our thoughts on others. If people are not receptive, we must remain reserved.

No divergent aims have yet arisen. If only this line has been

61

drawn, the hexagram changes to retreat, meaning that we should retreat from thoughts of giving up our goal to rescue the others. Thinking of changing our goals in mid-stream constitutes a "divergent aim."

Second Line: *Fellowship in the clan. Humiliation.* This line indicates that we harbor factional thoughts. For example, we criticize others but fail to correct ourselves; we feel we have special rights and privileges over others; or, we hedge on waiting the allotted time to achieve the rescue of those with whom we have inner connections.

If we distrust that our goal of unity can be attained, we soon settle for one of the factions. We ignore our obligation to do the correct thing, and instead do what is comfortable and enjoyable, or, although we agree with the *I Ching*'s principles, we continue in the comfortable habit of decadent tradition. In all these things we choose the clan (what is comfortable) over what is universally true and good.

Fellowship in the clan also refers to forming a unity with another while he remains incorrect; we form a faction with desire, thus exclude the Sage.

Third Line: *He hides weapons in the thicket...For three years he does not rise up.* This line may refer either to another's having secret distrust and bad motives, or to our distrust of him, or of the basic direction of the *I Ching*. True fellowship becomes more and more impossible because distrust is fortified by failure and failure is insured by distrust.

This line also refers to distrust of oneself. One feels unable to carry things to completion, or to correct oneself, or to be of service to that which is higher. Here, our ego makes a last-ditch effort to collapse our will so that it can resume control. It creates the illusion that we are powerless against it; this illusion becomes true only if we believe the ego's claim. To defeat the ego's power we need to ask the Sage's help; meanwhile, we should remain persevering. Patient acceptance of the situation will enable us to acquire the clarity needed to overcome the doubts put forward by our ego.

Fourth Line: *He climbs up on his wall; he cannot attack. Good fortune.* This line states that misunderstanding divides people. Because their problems seem insuperable, they give up on each other (they "no longer attack"). Although it is incorrect for them to give up on each other, it is better that they remain separated than to continue fighting.

This line also refers to being tempted to give up on our relationship with another person. It reassures us that in spite of all difficulties and mistakes, we will succeed if we persevere.

Fifth Line: *Men bound in fellowship....After great struggles they succeed in meeting.* Two people divided by the course of life are meant to be reunited at some other time when their troubles will be over. The answer to the inner question one asks, "Am I meant to resolve my problems with this person?" is yes, eventually, but now we must be patient.

The line also means that we are meant to resolve our problems with all people. We should give up on no one.

It also means that we should hold no one as an adversary. If in our inner eye we hold someone afar, we may be afraid of his getting closer. In various defensive ways we may separate him from us. We need to drop our braced attitude, (referred to in *The Power of the Great*, Hex. 34 as a goat), and adopt a just and moderate view of his mistakes and transgressions.

Sixth Line: *Fellowship with men in the meadow. No Remorse.* Here we see that the way of the Sage is the only path to follow. However, since we still hold doubts, we do not achieve the happiness that comes from a truly enlightened understanding in which we see with clarity the great power that is aroused by following the path of the true and the good. The way of the Sage appears to be more difficult than it is.

14.

Ta Yu / Possession in Great Measure

Li
―――
Ch'ien

(Now you understand.)

Possession in great measure refers to the state of self-possession and inner independence we have achieved through perseveringly and sincerely trying to find the correct way. In this state we unconsciously manifest the Higher Power.

Possession in great measure also refers to any improvement in our attitude or circumstance. Inner independence is a possession acquired from having overcome self-pity; the correct path is a possession acquired when we have returned from wrong-doing; a feeling of self-worth is a possession acquired through self-discipline and self-development. Other possessions include relief from money problems, and reuniting with someone from whom we have long been estranged.

This hexagram states unequivocably that if we truly possess a thing it cannot be lost or destroyed. What we have gained—the progress earned through our hard work—cannot be lost, in spite of temporary setbacks.

Disruptions in our relationships provide occasions for improving attitudes and for learning Cosmic lessons. Sometimes the situation resembles having lost one's credit card. When the card will be returned, we cannot know, but we are assured by this hexagram that renewal of a relationship is not dependent solely on our credit-worthiness, but on the other's as well; in any event, the relationship will be restored when the time is right.

Fire in heaven shines far.... describes the effect we have on others that comes from having attained the clarity of mind, detachment, and inner strength which the *I Ching* calls "possession in great measure." This effect is not something we can create through intention, or effort; it occurs when we are in harmony with the Cosmos.

One of our primary spiritual goals is to maintain 'great possession,' or harmony with the Creative. Such harmony exists so long as when, in our inmost mind, we conscientiously serve the true and the good. Although we may be required by our principles to withdraw from others and go on alone, we remain open-minded about them. In recognizing what is incorrect, we make no attempt to justify or overlook their wrong actions; we do, however, maintain a just and moderate view of them. We neither condemn nor mentally execute them, nor do we hold them forever in mental imprisonment. In the face of evil we take care not to become infected with the inferior thing, but retreat and maintain our standards without falling into alienation or vindictiveness.

Possession in great measure means that power accompanies our inner sense of the truth of situations. Recognizing that an evil is occurring carries with it the full impact of punishment mentioned in *Biting Through* (Hex. 21), and of imprisonment mentioned in *The Wanderer* (Hex. 56). It is important, in light of this power, that we make certain our thoughts remain moderate and just, for if they become infected with anger, feelings of retribution, or alienation, we abuse power, creating more obstructions, setbacks, and injustices. The power for good is inseparably connected to a moderate viewpoint and a modest attitude.

The attainment of possession in great measure is the result of continuous, conscientious effort. Through this effort we 'come to meet' the Creative halfway, and thus invoke its help. From putting forth 100% effort to undermine our ego, we form a 50/50 partnership with the Creative.

Once this partnership is formed, we must be careful not to abuse the power generated. The danger exists that having inner freedom, we may become too cool; having detachment, we may become too hard; having inner strength, we may think we have the right to feelings of disdain and alienation. Having a sense of the truth of things, we may interfere to "straighten things out." On attaining success we may think "we did it" all by ourselves. Precisely at the peak of great possession (a state of mind of which we are hardly conscious), our ego seeks to claim victory. We must not forget that our success is really a gift from the Higher Power.

While in a state of 'possession,' if we will sacrifice our right to justifiable anger, and relinquish any feelings of self-pity, along with the right to defend our point of view when challenged, we will succeed in remaining modest, thereby honor our teacher and guide, the Sage.

Another temptation, once we have begun to grow secure, is to seek vindication for our views and recognition of our way of life. This constitutes a return to dependency on others and a loss of the independence that leads to possession in great measure. Through achieving inner independence our way of life is empowered, and we unconsciously influence others. If we then seek to retain this influence, we once more lose our inner independence. If we resist the temptation to be dependent on the effect we are having (or are not having) on others, we will maintain our inner independence and the unconscious power associated with it.

First Line: *No relation with what is harmful; there is no blame in this.* Great possession means that we are now relating to the situation correctly, consequently the situation has improved and progress has been made. A correct viewpoint always confers feelings of inner independence. However, if inner independence fails to be combined with humility and reserve, others' egos are aroused. A display of independence creates envy in others, while exuberant self-confidence creates feelings of insecurity and inferiority. They then begin to challenge us in the "king-of-the-heap" game, and win it if they can generate any reaction by which we once again lose our inner independence. This can happen only if we allow our ego to glory in independence, or to indulge in exuberance and presumption. We should remain disengaged, neither responding to flattery, by which we presume matters to be better than they are, nor to challenges which make us feel defensive, causing us to contend, strive, and put ourselves forward. We must allow those who seek to engage us emotionally to go their own way. Only when they realize that such challenges lead nowhere will they make an effort to correct themselves.

Often this line refers to being tempted to halt our forward progress. We wish to stop and enjoy the good effect created by our inner independence and self-discipline. We fail to realize that the continued improvement of the situation is tied to our continued independence and self-discipline. We must not slide back into dependence and selfishness, which would reawaken others' egos. We need to keep steady and detached from them whether we make progress or not. At the heart of the *I Ching* way is 'going on.' We are not meant to stop and indefinitely picnic by the wayside, but get back on the path and go on.

It is a Cosmic rule that in seeking to hold onto joy (or progress) for the purpose of luxuriating in it, we lose it. Joy may be experienced, and feelings of close communion with another may be felt, but whenever we seek to prolong these moments, or dwell on them, or luxuriate in them, or possess them, we lose the inner independence on which such moments depend. They may only be received and experienced; we must always let them go, and go forward with no attempt to hold onto them, or to reproduce them.

Joy (or progress) is something we may neither construct nor possess; it is something which results from being in the right relationship to the situation. It comes as a gift from the Higher Power, in its own way, in its own time. We cannot make it occur, or make it stay. If we can accept such gifts when they come, and let go of them when they go, we will find ourselves blessed with more and more gifts.

Second Line: *A big wagon for loading. One may undertake something. No blame.* Although we have made mistakes, our recognition of these mistakes and our sincerity in trying to correct them means that we have obtained able helpers from the hidden world who will clear up the situation. As a consequence, our mistakes will not lead to embarrassment, or to a deterioration of our general situation.

Third Line: *A prince offers it to the Son of Heaven. A petty man cannot do this.* This line calls for sacrificing something we possess, such as justifiable anger, or a feeling of rights. Sacrifice, in the *I Ching*, refers to giving up emotions that comfort us—negation, desire, ambition, or anger—for the good of the situation. One such "right" is the careless presumption that God, or the Sage, isn't living up to "his bargain" to help us attain success. The Sage cannot react to such inner demands. Such culprits in our attitude perpetuate the vicious circle of no progress—the endless slipping of the "Wheel of Fate" when it is stuck in the mud of our emotional self-vindication.

This line also means to sacrifice the sense of power that comes from having possession in great measure as a state of mind—the intoxicating carelessness which causes us to seek a name, honor, and followers. Here lies the threat of the Inferior Man who would seize power and rule the world. We must guard against abandoning

67

the humility we need to keep steadily on our path.

Fourth Line: *He makes a difference between himself and his neighbor. No blame.* It is important not to get caught up in doing what the rest of the world does—react in customary ways to what is, from our perception, going wrong. We need to remember that in disengaging—turning the problem over to the Cosmos to solve—whatever is right will prevail, but not if we do not really let go. This is the difference between doing things the *I Ching* way and doing things the way one's neighbor might do them.

This line also means that we should not compete with people who seem to have more influence than we do. We need to realize that our inner sense of truth has a far greater influence than do those who rely on external means.

This line also refers to times when we see other people's inferiors getting away with things. Our ego then arises in the form of impatience and ire as we concentrate on "what should happen." In this activity our inferiors are enviously engaged. We need to disengage, and to cease looking aside.

We "make a difference" between ourself and others when we disengage and cease watching what they do. In looking aside we doubt their ability to succeed on their own, or to understand, or to do the right thing, or to be guided by the Sage. Looking aside causes us to deviate from our own direction.

Fifth Line: *He whose truth is accessible, yet dignified, has good fortune.* This line warns that in making our inner feelings available to others, we should avoid becoming expansively friendly. Our manner and independence are having the correct effect, but being too friendly would invite insolence, and a reversal of the good effects of our work.

Sixth Line: *He is blessed by heaven....Nothing that does not further.* If in the fullness of power (inner independence), we remain conscientious and careful (modest), we will keep envy and mistrust dispersed. Conscientiousness honors the Sage and expresses the principles of the *I Ching*. In following this way we find joy in a job well done.

15.

Ch'ien / Modesty

<u>K'un</u>
Kên

(Go forward constantly, conscientiously, despite mistakes.)

Mountain within the earth. The mountain wears down to become the plain. This is the image of modesty—a state of becoming—an attitude of patient conscientiousness in trying to do what is correct. The hexagram counsels us to rid ourself of ostentation (the heights) and to develop our character (fill in the depths). Ostentation often refers to indulging in some form of justification because we distrust following the truth.

Ostentation is involved when we carelessly presume that small bad habits or indulgences do not matter. For example, it is ostentatious to indulge in any form of careless abandon. During such moments we lose contact with our inner self, thereby lose our awareness, both of opportunity to serve the higher good, and of danger. Careless abandon occurs when we get caught up in striving to influence, or when we get lost in self-assertion. It is our responsibility, in serving the true and the good, to keep attuned to our inner voice.

It is also ostentatious to impatiently distrust that things will work out without our interference. Distrust causes us to contrive results, and to skip the small steps that lead to real progress.

It is ostentatious to follow the good only because it leads to a selfish goal. The transformation of character that occurs through ridding ourself of ostentation represents the attainment of modesty. Through sincerely correcting himself, the *superior man carries things to completion.* When we learn to follow the true and the good for no reason at all, we will have understood the true meaning of modesty.

Receiving this hexagram implies that we need to contemplate the many aspects of modesty. In practice, modesty means we allow ourselves to be led by the Higher Power without inner resistance. Resistance can take subtle forms. For example, our ego would have us memorize rules and create prescribed ways of approaching problems because in this way it can retain leadership of our personality. To avoid the ego's encroachment we need to remain unstructured and not allow ourselves to be seduced by plans and schemes.

Modesty means that while we hold to our values and principles, we remain receptive to our inner voice and open to the chance elements which provide the opportunity to say or do the right thing. Such opportunities always occur at surprising moments, particularly when we have an open, alert, and unstructured attitude. The second line of *The Receptive* (Hex. 2) notes that the ingredients are already on hand for dealing with problems that arise; we need add nothing or take anything away; we need only be alert to recognize these elements and utilize them when they show themselves. The *I Ching* also says in the fifth line of *Holding Together* (Hex. 8), that we should hunt only "the animal which voluntarily exposes itself," and not "slaughter all." This warns us against trying to achieve more than the situation makes possible. It is modesty to restrain the desire to make leaps of progress.

Striving indicates that our ego resists the situation, and distrusts where the path leads. It does not want to be 'called into action' by events and be the actor on the stage (the modest thing to do), it wants to be the critic in the audience who approves and disapproves of everything that happens. Modesty is to allow ourselves to be dependent on the Cosmos.

Another example of immodest activity occurs when we ask the Sage for guidance and then subject him to cross-examination. Modesty expresses itself when we resist the inner voices of doubt and hold an open mind. This does not mean we are expected to believe with blind trust, but rather that we remain open-minded and patient enough to give the Sage's counsel a chance to prove its trustworthiness. Modesty is inconsistent either with blind faith or blind disbelief. Modesty is found in simplicity and openness, and in an active resistance to negative habits of mind—the arrogant presumptions which shut us off, either from the help of the Sage, or from the potential for good that other people have, and from the possibilities inherent in the unexpected.

To give up on people is arrogantly to disbelieve in the power of the Creative to achieve the unlikely. Who are we to deny this potential by our doubt, a doubt which blocks its regenerating power? Only the Sage knows how to make things work to our true best interests; it is modesty to keep our minds open, and to recognize that the zig-zag path of the Creative works to the benefit of all, whereas the straight path created by our ego serves only narrow self-interest, and often works to the detriment of others.

First Line: *Only the superior man modest about his modesty may cross the great water* (achieve great things). When we have adhered perseveringly to what is right, we tend to become proud and disdainful of others, including the Sage. We tend to become more aggressive—demanding rewards, expecting good things to happen, and using power. Neither the Sage nor anyone else can adhere to the expectations of our ego without losing his integrity. If we work at our task with simplicity we will succeed. It is best to go forward and not allow our inferiors to keep looking back (or aside) with doubt and regret, as if we have expended energy to no avail.

This line also refers to having the modesty to be reticent; it is modesty to approach the business of helping others modestly; we do not hasten to offer ourselves, to intervene importantly, or to usurp others' space to learn. Modesty makes good use of silence and reserve. Modesty is to venture forth at appropriate times.

Second Line: *Modesty that comes to expression. Perseverance brings good fortune.* On a practical basis, modesty means that we remain disciplined and reserved when we would rather let ourselves go to enjoy the moment; we 'bite through' obstructions by holding strictly to our standards when we would rather be lenient and overlook others' insensitivity or misdeeds. We also disperse anger when we would rather give vent to it. When we hold with determination to these principles, a good influence on others cannot be prevented.

Following the good means that we carefully supervise and control the contents of our attitude so that we keep free from the fear and doubt which cause us to contrive and manipulate our way through life. This also means we stop listening to impatience, self-pity, anger, apprehension, and other emotions which dissolve our will to keep open and humble. We silence those deluded inferiors who enthusiastically seek ways to skip steps to achieve quick, visible progress. We withdraw from aggrieved feelings and from watching others for signs of change. We dispense with our super-visory attitude and cease going over old wounds. A modest attitude

71

accepts that it is the way of the Sage to achieve our goals by finding in events the correct way to proceed. We pre-structure nothing, but rely only on what we already have learned from the *I Ching* of duty and a correct sense of limits. We take our cue from events, and look to the essence of each matter put before us. This is to 'go with the flow.'

Third Line: *The superior man of modesty and merit carries things to conclusion. Good fortune.* This line often means that we should not pause in our progress to become indolent or resistant in attitude. Now is not the time to sit back and luxuriate in our gains, or develop an enthusiasm to carelessly risk them in the hopes of gaining still more. We should expect to make progress only by continuing our hard work. It is important that we avoid developing a wrong attitude toward what we have achieved (our possessions) by not allowing ourselves to be dazzled by a sudden relaxation in tensions.

Carrying things to conclusion also means that if we have persevered in doing what is right and then begin to reflect on it, pride arises. We may be tempted to think we are more than we are, setting ourselves above others pretentiously. Criticism then comes from the hidden world and we lose the help we need to complete our task. It is best to be rid of self-congratulation and egoistic feelings of superiority. Rather than looking back on what we have done, we should continue at our task.

Sometimes this line concerns tolerating within ourself a 'spiritual irritation.' We have done the right thing, therefore we become irritated with those who do not; this irritation stops our progress and prevents us from carrying our work to completion. We should carefully avoid self-righteousness, and wanting to achieve more than the situation allows.

Fourth Line: *Nothing that would not further modesty in movement.* We should strive only to control our inferiors' lack of discipline, especially their wanting to stop and luxuriate in the progress gained. We must also resist the baby in ourself who wishes to indulge in self-pity and doubt. Similarly, we need to unhorse the white knight who boldly seeks to do battle with evil in his rush to reach the goal. In such modest ways we serve the ruler and show an interest in our work. A sincere interest in culling out all that is inferior cannot but succeed.

Fifth Line: *No boasting of wealth before one's neighbor.* References to "boasting," "wealth," and to "riding in a carriage" generally refer to our assuming rights and privileges. We "boast" when we think we can do wrong, or indulge incorrect thoughts without incurring harmful results. In wanting a cozy relationship with someone, we abandon the inner independence and reserve that is essential to relating correctly to his insensitivity.

If such a person has reacted favorably to our reserve, this should not give rise to the rationale that he has finally corrected himself, so that now we may ignore any small signs that might indicate the reforms to be of a surface, or temporary nature. It is our duty to 'make certain of those around us' by paying attention to whether they are truly sensitive to us. We should also pay attention to any laxity which would cause self-indulgence. In a self-indulgent frame of mind we no longer see opportunities to relate constructively. In losing self-discipline, we also lose inner independence, therefore our creative impact. As the fourth line of *The Ting* (Hex. 50) puts it, "the Prince's meal is spilled and his person soiled."

To attack with force sometimes means that we must state our position straightforwardly, saying what we are, or are not, willing to do, or join others in doing. Such severity, however, must fall within the limits of modesty and objectivity, so that we are never personally offensive.

Sixth Line: *Modesty that comes to expression. It is favorable to set armies marching to chastise one's own city and one's country.* Modesty comes to expression when we discipline ourself for indulging self-pity, or for listening to false nourishment. The superior man really works at his modesty.

This line is similar to the top line in *Limitation* (Hex. 60), which mentions that there are times when only by limiting ourselves in the strictest manner can we avoid remorse. (Remorse occurs, for instance, when we continue to listen to the rationales of inner conflict.) The truly modest person is so conscientious that he is willing, if necessary, to set armies marching against his own inferiors, and to catch, and even "kill," if need be, the obstinate ringleaders of evil—vanity and pride.

Perhaps we need to ask if we are allowing a pride system to operate which would, if we listen to it long enough, shut out others as impossible, or conclude that the Creative is neither able nor willing to help.

16.

Yü / Enthusiasm

$$\frac{\text{Chên}}{\text{K'un}} \quad \begin{array}{c} \equiv\equiv \\ \equiv\equiv \end{array}$$

(The path of least resistance is nonresistance.)

Movement that meets with devotion refers to behavior that is correct and just. Such behavior is founded on the humility of acceptance, and on modesty and reticence, therefore it inspires willing adherence, and gives rise to the image of setting armies moving. Setting armies moving may mean that we have rallied good elements in people who are otherwise indifferent. It may also mean that help, in the form of timely, beneficial circumstance, comes from the Cosmos.

This hexagram discusses three kinds of enthusiasm: (1) inspiration to follow a path because we see with clarity that it is correct; (2) inspiration we create in others through being balanced and correct within ourself; and (3) the deluded enthusiasm that springs from our ego.

While receiving this hexagram may indicate that we have "set armies moving in our behalf," it more often indicates that our behavior, or attitude, has inhibited others' willing adherence, or has blocked the help of the Higher Power. Through listening to, or tolerating, our ego's wanting, wondering, or worrying, we develop enthusiasm for the solutions it proposes—a deluded enthusiasm.

Solutions suggested by the ego would seem to propel us straight to our goals; we become so entranced with the image of success that we are blinded to the ego's selfish, vain, and childish motives. This enthusiasm is the opposite of that which occurs when we realize that by working patiently and steadily on correcting and balancing our inner attitude, the obstructions which stand between us and our goals will disappear by themselves.

Balancing our attitude puts us in alignment with the Tao—the way in which flows the creative energy of the universe. It involves being open to the hidden and diverse ways in which the Cosmos works to benefit all. We patiently allow ourself to be used by the

Master Playwright in the creative drama. Whether we are needed to play a leading role or to work backstage, we remain ever alert to do the new thing required of us.

Ego elements are always present when we contrive solutions, strive to influence, adopt postures or attitudes, or press ourselves on others. Among the ego's more subtle activities are its efforts to "be devoted." Such activities are based on the idea that obsessive effort will work. No matter how single-minded or obsessive we become, ego-guided effort will fail. Sincerity in trying to find the correct way is required, but sincerity does not mean we lose our inner balance. To be balanced within is to mirror the Cosmos and the Tao.

The *I Ching* guides us toward the ordinary rather than the extraordinary. Our proper business is to relate correctly to the challenges of everyday life. Our ego, however, would have us believe that the first order of business is to work on the greater world problems. Everything put to us by our ego is grandiose. We are supposed to be heroes to the world. The Sage, on the other hand, would have us concern ourselves with the mundane. Instead of standing out, being recognized, seeking to be king-of-the-heap, we learn to do good invisibly. Instead of seeking recognition, we let go of our achievements. As Lao Tzu said, "The Sage does his work without setting any store by it, accomplishes his task without dwelling on it."

Once we accept our destiny to develop ourselves spiritually, our ego joins the effort and soon begins searching for a faster, more direct way to "get there." In doing so it applies monumental, self-chastising, and self-congratulatory effort. By contrast, the way of the Sage is reticent, self-forgiving, and modest. The goal is to follow the path with patient, modest acceptance. Indeed, the goal is only to follow the path, for there is no "there" to get to; there is only the path, and the job of treading upon it as well as we can.

It soon becomes evident that the problems we bring to the Sage are vehicles which the Cosmos uses to teach and correct us. Indeed, our everyday life provides all that we need in order to grow and find life's meaning. We need not travel afar, or seek exotic experiences. There is no need to retire to a cloister, seeking the perfect setting for spiritual development. Everyday life presents us with all the situations we need to develop patience, modesty, restraint, and an open mind. The path of self-development presents us with necessary periods of isolation from others. Later the isolation ends and we are put to use by the Cosmos. Thus, life seems to be an anvil, Fate a hammer for shaping our spiritual awareness.

Our ego would make spiritual development a hero's quest for the Holy Grail. It sees itself sharing mysteries with the select few. Such a deluded enthusiasm only repels others, and engages their distrust and resistance to following the good. To flow with time, to accept life modestly as it comes, to seek only to be sincere in one's way of life and true to oneself—this is the way of the Tao.

When deluded, monumental effort brings failure, we experience an emotional condition known as "darkening of the light" (see Hex. 36, Line 1). In this state of mind we are attacked by a series of childish emotions which trap us in a vise of negative thinking. Caught between fear and doubt, we contend with Fate and resist it, fearing that without renewed effort, or a change of course to find an easier way, we will be stuck in the losing position. We resort to inferior means because we doubt we can obtain help from the Higher Power. Doubt is like a shark that devours all the elements in our nature which we have disciplined to be patient and obedient. To stop this vise-like action it is necessary to decrease our childish emotions. We must cease listening to thoughts which harp on a perceived loss of face, or on a loss of influence. We must cease fantasizing how we appear in others' eyes. Such dependence on personal success comes from the ego. Unlike the Superior Man, who is willing to work in a background position, the Inferior Man insists on being recognized (see *The Receptive*, Hex. 2, Line 3). Instead of allowing the light to shine through him, he stands in its way. Finally, on perceiving that it must be decreased, the ego asks, "How much must I decrease myself?" The answer is: "Until there is no more resistance, until the ego gives up, and only humble acceptance and dependence remain." Only selfless humility sets armies moving in our behalf.

Once the difficult situation eases we need to be careful of the enthusiasm which accompanies a sudden release from pressure. We especially should avoid the deluded enthusiasm that powerful actions have been responsible for the results achieved. Our ego always believes that it alone has the power to manipulate events—a deluded and dangerous point of view.

Reverence for the ancestors refers to a thoughtful regard for the many people, famous and unknown, who have preceded us on the spiritual path. They were no better equipped than we are; they experienced the same trials and tribulations we experience. Attaining a certain enlightenment, they resisted adopting images of themselves as enlightened; they simply persevered and were faithful to the end. Through reflecting on their perseverance and patience, we are helped to keep steady on our path, and to bridge the chasm of our fears. We honor them when we correct our attitude and return to the true and the good within ourself.

First Line: *Boasting of aristocratic connections.* It is boastful to indulge incorrect thoughts or acts on the assumption that nothing harmful will result. All careless, arrogant attitudes have negative effects. We boast when we indulge feelings of irritation, alienation, or superiority; when we condemn others for their mistakes; when we peevishly think "shoulds" or "should nots"; when we decide to overlook others' incorrect actions in order to get along with them. The correct course, on observing other people's mistakes, is to disengage and keep still within. If we feel the need to display negative feelings, as when we resist or reject the situation, it is because we doubt that the Creative power will be aroused by retaining our innocence and purity of mind.

To think we have earned certain rights and then to stand presumptuously on those rights, this is also to "boast of aristocratic connections." It may be that we have earned something, but we may not presume, act, or think arrogantly, without regard to the limits of our path, or without regard to our responsibilities to the Sage, our teacher.

Second Line: *Firm as a rock.* The superior man is watchful to perceive the point in every situation at which he is tempted to become emotionally involved. He knows that this is the point at which his ego awakens, demanding to be acclaimed and verified. Precisely then he retreats and disengages. In this way he preserves his integrity, and keeps his inner balance.

Confucius's commentary on this line counsels us to "know the seeds...the first imperceptible beginning of movement." The "seeds" of involvement begin with slight moods of discontentment, vague feelings of restlessness, or swelling feelings of enthusiasm. If these seeds of action are not immediately recognized and resisted, they are swiftly followed by active discontent, or uncontrolled movement which sweeps us away from inner independence and

77

disengagement. Thus, we are counselled to withdraw in time.

Third Line: *Looking upwards* means that we look to Fate to rescue us, even though we argue on and on, plunging deeper into controversy, compromising our inner worth. Conflict may involve arguing with others, or refer to an inner conflict precipitated by adopting a set, negative view of a situation or person. Rather than looking to Heaven to bring these conflicts to an end, we must end them by ceasing to take part in them, by accepting that we do not know the answers, and by enduring the ambiguity of the situation until clarity returns; we resist indulging the petty irritations that prevent our good influence on others.

Fourth Line: *The source of enthusiasm. Doubt not. You gather friends around you as a hair clasp gathers the hair.* The source of enthusiasm lies in holding to our path, free of disbelief, because it is correct. We gather others to follow the good when our knowledge of the way is so strong that doubt can no longer invade our inner serenity; when we no longer feel any need to convince, contend with, or woo people; when we no longer try to employ giant steps or to skip steps in order to make swift progress; when we no longer try to achieve something without working for it. All such activity comes from the ego, which secretly holds to doubt and disbelief. Inner independence is the power that sets armies moving toward what is good. We can act correctly only when we have seen, with insight, that the correct attitude leads to success. If we are still guessing, or hoping, or if we are still attached obsessively to a particular idea, we do not see clearly, and thus lack the support of the Cosmos.

If any problem exists in our attitude, it is doubt. The hexagram counsels, "Doubt not." People cannot, and should not, fight against the debilitating power of our doubts.

Fifth Line: *Persistently ill, and still does not die.* The situation is difficult and uncomfortable. We are still under the influence of our ego, which strives to achieve results, or hedges to prevent them. However, our discomfort is useful in causing us to seek out the attitudes which block progress. The correct attitude is nothing short of relinquishing totally the resistance and longing put forward by the childish heart.

Sixth Line: *Deluded enthusiasm. But if, after completion, one changes, there is no blame.* Deluded enthusiasm refers to times when the Inferior Man (ego) leads our personality. The Inferior Man relies on action, outward display, schemes, obsession, and devices to force progress, and on retaliatory measures to right wrongs. The Inferior Man rules when we project a brusque or angry front, or when we seek to advance ourselves by wooing and flattering. Only when we have the strength to forsake the inferior means founded on fear and doubt, are we able to find the correct route to success.

17.

Sui / Following

$$\frac{\text{Tui}}{\text{Chên}} \quad \begin{array}{c} \rule{1.2em}{0.08em}\ \rule{1.2em}{0.08em} \\ \rule{1.2em}{0.08em}\ \rule{1.2em}{0.08em} \\ \rule{2.6em}{0.08em} \\ \rule{2.6em}{0.08em} \\ \rule{1.2em}{0.08em}\ \rule{1.2em}{0.08em} \\ \rule{2.6em}{0.08em} \end{array}$$

(Follow one's values, no matter how difficult this seems.)

Following has supreme success. What we "follow" is our sense of what is essential, just, and correct. To be loyal to the good and the true within oneself is to serve the Higher Power.

Only by being loyal and true to ourself are we able to be loyal and true to others, and in turn able to command their enduring loyalty.

As students of universal truth, we are automatically servants of the Higher Power. As such, we are meant to obtain a following among others. Through following what is true and good in our own natures we give others the confidence to follow what is good and great in theirs. Even though for a time they may servilely attach themselves to us, we must not be flattered and tie them to us. Instead of encouraging their dependence, we keep free of this attachment, and thus keep them free. Even if this means that they then fall into error by childishly attaching themselves to someone else, we pave the way for their eventual liberation from hesitation and fear to follow the good within themselves. This is the sort of following meant when the *I Ching* counsels us to rescue others.

This hexagram makes it clear that before we may engage others in following us, we must understand the principles of following. Leading and following are inseparably related. People may follow us without coming to harm only if we are directed toward what is good and correct. Our devotion to finding the correct way for ourself creates the inner independence needed to command from others their respect and loyalty. No law or legal obligation can enforce another's loyalty. Fear to do wrong either creates only a begrudging compliance, or a stubborn resistance. What we seek is a secure, willing, and heartfelt compliance with the good and the true.

Following the truth means that we "go with" our inner sense of truth the way an equestrian "throws his heart across the fence" before jumping. By clinging to truth we allow it to lead us to the correct solutions to our problems. We cling to inner truth (inner awareness) as if it were the North Star laying out a path across the ocean, guiding us toward that which we cannot see. In following what is high and good within ourself we are in partnership with the Sage who knows how and when to make the impossible succeed.

The greatness of truth enables us to follow it with joy. Often we do not follow our sense of truth. We fear that others will not understand us, and that we will become isolated, or that we will lose our chance to influence a situation for the better. We are also taught by our Western culture that to achieve our goals we must contrive, or force them to happen. This hexagram counsels that all good is achieved simply by following the good within. There is no need to contrive, interfere, or force ourself on others. When we do that we follow the inner child who whines and wants only luxury.

We often receive this hexagram because we become resistant in attitude, angry that the situation has not yet been resolved. We may have gone so far as to think of rejecting our fate to rescue the others, and to abandon serving the high and the good. We must not give up, even though we have momentarily lost our inner independence. We need to disengage from our emotions and renew our determination to follow the good, even though it seems that we have waited beyond a reasonable time for improvement. To remain engaged is to remain under the control of our ego.

We need to remember that we become impatient because of reverses. These reverses, we must realize, are due to some sort of personal indulgence. Basking in the comfort of progress we have gained, we sometimes grow egotistically expansive. This, in turn, opens the door to the re-emergence of egotism and transgressions by others, which, in our self-indulgent mood, we overlook. By overlooking their errors, we give them inches, and they take miles. We cannot afford in the slightest degree to relax into self-indulgence, or to appease bad habits in others (see *After Completion*, Hex. 63, Line 4).

First Line: *To go out of the door in company* means to remain open and accessible to people. The *I Ching* notes that we can only lead others if we ourselves follow the good. We achieve nothing if we shut ourselves off because they do not follow the path. Remaining open and accessible to "all sorts of people, friends or foes," is the "only way to accomplish anything."

Openness, however, does not mean that we abandon our principles. We cling to these principles, aware that events will somehow provide the means by which truth becomes self-evident. Thus, we do not throw ourself away in quarrels over "questions of current opinion," nor do we strive to explain the truth to a resistant attitude. We allow the opportunity for truth to emerge; if the situation permits, we may point to it, providing we have not abandoned reticence. As the second line of *The Receptive* (Hex. 2) puts it, there exists in every situation the means for its correction. We need only remain open for these means to show themselves. Most often, however, only our awareness is needed, for this awareness communicates to others on the inner plane.

Second Line: *If one clings to the little boy....*The "small boy" represents the childish part of ourselves. When we listen to its wants, dissatisfactions, and impatience, we lose our strong and persevering self. The small boy can be a conveniently hostile view of a situation, or compulsive energy which drives us to contending and contriving, and to using leverage because the small boy feels that force is necessary. The little boy acts when he ought not act, and in a cowardly manner holds back when the essence of the situation requires that he move forward. Our childish self seeks, as its right, to enjoy and protect the progress made, but this right must be sacrificed if one is to serve that which is higher. We must do what duty and fidelity to the truth command, even if doing so would seem to jeopardize all we have gained. In letting go of inferior means we let go of the small boy in ourselves. The path of the beautiful cannot be achieved by inferior means.

Third Line: *If one clings to the strong man....One parts company with the inferior and superficial.* What is inferior and superficial is a comfortable relationship that suits our prejudices, or an indulgent relationship in which we overlook what is incorrect, turning our backs on following and doing what truth requires.

In the pursuit of comfort people seek nourishment for their self-images at the expense of dignity and self-esteem. They give in order to get. Such relationships, in contrast to those based on respect, are superficial, and they cannot last. The ego, once fed, expands its appetite. When we see this truth with clarity, we are able to relinquish the easy road of comfort. Although doing so may entail a sense of loss, the loss is more than compensated for by inner growth and self-esteem. (Self-esteem is not something we can create by assuming ourselves to be "okay," as in "I'm Okay, You're Okay"; self-esteem always results from having made hard choices to follow the good, whatever the risk, and however alone and jeopardized that may make us feel at the time.)

Fourth Line: *Following creates success.* Danger arises from the success we have in influencing others. It is ironic that as soon as we attain an influence with others through pursuing the solitary path of conscious innocence, reserve, and inner independence, we begin to consider ways to keep that influence. Thus once more we become dependent on the relationship. This line counsels that "to go one's way with sincerity brings clarity." In not being turned aside by considerations and desires, we keep our ego under control.

To go one's way with sincerity also means not to erect barriers to forgiveness, as when our inferiors flatter us by saying, "those who have wronged us must meet with justice." We find that our ego goes along with us for a time, but then puts up its demands. To be sincere is to be completely free of ego demands, intent only on what is essential and correct.

This line can also refer to others being insincere with us.

Fifth Line: *Sincere in the good. Good fortune.* To follow our inner sense of truth wherever it takes us is to follow good with sincerity and devotion. Such sincerity meets with the assent of the Cosmos. The person who is sincere in following his inner sense of truth constantly asks himself what is essential and correct. In his heart he humbly asks the Sage to help him find the correct way. He keeps armed against evil by searching his mind for considerations, motives, and moods that would destroy a just and moderate view of things, or which would tempt him to break with what is essential in relating to others.

Sixth Line: *He meets with firm allegiance and is still further bound.* The Sage, having previously retreated out of reach, returns to help the follower. The sincerity described in the fifth line meets with response. The Sage helps the follower to find the correct way. The image of the correct thing to do and the correct thing to say comes of itself at the moment we need it because we keep attuned to what is essential and correct. During such times we have the impression of being a conduit for something beyond ourself. A sense of inner peace and comradeship accompanies this mysterious help.

Just as the Sage returns to help the follower, we return to being open-minded to those who seek our help.

18.

Ku / Work on What Has Been Spoiled

Kên
Sun

(Correcting decadent habits of mind, and tolerating what is spoiled in others.)

Work on what has been spoiled has supreme success. The images presented by this hexagram are a bowl in which worms are breeding, three days, and human decadence as the cause of corruption.

A bowl in which worms are breeding is an analogy of the false ideas that we or others may have about the way things work. False ideas come from incomplete perceptions. Receiving this hexagram tells us that some of the perceptions and beliefs we have been taking for granted are incorrect. It also tells us to seek out any decadent ways in which we may be relating to the Sage, Fate, other people, or to our general situation. This search should include the way we react to incorrect treatment from others. Before we can progress further it is necessary to recognize and correct our faulty ideas and attitudes.

Three days symbolizes the three steps of self-correction: (1) the diligence required to seek out the defects, (2) the sincerity required to resolve ourself firmly against them, and (3) the resolution required to guard against their return.

The *I Ching* tends to be concerned with faulty perspectives and slanders on the truth. For example, a person allies himself with his ego in suspecting that God is not good, that Fate is hostile, that human nature is naturally defective, that life is only meant to be suffering, or that others cannot find the correct way without our intervention. We often accept such attitudes because they are commonly held. Holding them results in indifference to suffering and insensitivity to life. By tolerating them within ourself we unwittingly influence others to adopt them.

Other faulty attitudes include taking comfort in a vindictive or hard attitude; enjoying something at the expense of principle; assigning attributes of the Inferior Man to God, the Sage, or the Higher

Power; assuming these attributes are natural within ourself; giving up on ourselves or others; and speaking or thinking carelessly on the assumption that what we think or say, even lightly, has no great importance. When our treasured ideas and beliefs come to mind during an *I Ching* consultation, it is best to ask whether they are correct. Often the idea or belief that comes to mind is the very thing the *I Ching* is telling us to question.

This hexagram also shows the correct way to respond to others when they are insensitive, indifferent, or unjust. To respond correctly we need to attain an impersonal, Cosmic perspective. This requires that we dismiss or disperse anger, and rid ourselves of personal considerations such as desire or envy. It is also important to avoid ignoring or dismissing the problem because we lack a way of dealing with it. It is essential to recognize defective attitudes as such, but in a just and moderate context. As soon as our viewpoint becomes correct, the power of inner truth is activated to correct the problem.

If we focus on having a comfortable relationship, or overlook evil because of desire, we "tolerate what has been spoiled," and are unable to relate to the problem constructively. Evil comes into our lives mostly because we make room for it through not being strict with ourselves.

It is possible to correct spoiled relationships by correcting our own lax attitudes. These lax attitudes create problems which accumulate until the whole is spoiled. By correcting the attitudes, the resistances which have built up over time give way. Suspicion and distrust subside and the excesses we have encouraged find no basis to continue. Gradually the situation returns to balance and harmony. In waiting for situations to return to normal we may not use force or pressure. If it is to be truly resolved we must allow others the space and time to see that sincere self-correction is the only path to follow. If we are consistent in maintaining our neutrality and disengagement, and in holding to what is correct within ourself, others will perceive what is correct in relating to us. Our attitude signals that envy and insensitivity are unacceptable. Even though someone who has been relating to us incorrectly begins to approach in a friendly manner, we should remain reserved and cautious so long as there exist contradictions in his behavior. We should not presume that our goal has been achieved simply because we hope so.

Finally, work on what has been spoiled applies to social behavior in general. Public officials intuitively know the minds of the people they serve. If the attitudes of the people are lax, if they are willing to sacrifice the long-term good for short-term gain, then public officials will represent them accordingly. If in their inner attitudes the people are firm in what is correct, public officials will know how they must govern; regardless of the form of government, evil finds its basis in the weaknesses of the people. When the people are strong in their inner direction, and firm in their attitudes, evil in government, and in society can find no place in which to grow.

First Line:...*what has been spoiled by the father. Danger.* Here, spoiled behavior comes from family tradition. For example, a father spends money without reference to family needs, simply because his father did it, or a mother manipulates her husband because her mother did the same thing.

Another example of a decadent tradition is the way a family may regard some people as "important," and others as "unimportant." We perpetuate such spoiled attitudes when we try to impress some people, and disregard others insensitively.

Another spoiled attitude is the traditional view that to solve problems we must either intervene powerfully, or else meekly accept insult and injustice. In another spoiled attitude, we cling to tradition because we fear to depart from the "accepted viewpoint," even though we may know it to be incorrect. The correct way cannot be understood until we have the courage to let go of the crutch of tradition. We need to be aware that the correct remedy may not fit any of our preconceived ideas of what is correct, yet when it shows itself, we will know it to be perfectly appropriate. In the meantime we should only do what is essential to the moment.

If this line refers to another's decadence, we must let him go, trusting him to find his way alone, even though it be dangerous. If we doubt his ability to grow and correct himself, our doubt will inhibit his ability to rescue himself. Doubt is an actively destructive force, locking people into the vicious circle of no progress. We doubt people when we watch with our inner eye to see if there is progress.

Second Line:...*what has been spoiled by the mother. One must not be too persevering.* The mother's influence represents instilled fears that cause people to answer to tradition and form rather than to their inner sense of truth. Most often this line refers to religious fears. Childhood fears are retained in the demonic forms of the childish imagination. Invisible to the adult who harbors them, they dominate his motives and define his view of success. So long as he cannot see these fears he will defend them and project them onto others, sometimes violently. We must be patient with such people, exercising *a certain gentle consideration*, keeping aware that unreasoning fears underlie their behavior.

Third Line:...*a little remorse. No great blame.* This line refers to our having over-reacted (even if we have only thought in an overly reactive way) in dealing with our own or other people's inferiors. We are remorseful on seeing the consequences of our behavior, but there is "no great blame," for as the commentary says, it is better to be too energetic in correcting wrongs than not energetic enough.

Fourth Line: *Tolerating what has been spoiled [leads to] ...humiliation.* If to enjoy someone we accept his wrong-doings, we fail to "nourish" him properly, and we reinforce his spoiled behavior. This habit leads to our own humiliation, for in tolerating what is wrong we throw ourselves away. We must be inwardly firm about what is right and wrong, remaining reserved as long as his inferiors rule.

It is the same in tolerating, or "going along" with custom because doing so is more comfortable than feeling isolated. We need to be free of fear to do what we see with clarity as essential and correct to do. Having done what is essential, we need to be free from fear of the consequences. We can rely on truth.

Fifth Line: *Setting right what has been spoiled by the father. One meets with praise.* Working at self-correction draws help and praise from the Cosmos. Here, what has been spoiled refers to our tendency to be weak in dealing with self-indulgence, self-importance, and careless indifference, either in ourself or in others. For example, if we hesitate to withdraw when the situation requires it, we need to ask why we are afraid to do so. Are we afraid to let people go, to walk on alone, to endure? Does withdrawal seem too harsh, or ineffective? Do we believe that we ought to ignore evil in others? Do we do what they want, though it makes us uncomfortable, and we believe it incorrect?

First, we are obligated to recognize and admit to ourself when a thing is incorrect, otherwise, in our inner attitude we condone it. Second, we have no obligation to do what others want simply because they want it. We are not required by the Cosmos to respond, or to do anything to meet their expectations. It is incorrect to do things which make us feel uncomfortable and unbalanced. To rectify the situation we need only disengage from the feelings of obligation we have assumed, become firm in our inner attitude, and allow ourself to be guided around the difficulty. With this attitude the problem will resolve itself.

Receiving this line tells us that in rectifying what has been spoiled we have resumed the right path. Through correcting ourself we engage the power of the Creative, and thus have the correct effect on others. In renewing our attitude, the bad effects of our mistakes are nullified.

Sixth Line: *He does not serve kings and princes, sets himself higher goals.* Here, pursuit of our path has caused us to withdraw from others, or to withdraw from the conventional way that society does things. Withdrawal is correct, for only when we are free and firm in following our path can we meet each situation correctly. Once liberated we must guard against feeling critical, and against any temptation to give up on people or to abandon our duty to rescue them. We withdraw to keep ourself correct, and to deny other people's egos a basis for continuing the evil process.

We should not be afraid that self-development will lead to permanent isolation from others, or to impoverishment; these are oppressed views. By developing ourself the rescue of others will become possible. Only through self-development and serving that which is higher (universal truth), can we attain unity with others.

19.

Lin / Approach

$$\frac{\text{K'un}}{\text{Tui}}$$ ☷☱

(Better times approach.)

Approach has supreme success. Perseverance furthers. When the eighth month comes, there will be misfortune. Through developing a balanced, sincere, and conscientious attitude we acquire the assistance of the Sage, who approaches to help; as a result, times change for the better and tensions ease.

Along with this good news, however, the hexagram warns that we should arm ourselves against the tendency, when times have improved, to revert to a careless, self-defeating attitude. When tensions begin to ease, an arrogant self-confidence returns and we forget that the source of our good luck has been our simplicity, humility, and dependence on the Higher Power.

We should also avoid assuming that because we have invoked the Sage's help, that this help will continue indefinitely, or that we have earned it "forever." Little by little, as we grow careless, we no longer pay attention to encroachments by our Inferior Man (ego-self-image); we also give more latitude to our inferiors so that they lose their discipline; as we lose our sense of limits, we lose the help and support of the Sage. Thrown back on ourself, we allow our ego to resume the lead through returning to old habits of manipulating events, striving to influence, and interfering in other people's lives. All this can be avoided if we will conscientiously maintain inner discipline during good times.

This hexagram suggests the principle which occurs in a number of other hexagrams (notably *Peace* (Hex. 11), *Shock* (Hex. 51), and *After Completion* (Hex. 63)) which is best described by the image of 'going on.' Here, going on refers to an attitude that whether situations get better or worse, we remain emotionally detached and inwardly independent. That times are better should not indicate that it is time to let down our discipline, renew bad habits, or luxuriate in self-indulgence. We enjoy the moment, but we do not get lost in it;

we go on, almost without breaking step. This attitude is the embodiment of modesty (see *Modesty*, Hex. 15), because it requires a continuing conscientiousness. Going on fulfills the requirements for making progress (see *Progress*, Hex. 35) since it requires that we work at "brightening our bright virtue." Because we do not allow ourselves to indulge in an emotional high, we avoid a resulting emotional low, thus we maintain the inner steadiness that characterizes the Sage, a steadiness which enables us to achieve all our purposes (see *Duration*, Hex. 32).

First Line: *Joint approach. Perseverance brings good fortune.* Good times approach because, through making ourselves correct, we have achieved an alliance with the Sage. We should not, however, allow this improvement in conditions to give rise to hope and enthusiasm, which would cause us to lose our inner equilibrium. We make progress only so long as we persevere in trying to maintain a correct and firm attitude.

Second Line: *Joint approach. Good fortune. Everything furthers.* Although times change for the worse, we should not despair, but remain constant in resoluteness and inner equilibrium. This is possible if we remember that the Creative knows how to make use of every situation. Here, joint approach means that when we are in alliance with the Creative, both good and bad times further.

Third Line: *Comfortable approach. Nothing that would further. If one is induced to grieve over it, one becomes free of blame.* A comfortable approach refers to times when we forget to be careful of our inner thoughts; we relax our reserve and conscientiousness. This line signals us to be extraordinarily careful to keep our thoughts pure, and to maintain our reserve and caution in relating to people. When our influence increases, we tend to forget our limits; we luxuriate in feeling good about the progress made, presuming that our work is finished. In alliance with the Sage we have a responsibility to be strict with ourselves and firm in inner discipline and independence.

Fourth Line: *Complete approach. No blame.* While we must maintain a firm attitude, we must also take care to remain open-minded about others, just as the Sage is open-minded about us.

91

We also need to be open-minded about ourself: we can succeed; we can do what needs to be done.

Fifth Line: *Wise approach. This is right for a great prince. Good fortune.* After turning matters over to the Sage, we must not interfere because we suddenly develop doubts about what we cannot see. Sympathetic forces may be attracted only through modesty and restraint. It is wrong to take everything into our hands to achieve, or block. We need only allow things to happen without interfering.

Sixth Line: *Greathearted approach. Good fortune. No blame.* When we are firm in our principles, yet open-minded and compassionate, we attain a greathearted approach to life which is free of impatience with others' imperfections. This attitude invokes the help of the Sage. As the Sage humbles himself in a greathearted way to help us, a greathearted humility enables us to help others.

20.

Kuan / Contemplation (View)

$$\frac{\text{Sun}}{\text{K'un}} \quad \begin{array}{c} \equiv\equiv \\ \equiv\equiv \end{array}$$

(By one's thoughts one commands.)

This hexagram refers to attaining, through contemplation, the 'inner truth,' or Cosmic view of a situation. Receiving it means that we should ask the Sage for help in penetrating to the essence of the matter.

Once we become detached, either through contemplation or meditation, from the situation we observe, our understanding is able to reach the Cosmic level where our perspective is based on the principles of universal justice. On attaining this perspective our attitude comes into harmony with the Cosmos and influences the situation in a hidden, dynamic way, without conscious intention. The effect is so powerful that it unaccountably causes those in error to change their point of view. We need not say or do anything because our thoughts, having attained this perspective, command.

On attaining the inner truth, or Cosmic view of a situation, all duality disappears. In the duality of life, love and hate, like and dislike, justice and injustice, are inseparably paired. At the Cosmic level, however, this duality disappears. Love encompasses, yet is beyond self, hate, fear, attachment, rights, and desires. The territorial claims that accompany dualistic love are sublimated, yet satisfied in the higher truth. Adversative positions cease to exist and concepts of territory, possessions, and rights take on new meaning. In penetrating to the essence of the matter Cosmic justice may bypass territory, possessions, and rights. At other times, however, the essence of the matter can revolve around such mundane considerations. We cannot assume that the Cosmic view, in any given situation, will mimic our traditional concepts of justice, or of what is right. In contemplating each situation it is necessary to approach it with an entirely open mind, asking the Sage to guide us to see the matter correctly. When the view of the Sage penetrates through to us, we experience judgment that is not judgmental; patience, tolerance, and understanding replace petty likes and dislikes, and feelings of retribution. We are no longer insular and self-oriented, but see the underlying fears and wounds that create the weakness of spirit which plagues mankind.

The ablution has been made, but not yet the offering. Full of trust they look up to him. We understand, at least partially, but we do not act accordingly. We still have an inner opposition that obstructs following the good with true sincerity. It may be that we view another as an adversary. If we can "sacrifice" this view, or any similarly rigid definitions of the situation, or the people in it, we will unlock the elements which create opposition.

To search out and rid ourself of obstructing ideas is to perform inner cleansing, thus make an "offering." It helps to place obstructing ideas or attachments on a visualized inner altar, as a sacrifice to the Higher Power.

In observing people, we should not dwell on what is wrong with them, but realize that growth always involves mistakes and errors. We need to view others' wrongdoings in the context that everyone has false ideas of the way things work; because of these ideas they suffer eclipses of personality.

We also need to remind ourselves that the process of growth requires that things must expand fully before they can contract; a person who follows a dead-end road can give it up only if and when he clearly sees where it leads. Sometimes this means he must follow it to its very end.

By remembering our mistakes and deluded enthusiasms we are able to keep a modest, moderate, and just perception of others' mistakes, and we are able to keep our minds and spirits pure, and ourselves in balance.

The power of inner concentration...enables them to give expression to these laws in their own persons. The power of influencing others is increased by detachment and inner-independence, and diminished by attachment and doubt. The more we are firm in inner independence, and the more consistently we maintain our inner purity and beauty of spirit, the greater our influence becomes to achieve the good.

Sometimes, receiving this hexagram means that the problem referred to is hypothetical, meant to teach us a general principle. The lesson may be learned by contemplation rather than by having to go through a disagreeable experience. It also means that the lesson is applicable to all situations.

First Line: *Boylike contemplation. For an inferior man, no blame. For a superior man, humiliation.* We cannot expect others to follow the *I Ching* way, but we are certainly meant to follow it ourselves.

We are not meant to know everything. The ruling Sage is at work. His actions are beneficial even though we cannot understand them, and even though, taken piecemeal, they sometimes seem detrimental. This line implies that all events are part of larger events and forces now at work. The adversity we often see as Fate being against us is beneficial, because through it we grow spiritually.

Second Line: *Contemplation through the crack of the door.* Because we have been doing things correctly we expect to make great strides of visible progress. Just as our small, personal failures do not cause the general situation to fail, our personal successes do not immediately show as visible progress. All truly successful work occurs as minuscule progress. This slow progress, unlike quick, visible progress, endures. The person who develops himself must learn to trust the hidden power of his work, and to rely on progress that he cannot see. We also need to realize that the progress achieved has been sufficient to safeguard the situation. Receiving this line reassures us that this is so.

This line also refers to times when we are treated insensitively and to our taking the situation personally. We need to put the shortcomings of others into perspective: although our inner thoughts affect them and create progress, they continue to err because of pre-existing inner conditions and habits of mind. Continued progress depends on our remaining moderate, just, and impersonal in attitude. Because true progress is necessarily slow, we need to remain patient.

Third Line: *Contemplation of my life decides the choice between advance and retreat.* We may openly communicate with people (advance) when we feel no resistances and people are open to us. We must be careful, however, to avoid careless self-confidence, self-importance, and attachment, which manifest themselves as self-assertion. Checking ourselves (retreat) is necessary when we feel any attachment, urgency, impatience, or enthusiasm, for when the emotions enter we lose our connection with inner truth.

We need not worry about the time required to make progress; if we retain our humility everything will happen at the correct time. If we observe the principle of advancing with the openings and retreating with the closings, we will have placed the limits on ourselves which are essential to having a creative effect on people.

Fourth Line: *Contemplation of the light of the kingdom. It furthers one to exert influence as the guest of a king.* When we are in a position of influence we serve the Sage best if we retain our modesty, venturing forward only when and as far as openness and receptivity in others allows. Regardless of whether we like someone or not, it must be as if he were king and we his guest. We must not lose our dignity by being luxuriously expansive (giving way to our ego), or by losing contact with our inner voice so that we allow ambition, presumption, eagerness, and self-assertion to take over. We attempt to create an influence only because we doubt that openings will arise. If we can be content to allow any part we may play to arise of itself, we will rid the situation of the negative effects of doubt, and we will keep our ego out of the situation so that something constructive can be achieved. All that is important is that we remain receptive (see *The Receptive*, Hex. 2).

For the *I Ching* to be of help it must be honored, not used as a means to selfish ends. We make it inaccessible when we demand that it solve problems our way, on our timetable, and without any setbacks, or if we allow our ego to interject, "I'll try it but it probably won't do any good," or if we accept the answers that please but reject those that imply criticism. We honor and invoke the Sage's help when we remain modest and conscientious. When we forget to be conscientious, blame attaches to our progress.

The light of the kingdom is true and complete. The principles of the *I Ching* are to be applied to all situations; to do so lessens suffering in the world.

Fifth Line: *Contemplation of my life. The superior man is without blame.* Contemplation helps us understand the light of the king-dom—how things really work—and to find the path that is free of blame. This line refers perhaps more to meditation than to contemplation, for it is mostly through meditation that we are able to hear our inmost thoughts and contact our inmost feelings. In meditation we are able to see how our thoughts have power for good or for evil; we are able to see that correcting ourselves frees us from blame.

This line also states that our thoughts have hidden power; we may achieve great and good things simply by maintaining an open mind, and a humble acceptance of events. We regard every event and circumstance as capable of being used by the Creative to benefit all.

Thus it is said, the way of the Sage is true and complete.

Sixth Line: *To know how to become free of blame is the highest good.* Danger always approaches and we make mistakes; to see these mistakes and resolutely correct them is to know how to become free of blame. We sacrifice all emotional responses to which we feel entitled, for the general good. The Superior Man gives up doubt, returns to acceptance and perseverance, and ceases considering forceful ways of dealing with externals. The Superior Man corrects himself.

21.

Shih ho / Biting Through

$$\frac{\text{Li}}{\text{Chên}}$$ ☲ ☳

(Getting to the truth of the matter.)

Biting through refers to getting to the truth of the matter. An obstruction is pictured as preventing the lips from coming together, blocking access to nourishment. Nourishment, in this case, refers to attaining unity (harmony) with another person, the truth, or the Sage. This unity, or harmony, is vital nourishment for us as human beings. Before we can attain it we must discover what obstructs it. On discovering the obstruction, we experience a breakthrough in our understanding, "biting through," the obstruction.

Inasmuch as any idea, attitude, belief, or behavior pattern obstructs human unity, that idea or belief is based on a misunderstanding of the Cosmic truth. People misunderstand the truth because a "culprit" exists—an idea which "slanders" the truth. The most common slanders are false ideas about the nature or identity of God, human nature, the way we should respond to evil, and the way the Cosmos works.

On discovering something to be untrue (evil), unjust, or simply a mistake, we are meant to resolutely and firmly "bite through" it by acknowledging it, within ourselves, to be the case. We acknowledge it to be incorrect or wrong in no uncertain terms. We do not deny the truth because it is uncomfortable or inconvenient.

Acknowledging a thing to be right or wrong automatically and unconsciously conveys our perception to others with no conscious effort on our part. If we waver because we want to excuse something, or because we prefer not to be involved, or because we think it isn't "that bad," we send the perpetrators the misleading message that however they behave, it is all right; we send those who may see our behavior as an example, the message that it is not important to come to a decision on such matters. We do not have the right to do this.

Once we have acknowledged a thing to be wrong we must deal with the next question: what are we to do about it? The hexagram

98

answers that we must "let justice be administered." This means that once we have acknowledged the presence of an evil element, we turn it over to the Cosmos for resolution and correction; then we withdraw and think no more about it, so as not to become infected by it. Turning the matter over to the Cosmos activates the power of truth. However, if we consciously dwell on the problem in an alienated way, if we try to have some intentional effect, or if we intervene by powerful means, the power of truth cannot come to our aid. Involving ourselves in the matter means that our ego, which distrusts the corrective power of the Cosmos, has entered as the white knight in shining armor to do battle with the black knight of evil. The intervention of our ego bars the Higher Power from helping us. So long as we remain engaged with the problem, the Higher Power is not free to act.

The hexagram states that we must be energetic in biting through the obstacle to unity. It takes great energy to withdraw. Forgiveness means that we try to understand how people are motivated to do wrong. It is to understand the power that fear, doubt, and bad habits of mind have over people. It is also to understand that the Creative is capable of penetrating people's hearts and of enlightening their minds.

It is customary to think that to forgive also means to forget; this is not the way of the *I Ching*. We forgive, but we do not forget, just as in studying history we try not to forget its lessons, for to do so is to grow arrogant and complacent. We remain aware that people will continue to be subject to their fears and bad habits until they have acquired the insight and discipline which will enable them to break free of them.

We do not need to steel ourselves against a person by defining what kind of person he is, just to keep aware that he has not yet corrected himself. Nor do we need to supervise his progress in order to measure where, along his path, he is. Such attitudes make it impossible to hold an open mind, or to give him the space and time he needs to correct himself. We need only keep attuned to his attitude of the moment to discover when he flatters and when he is sincere. We reinforce his sincerity by relating to him sincerely, and we withdraw when he flatters or is insensitive and indifferent. This is to follow the principle of advancing with the light force and retreating with the dark force. The principle of "biting through" is to train others by responding correctly to the ebb and flow of their superior potential. If we do this consistently, we will have a creative impact.

Withdrawal is the way the Sage of the *I Ching* 'bites through' our ego; withdrawal is the way we are meant to deal with other people's egos. So long as we are sincere, the Sage who speaks through the *I Ching* relates to us. When we are arrogant, he disengages, leaving us to the whims of chance. In this manner he disciplines and punishes our inferiors. This withdrawal is that of the wise teacher, free of emotion. It is moderate, and lasts only for so long as we remain arrogant. Similarly, when the occasion demands, we are meant to withdraw from others into a polite reserve, even though they may try to engage us again through flattery, or to upset us through outbursts. (They do this because their egos have perceived a loss of power when we cease to interact, and they seek to regain control.) It is important not to be jarred off balance by these challenges. We must remain resolved and reserved until the others have become humble and sincere; even then we must remember that habit is strong so that when tensions ease, we do not become careless and forgetful.

To withdraw is to punish, called "biting through" in this hexagram. The sole purpose of punishment is to restore order, therefore we may punish only until order is restored. We are not meant to create what the *I Ching* calls a "massacre," whereby we track down and bring into the open every last bit of evil. Evil may not be overcome in a wholesale manner; we may undermine it only through small steps. After each step we must return to simplicity, serenity, and sincerity. The use of power is not unlike taking hold of a tiger's tail; no sooner do we perceive the punishing power of withdrawal than our ego may seize it ambitiously. We must not exercise the power of withdrawal willfully or vindictively, for it is not our ego's right or place to punish others. To allow it to do so creates bad results.

If 'biting through' is in reference to the Sage's dealing with our ego, we need to search our inner attitude for ideas which exceed a moderate and just view of others' transgressions. It is excessive to take a hard line by viewing them as hopeless, which in *I Ching* terms is to "execute" them. We need to "kill," or firmly reject all ideas which slander the truth.

Since this hexagram is concerned with justice, it is also concerned with spiritual equality. If we think we were born better and therefore deserve more privileges than others, we harbor a "traitor" in our inner attitude. Such an idea becomes the basis for indifference to suffering. We should not overlook the possibility that the Sage may be biting through our attachment to such pretenses.

'Biting through' also means that we maintain an open mind and a proper perspective of the situation: we remember that we began our self-development only because we wanted to achieve something personal and selfish. Even as our path away from selfish, childish behavior continues to be a long and difficult struggle, it is the same with others. Like ourself they will come to see that they are following dead-end paths, that they need help to find the correct way, and that to achieve true human unity they must rid themselves of personal, selfish motives. Such higher truths serve as the basis for an open-minded, moderate point of view.

First Line: *His feet are fastened in stocks.* While receiving this line may refer to the correct limits for punishing others (a mild penalty for the first offense), it more often refers to the unpleasant experience we have just had. We should develop a correct perspective of this punishment; it is not so much that the Cosmos punishes us as the fact that proceeding in the wrong direction (towards a dead-end) is by its nature self-punishing. Fortunately or unfortunately, it is only by making mistakes that we learn to correct ourselves.

Second Line: *Bites through tender meat.* Punishment of others has been carried too far, and we lament the bad effect. No great harm has been done, however, because the punishment was just. To withdraw in anger, or with feelings of negation, is to carry the punishment too far.

As in the case of the first line, this line often refers to our being punished by the Sage for having an obstinate attitude.

Third Line: *Bites on old dried meat.* Our ego lacks the power and authority to punish others. When we are not truly disinterested in withdrawing from them, but do so to avenge ourselves, we arouse a poisonous hatred. The only purpose of punishment is to prevent excesses; therefore, punishment must not be excessive. Also, punishment should be concluded quickly so as to invoke no "lawsuits" wherein their egos respond to ours in retribution.

Lawsuits are conflicts (or wars) between people which may exist on a subconscious level for years. A lawsuit is initiated when one person's ego attempts to punish another's. From that time forward the person punished seeks retribution. Retribution often takes the form of an attack on one's inner independence, thus the lawsuit becomes a king-of-the-heap game which can only be ended when the one attacked ceases to punish or react. The reference to "old dried meat" suggests that a long-term lawsuit may already exist on a certain issue, and that we must free ourselves from an established reactive pattern.

Fourth Line: *It furthers one to be mindful of the difficulties....* Here we begin to see success in our effort to withdraw (punish) and remain reserved; consequently, the other person has begun to relate to us correctly. However, this is only a first step. We must avoid the temptation to rush back into a comfortable, careless relationship that would collapse our work. We tend either to be steeled in perseverance or relaxed in an easy relationship with others. If we can remain neutral and persevering, being neither soft nor hard, but cautious, careful, and strict in inner discipline (all the while remaining open-minded to the extent that our disbelief remains suspended), we will correctly "bite through" the obstacles to a correct fellowship.

When just this line is drawn, the hexagram changes to *The Corners of the Mouth* (Hex. 27). Since this hexagram refers to the thoughts we allow to inhabit our mental space, the counsel is to be particularly careful about relaxing our standards. Our inner thoughts create or cure the "difficulties" mentioned in this line.

Fifth Line: *Bites on dried lean meat. Receives yellow gold. Perseveringly aware of danger. No blame.* We would like to be lenient with another person, but our duty is to be impartial. To accept an alliance merely because the other person wants it is incorrect, particularly if the other has not become firmly committed to following the good. He must realize, through his own perception, that a firm commitment to the good and the beautiful is the only vehicle to an alliance. Unity between two people can occur only when both their wills are independently directed toward the good.

The line also counsels us to *be like yellow gold.* This means that because a person seems to have a better attitude we should not interfere to lead him out of his difficulties. It is dangerous to shield people from the results of their poor attitudes, or in any way excuse and justify their wrong actions. We may help them (if they are open to us) only when they exert the effort to help themselves, and when they work actively at correcting their mistakes. Simply to let them off the hook in our inner attitude is to engage in magnificence, and to interfere in what the Creative is doing to correct the situation.

Sixth Line: *His neck is fastened in a wooden cangue.* Our obstinacy to do things our way rather than to be led results in humiliation and remorse (a wooden cangue). The way out requires gradual progress and a humble return to the correct path. We could have avoided the error had we remembered that the Sage knows how to make evil circumstances work to the good; it was not necessary to intervene.

This line may also refer to another who has got himself trapped by having used wrong means to pursue what may also be wrong ends.

22.

Pi / Grace

$$\frac{\text{Kên}}{\text{Li}}$$

(Self-important intervention.)

Grace refers both to false grace and to true grace. False grace refers to presumptive behavior and adornment of the ego-self-image. True grace refers to possessing an open mind, humility, simplicity, and acceptance.

Anything having to do with pretense, such as projecting a front or image of ourselves, or employing a personal style or technique in dealing with people, constitutes the ornamentation, or brilliance of the ego-self-image. A cutting wit, bravado, intimidation, assumption of hierarchy over others, egotistical display of self, a show of firmness (as opposed to being firm within), all involve brilliance. The ego-self-image is a false self created out of bravado and defensiveness. This self sees the world in a limited, self-oriented way, and is frequently preoccupied with how others perceive it. Achieving results through brilliance is the opposite of the *I Ching* way of influencing through the power of inner truth (see *Inner Truth*, Hex. 61), and through the unnoticed, background position mentioned in *The Family* (Hex. 37).

Brilliance also refers to contrived solutions to problems. We contrive solutions to problems because we distrust or discount the willingness or ability of the Creative (the Unknown) to make things work; we fear we must act on our own, or that we must intervene to save the situation. This fear arises because our ego perceives that everything should move in a straight line toward the solution it thinks is correct. It is unable to realize that the Creative works things out by using every direction the situation takes. The Creative, it may be said, works in zig-zag fashion, tacking this way and that, confounding the supervisory ego, and its everlasting search to control.

Brilliance also refers to fixed (conventional, habitual) approaches to problems, as when we demand that people do what we want. It also refers to fixed ideas, as when we have a set view of things, and we are not open to new perceptions. We may see a situation as "disastrous," while from the Cosmic point of view the turn of events may be the only way things can turn out correctly—something we realize later, through hindsight. (The ego always wants to know in advance, and with certainty, what will happen.

Brilliance can also refer to a fixed approach to how wrongs are to be righted, as when we require that those who have offended us grovel before us, or climb over a capricious list of hurdles before we will trust them again.

An implied contract between two people, by which they promise to assuage and tolerate each other's egos, is an example of a brilliant relationship which works quite harmoniously for a time. Sooner or later, though, the tyrannical baby in each person, by being thus cultivated, becomes overgrown and causes trouble.

Still another form of brilliance concerns our perception that some people are important, or unimportant, simply because our family, or clan, or social group has pronounced them so. Similarly, it is brilliance to think it important to be understood, or to "do something" about a situation. Our importance lies in perceiving the matter in its essentials, and to turning the matter over to the Cosmos, not in being the focus of action. When we turn the matter over to the Cosmos we activate the power of the Creative to right the situation. True grace is to let go unconditionally because we realize that only the Unknown understands how to bring about the correct solution.

True grace relinquishes all the ways in which our ego defends itself. In the work of self-development our relationship with the Unknown is explored, enabling us gradually to relinquish our defenses against it, and to allow things to happen without interference or manipulation. We cease striving to make things happen, or to prove ourselves through adornments of intellect, title, rights, or other forms of self-assertion. We realize the true power and grace of simplicity, acceptance, and dependence on the Higher Power.

The "fire that breaks out in the secret depths of the mountain" symbolizes the beauty of spirit that creates affection. Beauty of spirit is important but we cannot rely on it to make things work correctly. More earnest effort is needed to keep ourself clear and correct. The two strong lines in the lower trigram represent the foundation of equality, justice, dignity, and respect that must be properly in place before unity with another can exist. Although in our simplicity we would rather open ourself expansively to people, we must nevertheless be inwardly strict and require a correct sensitivity and receptivity before we relinquish our reserve.

We often receive this hexagram when we plan to do something instead of waiting patiently for the chance by which we might make progress, to show itself. There is danger that the indulgent and luxurious elements here called brilliance, have crept into our attitude. The hexagram calls us back to the true grace of simplicity— acceptance of the fact that we can achieve nothing of value without the help of the Sage, and that reliance on planning and contriving blocks this help.

Receiving this hexagram can also mean that another's improvement looks better than it really is, and that we should not be fooled by appearances. The change we see is only of a surface nature ("he molts in the face," as it is put in *Revolution*, Hex. 49), made in response to pressure rather than from his insight and firm choice to follow the good.

First Line: *He lends grace to his toes, leaves the carriage, and walks*. The carriage represents using brilliant means to make progress: when we ought to be walking, we are riding; instead of following, we lead. We contrive solutions rather than allow them to evolve from the situation; we force our way rather than persevering in non-action and detachment; we strive instead of turning things over to the Sage and Fate to correct; we try to order everything to our liking instead of remaining open and innocent.

Sometimes, because we are parents, teachers, or owners, we feel we are entitled to assume rights that supposedly go with those roles. True grace is to recognize the impotence and egotism implicit in feelings of entitlement. Being a parent or owner does not mean we automatically know what is correct, or that we have the right to use wrong means to make progress. We should rely instead on simplicity and humility to find the correct way to proceed.

We also ride in a carriage when we skip steps to accept unity before the correct conditions are firmly established. This is to use dubious means to achieve our goals.

The carriage also refers to ways in which we defend ourselves. We should avoid pretending that we are brilliantly wise and all-knowing. We should accept instead that we do not know the answers. If we allow ourself to be led blindly, inner truth will surface, in response to the needs of the moment, to show us the correct way. To allow ourself to be defended by the Unknown is to leave the carriage and walk.

Second Line: *Lends grace to the beard on his chin.* In this line the chin refers to the essential element, while the beard refers to the nonessential but decorative element. Receiving it often refers to being concerned with how our actions appear to others rather than whether they are essential and correct. Thus, by harboring doubts we lend credibility and power to what we think others think. If we dismiss these doubts, people will cease questioning the validity of what we do.

At other times this line refers to our being more interested in how a person appears than how he behaves. Or, we judge another because of the symptoms of his behavior (his defense system) rather than because of the root fears which dominate him; therefore, we fail to understand him. In other words, we follow desire and our inferiors (the beard) rather than our superior nature (the chin).

The beard also symbolizes false grace in the form of our (or someone else's) self-image—the studied (or customary) way we handle people and problems (our array of defensive actions). It is as if we have an inner mirror in which we say, "See, this is how I handle this," or "This is the kind of person I am."

In terms of achieving results, this line also refers to paying too much attention to outer form and to appearances. We care more about achieving a result (the beard) than how it is to be achieved (the chin). In the *I Ching*, how you achieve something is more important than whether it is achieved. Sometimes too, the line means that we follow the path because we know it will lead to our goal, instead of purposelessly, because it is good and correct. The beard also refers to times when we want unity before the conditions for unity are correct; thus we are content to use wrong means. The student of the *I Ching* eventually realizes that the goal cannot be separated from the path. How and when we say or do things is as important as what is achieved.

Finally, the beard refers to times when we focus on external appearances (the beard), doubting the *I Ching*'s reassurances that things are progressing on the inner level.

Third Line: *Graceful and moist.* Because all seems well for a change we relax and enjoy ourselves, forgetting our obligation to be reserved with the person who has not corrected his attitude toward us more than superficially. Or, because the situation has improved, we regain an arrogant self-confidence to take up issues and try to force progress instead of letting things develop naturally. When we give up discipline in this manner, we lose the penetrating power of inner truth.

Fourth Line: *Grace or simplicity.* We are tempted to rely on charm, a sense of power, intellect, or a studied approach to things, all of which comprise the brilliance referred to in this line. Brilliance refers to plans and planning, as when we imagine a stunning way to handle an injustice. We return to simplicity when we recognize that we do not have the answers. We should also free ourself from the doubt implied in thinking we need to possess the answers. Acceptance not only means that we accept not knowing, it means that we relinquish our ideas of how to handle problems; we simply follow the way dictated by truth, advancing when the way is open, and retreating when the way is closed. We ask the Cosmos for help and work with it as the opportunities and changes present themselves. Instead of the brilliance of questioning, we fall back on the simplicity of acceptance.

Another aspect of brilliance is thinking that we are good because we like or know what is good. We cannot "be" good. We can only follow what is good by asking ourself in every situation, "what is the correct response, the correct way?" To adopt the idea that we are good, or enlightened, is brilliance. It is enough to follow the good and retain our humility.

Sometimes simplicity means that we return to being reserved with those who mistrust us, or who are insensitive to us; we proceed on our way alone. Until the other person has become devoted to finding the truth within himself, this is the only true relationship possible. Otherwise we cling to empty form and pretense (brilliance), and ignore the substance of the relationship.

Sometimes we distrust being silent and reserved. There is nothing wrong with having nothing to say.

Fifth Line: *Grace in the hills and gardens.* Returning to simplicity requires that we renounce our defenses of self. This ego decrease makes us feel exposed and jeopardized; however, our courage and self-sacrifice is noticed by the Sage. He recognizes and respects our sincere effort to do what is correct.

Sixth Line: *Simple grace. No blame.* In discarding ornamentation and the security of a fixed order, and in disciplining the clamoring, demanding voices of the inferior self, we begin to see the beauty and correctness of the way the Cosmos works, and of our limitations. Through relinquishing the use of power (leverage), we find the correct way to make progress—through the true grace of simplicity, sincerity, and serenity. While we follow the guidelines of being straightforward and square, we allow ourself to be guided by the needs of the moment. We adhere to the sparse line of the essential, venturing forth only reticently with the openings, ready and willing to retreat the moment others are no longer receptive, or if we begin to be emotionally involved. Thus we also do what is great.

23.

Po / Splitting Apart

Kên
K'un

(Disbelief in the power of non-action, or in the power of "just being.")

It does not further one to go anywhere. Doubt and fear have already caused us to split from our path, or threaten to do so.

The primary doubt is whether we will achieve our goal through following the path of docility and inaction, and by simply clinging to the power of truth to correct the situation through 'letting it' in our attitude. We are afraid to allow matters to take their course. We think we have to influence the situation through some action or plan. Even to contemplate intervention is to "split apart" from our path. When we split from our true path, we turn matters over to the Inferior Man and the inferiors.

We often receive this hexagram when we think we must arm ourself against a situation which will be embarassing, will compromise our principles, or lead to new difficulties. To take preventative action, or even to contemplate doing so, is to split apart. We need, instead, to trust that we will receive the protection we need, for so long as we insist on defending ourselves, the Higher Power will leave us to our own devices. Through distrust we isolate ourself from help. Whatever we do through our own devices will prove either inadequate or defective, so that at the worst we will have had a destructive effect, or at best we will have prevented the situation from progressing. Going with the flow (*wu wei*) enables the Creative to do its work.

Splitting apart can also refer to times when we lose our conscientiousness and drift into abandoning our responsibilities. Abandonment occurs when we let people go, but not in kindliness. As it is put in *Youthful Folly* (Hex. 4), we should bear with fools in kindliness. Abandonment also occurs when we give people up as unable to rescue themselves, or when we think they will never relate properly to us.

We also receive this hexagram when we have returned to the correct path after having split apart from it.

This hexagram may refer to other people's splitting from their paths. During such times we should submit and take no action or role; instead, we should be docile, go our own way, and leave the evil thing to collapse of itself. Even though those from whom we disengage may suffer adversities, the adversities will provide them with the opportunities needed to learn what is correct. The Superior Man does not fear adversity. He understands that it is often the only means by which we may grow and correct decadent attitudes towards life. Thus life, with its adversity, is the workplace for developing our higher consciousness. This does not mean, of course, that we should court adversity, or be glad when others have it. Adversity is to be avoided, if possible, but when it does occur, we should view it moderately, and derive every possible lesson from it so as to avoid needing to have the lessons repeated.

First Line: *Followers of the ruler are destroyed.* Doubt and fear have undermined a firm and persevering attitude. We feel impelled to force matters to a conclusion. The first evidence of this doubt is our holding to grievances and injuries, storing them up as conditions that must be rectified. True, they must be rectified, but not in response to our ego's demand. We must leave the work of correction and punishment to the Sage. Meanwhile, we relinquish inner resistance, develop an open-minded acceptance of the way the Cosmos works, and trust that it does whatever is necessary to benefit and balance the whole.

Second Line: *Those who persevere are destroyed.* Clear indications of danger occur when we think, "I don't care what happens." When we insist on coddling anger or other negative emotions, the danger and difficulty of our position is increased.

This line also refers to times when, after returning to acceptance, we are tempted to do something to improve relations. We should return to neutrality and disengagement.

Third Line: *He splits with them. No blame.* Here, we retreat from the evil influences which occur in the first two lines. We remember the help of the Sage and gain the stability to oppose our clamoring inferiors.

111

This line may also indicate that someone else is "splitting" from wrongdoing to return to the correct path.

Fourth Line: *The bed is split up to the skin. Misfortune.* Even though we correct our attitude, the trajectory of events launched by our "splitting apart" must run its damaging course. Nevertheless, the damage has reached its peak.

Fifth Line: *A shoal of fishes.* When our attitude becomes correct, a change in conditions is brought about, much as when a shoal of fishes changes direction in unison. When we give up striving to force change through conflict and leverage, the inferior element capitulates and ceases resisting and competing. Acceptance leads to success.

Sixth Line: *There is a large fruit still uneaten.* The correct path, which throughout the splitting apart has been held in doubt, is now vindicated in our mind.

Evil in others always feeds off the evil it finds in us. Fear and doubt are sources of the dark energy. If we hold perseveringly to neutrality, evil becomes exhausted and dies. When it dies, good is the seed of the new that remains; a good effect on others is the "large fruit" that has been produced by our work and perseverance.

24.

Fu / Return (The Turning Point)

K'un
Chên

(Retreat from the dark power of pride and desire.)

We receive this hexagram the moment we glimpse that we have departed from (or have been about to depart from) the correct way. Thus, we have the image of the dawning of the light.

Through wavering and doubt we have fallen (or have been tempted to fall) back on old belief systems, methods of defending ourselves, strategies for dealing with problems, structured ways of relating to others, or a careless approach through being indolent. Either we have avoided the work of maintaining self-discipline, or we have failed to pay attention to our inner attitude.

We receive this hexagram when we have barely glimpsed the problem. It is meant that we should then throw full light on this glimpse so that we may bring it into the full light of consciousness to initiate corrective action.

Return not only refers to the dawning glimpse of light which returns after being absent, it means that we should return to the correct conception and the unstructured path. We retreat from resistance and return to inner discipline, humility, and acceptance. We relinquish all the reasoning that causes us to argue, make claims, or use leverage and force. We quiet the clamoring voices of the inferiors (see *Keeping Still*, Hex. 52), and prohibit our ego from looking at the situation, and from indulging its petty feelings of annoyance. In this way we displace its influence and make room for Cosmic understanding.

Above all, we retreat from the power of pride. Pride arises when we see that we have erred. If we do not resist pride at once, we will remain locked in the grip of the dark force. Pride not only keeps us from having a good effect on our situation, it causes us to resist asking for help and enlightenment, and thus isolates us from the Sage. Pride also "darkens our light" and plunges us back into the eclipse. We must relinquish pride, and humbly ask for help.

113

We also need to retreat from old motives to create "desired effects." Following the path of desire will never accomplish the enduring unity, based on justice, that we really seek. To retreat from desire is also to retreat from ambition and impatience. We return to progress made by tiny steps, carefully taken. We return to the true grace of humility and dependence on the Higher Power.

First Line: *Return from a short distance.* Alienation and doubt are beginning. Thoughts of abandoning the path creep into our mind. We should turn them away before they become firmly established, while we are still able to see their bad effects; once we are in their grip we can see nothing.

Second Line: *Quiet return. Good fortune.* Pride has been aroused because of other people's transgressions, and because we feel abandoned by Fate. We should sacrifice pride, let go of the situation, and return to serene perseverance. We have not been abandoned by Fate. Were it not for adversity and challenge, we would not grow.

Third Line: *Repeated return. Danger.* Return from leaving the path of patient perseverance; retreat from the inner demand that either the situation improve or we will abandon it. A hard, resistant attitude must be sacrificed in order to go on perseveringly.

Fourth Line: *Walking in the midst of others, one returns alone.* We let go of the temptation to adopt the hard, resistant attitude indicated in the previous three lines, and return to dependence and humility.

Fifth Line: *Noblehearted return. No remorse.* There need be no remorse if we are willing to look within, recognize our errors, and return to the path.

Sixth Line: *Missing the return. Misfortune.* If we miss the moment of return, our accumulated good work will certainly be undone. This obstinate attitude is perhaps the greatest danger we must face during self-development, for it arouses the forces which attack all imbalanced attitudes.

25.

Wu Wang / Innocence (The Unexpected)

$$\frac{\text{Ch'ien}}{\text{Chên}}$$

(Maintain a blank mental screen and be alert to the unexpected.)

If someone is not as he should be, he has misfortune. The commentary defines innocence as being free of forethought and reflection. Forethought refers to anticipating what lies ahead, while reflection refers to afterthought in which we evaluate, from our ego's (or vanity's) point of view, our role in what has happened (whether we have won or lost, or have been affirmed or rejected). The type of anticipation and reflection referred to here is not that of objective contemplation, whereby we dispassionately attempt to evaluate whether what we have done was correct; it refers instead to the restless activity of the ego to see if, in its magic mirror of approval, measurable progress has been made toward attaining what it desires. The ego likes to interject itself as the one persevering, and to see itself either as "the fairest," the smartest, or the most correct one of all. It also demands of the Cosmos that life proceed in some "reasonable" or calculable manner, demanding that events proceed in a straight line toward the goal; it distrusts and disdains the zig-zag path of the Creative.

We lose our innocence when we 'look forward,' 'look backward,' or 'look aside.' We look forward when we seek to protect ourselves from imagined consequences of present situations, or when we look for ways to undo what we have done, or for new ways to advance ourselves. We look backward when we congratulate or blame ourselves (or Fate, or the Sage) for events in the past. We look aside when we compare our situation, or rate of progress, with that of others. We must not engage in such looking, but pay attention only to the needs of the moment.

Looking aside gives rise to envy, resentment, and even hatred if we perceive that our road is more difficult, or that others' inferiors seem to be getting away with things our path prohibits us from doing.

We experience another type of envy when we look aside at others who have qualities we would like, or have liked, in some former time, to possess. We are almost always unaware that our strange attraction to people of power, wealth, or fame, is due to envy caused by old, hidden doubts about our being able to achieve a full and rich life.

The sort of looking aside, forward, or behind that is done by our childish heart constantly engages us in measuring, hoping, anticipating, expecting, and dreading. Such looking comes from fear of the Unknown, and from doubts about ourself and the Creative; it leads us to conjure up imaginary problems and to evaluate situations incorrectly. It makes us decide how much effort we are willing to put forward to achieve success, and so leads to a tentative and conditioned commitment to the good. Such evaluations give rise to fantasies in which we envision events proceeding in specific, goal-oriented ways. Our inferiors then demand that we do whatever they think is necessary to make events march in that direction. All this defending, contriving, and hedging is the opposite of what is meant by acting from innocence. Acting from innocence is acting from a pure, clear, and empty mind, and from an unconditioned commitment to good. When the darkness of doubt prevails we must retreat into a blank state of mind, dispersing all negative reactions to the way things appear to be moving. To maintain our innocence we must let go of the present and allow changes to proceed as they will. Acceptance is the correct state of mind about today, innocence the correct state of mind about tomorrow.

Since we no longer have the natural innocence of youth, and since our minds have been conditioned to think that this or that is so, we must put forth effort to attain and maintain *conscious innocence*. By keeping our minds open and free in the manner of a blank screen, we are able to attain the Cosmic perspective and understand the true nature of good and evil. When all roads seem blocked, a new way can become visible; in the depths of the storm, we are able to remember the rainbow. In a state of innocence we are able to meet unexpected events with the help of the Creative, which always points out the correct and appropriate response. If, however, we cling to old prejudices, hide behind old defenses, and adhere to grooved patterns of reaction, these habits of mind will forcibly and unexpectedly intrude to destroy our ability to respond creatively and innocently.

Innocence refers to being pure in heart. Effort is required to maintain purity: we avoid trying to skip steps or use wrong means to accomplish our goals; we avoid rationalizing incorrect solutions to problems; and we hold to inner independence so that we are not lured aside by flattery or desire. Working at keeping our innocence benefits everyone around us.

Innocence also connotes acceptance of the "undeserved misfortune" mentioned in the third line. We accept what happens without losing our principles or giving up our goals. We accept that our standards are being tested by others' egos, or by the fires of adversity. When people see that we remain firmly disengaged, their envious testing gives way, and progress is made toward the good. Distrust of the true and the good is a defensive crutch to keep away hope and frustration. There is a certain safety in having a "turned-off" view; one never gets disappointed. But this view blocks the inner freedom which produces true joy. It is difficult for people to take the risk of giving up a defensive attitude.

Finally, innocence refers to an unstructured mind. An unstructured mind meets events, good and bad, with equanimity. It neither jumps to conclusions with enthusiasm, nor turns away from experience with fear and dread. It does not seek protection in grandiose belief systems simply because they seem to resolve ambiguities comfortably. This is not to imply that we have no point of view. Through the teaching of the Sage we greet a shocking, unsettling event as a jog in the path; we regard obstructions as opportunities to think in new terms. The unstructured mind asks of each new experience, "What can I learn from this?" To the unstructured mind life is a teacher. Free of negation, the unstructured, innocent mind remains independent and free.

First Line: *Innocent behavior brings good fortune.* Our original impulse is to remain detached, reticent, and disinterested. Receiving this line is a reminder to stay detached and to make no plans to hedge against what might or might not happen; such behavior, which is true to our original nature, brings good fortune.

Second Line. *If one does not count the harvest while plowing....* If we dread a bad result from what we are about to do (or have just done), or if we begin to wish the situation were better, then our attention is drawn from what we need to be doing at the moment, which is often to remain disciplined and resolute. Diverted into wishing, we are unable to act spontaneously as the moment demands; instead, we act in a conditioned way to attract the desired result. In listening to selfish considerations offered by our inferiors, innocence is lost. Innocence relates to the situation from a blank and unconditioned mind. Focussing on what is essential and correct, and perseveringly holding to reticence and modesty, we advance with the light (respond to sensitivity) and retreat with the dark (withdraw when insensitivity prevails). In this manner we are able to keep our simplicity, sincerity, and serenity. With our inner center of gravity thus in place, our effect is creative.

Pulled by hopes and expectations, we try to manipulate the direction of events and become disappointed if things do not work as we would like, or on our imagined schedule. Disappointment then collapses our will to persevere. In looking at the goal rather than at the needs of the moment we suspect, with every new obstacle, that Fate is working against us; we are unable to see that we are working against ourselves. Expectation and mistrust put us out of harmony; out of harmony, events no longer work for us. It is important to return to an open mind, to cease measuring progress, and to stop assuming that things are regressing. Such a goal-oriented viewpoint is a major obstacle to success.

Third Line: *Undeserved misfortune.* Situations occur which are negative and it is not our fault. Nevertheless, we must adjust to them with acceptance. To fail to do so will only bring further misfortune. We should not let negative events destroy our innocence.

Fourth Line: *He who can be persevering remains without blame.* "Not listening to others" may refer to feelings of alienation by which we blame others, the Sage, or Fate for presenting us with galling difficulties. "Others" includes the voices of dread and anticipation put forward by our inferiors and sometimes by other people who fear for us. Listening to them causes us to act hastily and incorrectly; therefore, the line counsels us to remain persevering. Dread of losing is as faulty as wanting too much to win. Dread causes us either to press forward to force change, or to hold back unduly so that spontaneous action becomes impossible. If we allow ourself to be guided by what is essential and correct, we will find the best way to be of help, and the right time for helping.

Fifth Line: *Use no medicine in an illness incurred through no fault of your own. It will pass of itself.* This line reassures us that we may safely remain innocent (unconcerned). It also reminds us not to concoct any remedies, but to remain unstructured and disengaged.

Sixth Line: *Innocent action brings misfortune.* Sometimes our sincere actions are misunderstood. We need to accept this fact and withdraw, to give the other person space to find the truth. We can work successfully with a situation only as long as it works with us. We can go only as far as openness in the other person allows. Waiting quietly, without ulterior design, means truly to disengage, without trying to explain. We need to remember that time is the vehicle of the Creative, and people need time to have inner truth penetrate through to them.

Just as both the dark and the light are necessary for us to see, we must allow people to misunderstand. Only by making mistakes can human beings see that their mistakes cause suffering. Only then can they commit themselves to the good and the true. Misunderstanding is the necessary prelude to understanding.

26.

Ta Ch'u / The Taming Power of the Great

Kên   ☰☰
Ch'ien   ☰

(Dealing with crescendo-of-awfulness situations.)

In the creative process there is often a buildup of tension so that the situation we are enduring seems to get out of control. In the course of self-development we develop an inner power and independence which creates envy in others, particularly in those whose egos (fears) are firmly in control. This envy causes them to test us to see if we can be driven off-balance, or if we can be driven away from serenity to become doubtful and fearful. This effort succeeds if they can arouse our fears, spur us to anger, or otherwise cause us to become disturbed by their inferior behavior. This challenge to our inner independence succeeds if we give up our requirements of what is just and correct, or if we become involved in controversies they initiate. If they succeed in such efforts, they will feel satisfied that our virtues are not real, that they are no longer obligated to grow and change, and that they no longer have a 'Cosmic obligation' to deal correctly with us, or with the issue at hand. If we maintain our inner independence, firmness, and integrity, the testing will continue through a 'crescendo-of-awfulness'—an almost unendurable tension—then end. At this point the aggressors become repulsed by their behavior, and they make an important forward step in correcting themselves.

During the awfulness everything looks hopelessly stuck, as if the Wheel of Fate cannot be budged. Only our steadfastness frees it to bring about progress. By "keeping still" during the buildup of tension, and by keeping free of worrying and wanting, we "attain the way of heaven," as it is put in the 6th Line.

Crescendo-of-awfulness situations may be caused by envy, or be the residue of major conflicts which the *I Ching,* in *The Wanderer* (see Hex. 56), calls "lawsuits." Inner lawsuits arise when one person gives up on another. This giving up is evidenced when we undertake defensive or aggressive actions, erect permanent barriers, or maintain a series of impossible requirements which the other person must fulfill before we will forgive him. Requirements which relate to satisfying our injured pride are impossible to fulfill within the limits of spiritual dignity, and differ from requirements that others relate to us in a just and correct manner. Ego-generated barriers and demands cause retaliatory responses (inner lawsuits). Many divorces begin with inner lawsuits which persist an entire lifetime. National or racial conflicts persist for generations. When tense and trying situations occur we should ask whether we carry grudges, harbor prejudices, or list demands that have to do with injured pride.

For crescendo-of-awfulness situations this hexagram counsels us to *hold still, hold firm,* and *hold together.* Holding still refers to keeping our inner thoughts quiet and neutral; we neither seek a comprehensive solution, nor to know the outcome. (Our ego, in striving to maintain control, cannot endure the ambiguity of not knowing.)

Holding firm means we do not doubt our inner sense of truth, or abandon what we have learned in our *I Ching* experiences. We hold firm to what is correct. If we waver, by doubting what we know, or by worrying about what the outcome will be, we begin to defend ourselves. Efforts at self-defense, however, are only bravado. The more we struggle, the more we undermine ourselves. In this predicament we must hold firm. This means we brace ourselves against our own anxiety, as if we were standing in the surf, allowing a large wave to go by; the power of the false dragon, like the energy of the wave, dissipates if we are determined to stand fast. Its power lies solely in its ability to arouse our fears and doubts. Our power, on the other hand, grows to the extent that we are willing to trust the Unknown.

Holding together means that in spite of all challenging forces we do not give up on others' superior potential, or on their ability to perceive and correct their errors. Too conveniently we brand society's worst offenders as subhuman; no one is outside the human family. Each of us has the potential to be the worst sort of human being, given appropriate conditions. The more we deny that there is an understandable reason for others' behavior, and the more we condemn them as impossible, the more we trap them into wrongdoing. Our rigidity aids and abets their misunderstanding of the truths of life. A just and correct point of view is always moderate.

Perseverance furthers. A determined, independent attitude tames strength (in this case the negative power of fear and doubt). Here, strength refers to mindless energy to do something to ease the tension. Through persevering—not responding to this pressure—

great power is produced. We also develop strength of character, and thus "nourish people of worth." In strengthening our inner selves, we strengthen the superior potential in others. The counsel to "not eat at home," means that we resist doing the easy, comfortable thing. "The firm ascends to the top" means that through remaining firmly persevering we transcend the challenges, thus honor the Sage.

Heaven within the mountain means that although we have the correct ideas in mind, "the heavy burden of knowledge must be shut away in silence" until the doors of receptivity in other people open, and a "real influence" can take place. Throughout the first five lines of the hexagram the time is not ripe, but the last line indicates that the time has come when obdurate resistance gives way and an outlet is offered for the release of stored-up energies. This change in conditions occurs through no effort on our part; if we try to make it happen, we "fly before being fledged," as it is put in the first line of *Preponderance of the Small* (Hex. 62).

Giving "actuality to the past" refers to others who disciplined and developed themselves, who held to their principles in the face of adversities. When we hold to our principles and control our ego, we share their experiences, and thus give actuality to the past. Remembering them helps us to be strong. The correct way to study the past is not just to consult the *I Ching*, but really to discipline our inferiors and apply the counsel of its lines.

First Line: *Danger! It furthers one to desist!* Fear and anticipation have jarred us off-balance so that we stand ready to engage in conflict and striving. Our energy is no longer centered, but directed forward. It is time to keep still within, not to act; keeping still enables us to compose ourselves. The assault of the false dragon makes us want to use any means to do what justice and right seem to demand, but doing anything now would complicate things, requiring us to retreat. For the moment we must endure the inappropriate and evil situation, to give those responsible for it the space they need to correct themselves.

We should also avoid doubting what we know to be true—that those misbehaving are in the wrong. We must not excuse them, but rely on the Unknown to show the way past the difficulties. We should not seek a comprehensive answer to the problem as this would only create self-conflict.

Second Line: *The axletrees are taken from the wagon.* Although we may be tempted to force our way, circumstances prevent it. Being thwarted, we should compose ourselves and remain content to wait. Self-discipline allows creative energy to build.

Third Line: *A good horse that follows others. Awareness of danger, with perseverance, furthers. Practice chariot driving and armed defense daily.* To move past a hindrance in our attitude it is necessary to meet and deal with it several times. This is to "practice chariot driving." Adversity is the vehicle which arouses the fears and doubts we need to face. At first we develop only an intellectual perception of the correct response. Repeatedly dealing with the problem makes our intellectual perception "knowledge of the heart."

A "good horse" refers to our willingness to be led through such "practice." Through this process we face our fears, and endure being jeopardized emotionally until we are able to see that the things we fear are harmless.

We are unable to follow like a good horse if we stubbornly hold to emotions such as doubt, desire, or anger at injustice, which cause us to be rigid, like a balking horse. We are helped to gain power over them if we remember others who have endured similar practice. Until our emotions have been thoroughly dispersed, however, we should remain aware that they will mount other attacks. We will need to remain alert. Meanwhile we must not allow ourselves to be worn down by hindrances.

Fourth Line: *The headboard of a young bull. Great good fortune.* The bull refers to the unreasoning energy that arises from hidden emotions such as desire, fear, or anger. These energies manifest themselves as capricious impulses to extend or defend our point of view, whereby we press ourselves on others. Sensing our lack of inner independence, those we wish to influence remain unreceptive. Through realizing the futility of efforts driven by our emotions we "put a headboard" on the energy they generate, thus forestall their "wild force." The "headboard" of understanding enables us to withdraw and wait for the right time to have an effect.

Fifth Line: *The tusk of a gelded boar. Good Fortune.* Here, wild force refers to energy fueled by desire. Only by inhibiting our heart's desires can we achieve the inner freedom and independence that automatically has a good effect on the situation.

Sixth Line: *One attains the way of heaven. Success.* The buildup and thrust of power is moderated by modesty and perseverance in inner equilibrium. When the obstructions in our attitude are thus overcome, creative energy is released and another step in correcting the general situation is achieved.

27.

I / The Corners of the Mouth (Providing Nourishment)

$$\frac{\text{Kên}}{\text{Chên}}$$

(Watch how you nourish yourself on fantasy, wanting, wondering, worrying, and on feelings of alienation. These constitute a bowl of worms.)

Pay heed to the providing of nourishment and to what a man seeks to fill his own mouth with. In its general sense nourishment refers to obtaining the necessities of life. This hexagram acknowledges our dependency on the Higher Power for these necessities, and counsels that to obtain them, we must develop a correct attitude. If our attitude is modest and unassuming, aware of our dependence, we will always receive what we need.

Nourishment also refers to what we feed ourself—the food we eat, the thoughts we think, and the information, facts, and fantasies we entertain. Just as we should take care that what we eat is wholesome and well-balanced, we should have a similar regard to what we allow to enter our minds, for just as food and drink affect us, so do ideas. Everything we study in school, read in novels, or watch in the media shapes our inner attitudes in one way or another.

Most important are the ideas we entertain through fantasy. These become absorbed into our thinking by default unless we are decisive about them. For this reason the hexagram warns us to take great care not to indulge idly in fantasy. We customarily think this activity harmless; however, seemingly harmless indulgences not only shape our fate, but they also determine how we nourish others. If we maintain an independent yet humble attitude, we have a good effect on others. But if we allow envy, self-pity, hardness, alienation, wanting, dreading, suspicion, and distrust to worm their way into our attitude, our effect is detrimental.

Negative elements always enter our minds because we listen to them. Often such elements come from our ego which stands, as it were, just out of sight behind us, where it can insinuate into our ear the flattering scenarios which justify its plans and schemes. By such means it slips unobtrusively into command. These scenarios arouse all sorts of fears, doubts, and their consequent emotions; although they have no relation to reality, we seriously base our actions on them.

Through fantasy we become convinced that certain people, situations, or times in our lives are more important than others. Being convinced of the importance of something disturbs our inner balance. We begin anticipating and watching for the effects we seek. Ambition follows; then, perhaps, we use leverage when the desired results are not achieved. A similar problem occurs when we wish to correct what we perceive to be mistakes in important matters. Ambition and fear cause us to lose inner independence. Instead of trying to remedy the external situation, the *I Ching* would have us correct our inner attitude, and cease indulging in fantasy.

The effort required to correct our attitude is always considerable, but we are not meant to become so focussed on improvement that we lose our receptivity. In all such circumstances we need to detach from the situation until we have re-established our balance. Even though some situations and people are more important to us because they constitute our particular sphere of responsibility, this importance exists only to a point. Holding something as either too important, or of no importance, goes too far. It is important only that we act and react in a manner that is sincere, modest, and essential, paying no heed to whether people like or dislike us. Beyond doing our best, we must allow to happen what will happen.

It is said in this hexagram that the great man nourishes and takes care of superior men in order to take care of all men through them. The most important means of obtaining nourishment from the Cosmos is the practice of meditation. Tranquillity is restorative. *The Taming Power of the Great* (Hex. 26) counsels us to practice self-renewal; this means that daily we should bring ourself to tranquillity. This is done by cleansing our *Ting*—our inner container for nourishment. Self-cleansing means to clean out all thoughts and allow mental activity to subside. Creating inner space allows the light force to enter with its restorative effect. Being recharged, we radiate peace to others, strengthening and nourishing what is high and good in them. The creative energy flows through us abundantly, giving rise to creative ideas, correct perceptions, and the Cosmic view. Thus we find the correct solutions to problems. By placing himself in this state, every great writer "invokes the muse," every inventor sees his invention, and every problem-solver finds the "next step" in solving his problem. Genius is the ability to receive from the Cosmos, not, as our egos keep hoping and insisting, an ability to contrive and think things up. Contriving generally produces only contrivances.

First Line: *You let your magic tortoise go...misfortune.* Through the invasion of doubt and envy we fall into self-pity and discontent, losing our inner independence (magic tortoise). To doubt is to be oppressed by feelings of hopelessness; these soon pervade everything we do. Envy and wanting are communicated to others on the inner plane and give rise to their contempt. We should not allow ourselves to want, or to entertain mental images which compare us with others, or which show our situation from a negative viewpoint, or which otherwise undermine our trust in the Unknown. It is important to restore our inner independence and self-reliance.

This line also refers to times when we allow our inferiors to become annoyed with people who have not disciplined their inferiors. This annoyance soon gives way to feelings that they are tiresome bothers, and that they are hopeless. Our undisciplined inferiors view self-development and discipline with resistance. As soon as we listen to their complaints the ego resumes leadership of the personality. Our inferiors secretly long for a life free of responsibilities. They do not yet see that the "easy way" is a delusion, and that the hard way of modesty, forgiveness, and conscientiousness is infinitely more satisfying because we do not become enmeshed in self-conflict. To fail to forgive others pinches and truncates the soul, and sets into motion the oppression of a false path.

Second Line: *Deviating from the path to seek nourishment from the hill. Continuing to do this brings misfortune.* Through a feeling of weakness we do things in a careless way. For example, we hope to have a better influence by going along with someone else's wrongdoing; then we trust the Sage to provide protection from the consequences. Accepting the Sage's help while not making a true effort to be correct is unworthy; it leads to misfortune.

Third Line: *Turning away from nourishment. Perseverance brings misfortune. Do not act thus for ten years.* The commentary to this line mentions that the gratification of physical desire and the "mad pursuit of pleasure for the satisfaction of the senses" can never lead to our goal. We often receive this line when our inferiors complain that the path of the Sage is too ascetic, and that if we follow it "we" (our inferiors) will never find the happiness we seek. The line, however, is simply a statement of one of the fundamental truths of life, that happiness cannot be attained through the pursuit of pleasure and the gratification of the senses. The lures of seduction are false paths; although they seem to promise happiness, the promise is never fulfilled, because here we are dealing with delusion. What the line predicts is true: to seek nourishment of the lower self at the expense of the higher self always brings misfortune and suffering, if not now, further down the road.

We should also be aware that receiving this line may indicate less obvious forms of "nourishment that does not nourish." For example, it may refer to our seeking to have our ego-self-image (or self-importance) recognized by others. We do this when we argue to prove we are right, or when we strive to change a circumstance to what we think it should be. Emotional dependency on others, or on the situation's progressing in a certain way, leads away from our goal. Trusting that events lead in the correct direction, despite their appearances, results in inner independence and strength of character.

A less obvious form of bad nourishment occurs when we seek to have our lives perfectly secure and unchallenged. Our relationship with the Unknown, and our freedom from pacts and certainties, enables us to be of use in the world. This usefulness nourishes us with inexhaustible nourishment. Therefore, we should not seek to know everything comprehensively, or to have consummate power; we should seek only to keep detached and open-minded in response to the challenge of the moment.

Fourth Line: *Turning to the summit for provision of nourishment brings good fortune.* We turn to the correct source of nourishment when we seek mastery over our inferiors. This effort leads to the help we need to "bite through" obstacles to unity with others.

Fifth Line: *Turning away from the path, one should not cross the great water. To remain persevering brings good fortune.* We lack the strength to nourish others through being reserved and self-reliant. The Sage cannot make us strong. Although we are dependent on his guidance, we must do the work of disciplining our inferiors. We automatically nourish others in a beneficial way when we nourish ourselves correctly, but when we feed our inferiors on negative thoughts and fantasies, our strength is undermined.

Sixth Line: *The source of nourishment. Awareness of danger brings good fortune. It furthers one to cross the great water.* The source of true nourishment is the Sage, who supports and helps us. All benefits come from the Sage's intervention on our behalf. The danger referred to is that when things go well we tend to grow comfortable and careless, forgetting our dependence on the Sage. Not only do we forget our dependence, but we also forget the responsibility that accompanies the help we receive. Our responsibility is to work to rescue the others to whom we are connected by inner ties. We rescue them by remaining conscientious in serving what is high and good within ourself. A careless, presumptuous attitude always incurs danger.

"Crossing the great water" means that it is time to pull ourselves together by displacing the influence of our Inferior Man, and by disciplining our inferiors. We do this by attending to our inner nourishment; this means we sort out and resolutely discard all thoughts, fantasies, false comforts, and self-deceptions that are unworthy of inner dignity. Among the most vain self-deceptions is the fantasy that all progress is of our making. We serve the Sage when we remember that in all situations the Sage, as a third party, is present; when success occurs, it is always due to having engaged the help of the Higher Power. We need to remember how we have been helped, and not forget that others, who have not yet discovered this wonderful nourishment, have potential for good. We forget their good potential when we become preoccupied with their mistakes and bad habits of mind. In detaching and proceeding on our path, we renew our humility and once more become true to ourself. Being true to ourself we are in harmony with the Cosmos. Only by nourishing ourself with humble thoughts can we surmount the dangers (cross the great water), and continue to transmit to others the good nourishment we receive from the Sage.

The Sage is readily available to all who seek his help, without exception. Anyone who is sincere and open-minded will find himself aided and nourished if he consults the *I Ching*. Moreover, we must not be deluded by the false tradition that the Sage can only be consulted by this or that means, or only so often, or only if we are of a certain age. The Sage, source of our nourishment, is always accessible and responsive to the sincerity and humility of an open mind.

28.

Ta Kuo / Preponderance of the Great

$$\frac{\text{Tui}}{\text{Sun}} \quad \overline{\overline{\overline{}}}$$

(It is a time of great opportunity, therefore a time to take great care.)

There are powerful moments in life which present opportunities to make progress. Everything is in a state of flux, ready to establish a new direction, either towards improvement, or towards stagnation. This is the moment we have been preparing for. Although this moment may seem too big, or the situation too difficult for us to handle (the "weight of the great" being excessive), if we concentrate all our energies on being conscientious and correct, meeting every event, good or bad, with acceptance, we will win the help we need to conquer the difficulties. The time is like that described in Hemingway's *Old Man and the Sea*, when the old man finally hooked the big fish of his life. Landing it required his greatest attention, discipline, and courage.

The weight of the great is excessive means that the pressures exerted by the situation are great. The danger, symbolized by the sagging ridgepole, is that through allowing ourself to be influenced by these pressures, we may lose our inner equilibrium. A straight and firm ridgepole symbolizes our will to go on in a balanced and independent way. "The ridgepole sags" when we become infected with doubt. On seeing the difficulties of the situation our inferiors become alarmed. They try to determine what will happen next. Their fears produce an energy to react. If they take control of our personality, firmness will degenerate to hardness, withdrawal to retaliation, and perseverance to ambition to overcome the situation with sweeping effort. On perceiving success, they want to stop and luxuriate in enjoyment and self-congratulation; on perceiving renewed difficulties they want to give up altogether. With each change of direction our ego threatens to collapse our inner equilibrium and independence. The remedy is to cease anticipating, and to return to dependence on the Higher Power. We cease allowing ourselves to

131

press forward, or to think of giving up.

This hexagram also refers to strong elements in others that make them assault us with their fears, mistrust, doubt, or desire. ("Strong" refers to impetuous movement to resolve what is ambiguous.) Being thus assaulted we feel pressure to forego modesty and patience. We can meet this challenge if we remain detached and allow the changes to proceed as they will. Then our way of life will slowly penetrate to others without pressure, explanation, or demonstration. Such "gentle penetration" allows healing and attraction to occur naturally. To be truly rich is to remain modest; to be truly powerful is to remain reticent. Through modesty and reticence we achieve a real superiority over the situation.

First Line: *To spread white rushes underneath* means to take great care. We remain alert to each change in the situation. We cautiously, even hesitantly, proceed if the situation opens; we retreat the instant we feel the slightest resistance.

Extraordinary times often refers to an ongoing situation or relationship with a particular person or persons. This relationship calls for extraordinary caution to extend over a long period of time, until the causes of the difficulty are resolved. One is dealing with entrenched habits, fears, doubts, and areas of inner burnout. These problems can be healed only slowly. Trust can be re-established only gradually. To admonish people, or contend with them, or act on the offensive, or indulge ourself in any way during such "extraordinary times," is to violate the principle of extraordinary caution.

Second Line: *A dry poplar sprouts at the root.* This image refers to a time of renewal and growth. Our relationship with another is entering a phase of renewal. Such times require great care. The situation is similar to starting a wood fire. If, at the beginning, we crowd the slender flame with too many branches there will not be enough air for the fire to become established. Once it is established, we cannot ignore the fire, or forget to feed and tend it. It is the same with relationships: we cannot afford the luxury of relaxing into egotistical self-indulgence. It is important that we remain alert and careful, taking care not to presume that people are more developed and ready for close communication than they actually are. We should not exceed the potential of the situation.

Third Line: *The ridgepole sags to the breaking point....* This indicates that we have failed to exercise great care. The entire structure of our work is threatened, and we are thrown into doubt and dismay. If after this warning we persist in a careless, presumptuous attitude, catastrophe is assured.

Fourth Line: *The ridgepole is braced.* We have won other people's respect for our way of life through being modest, approachable, and independent. We must not then allow our ego to glorify itself by trying to show them that we have been right; we should remember that we have been guided and helped by the Sage. We should avoid thinking that others are incapable of understanding and finding their way. Instead of trying to draw people to us personally, through the appeal of wit, charm, appearance, or success, we should rely on the power of our example and rectitude. Even though the "ridgepole is braced" we should not discard reserve and caution, or relax into careless self-importance.

Fifth Line: *Withered poplar puts forth flowers.* Renewal of the relationship cannot succeed until we have resolved the misunderstandings which originally disrupted it. Although everything seems fine on the surface, and each person tries to relate properly, the basis for renewal is still inadequate. If we try to take advantage prematurely of our good work, we find that the selfish motives and decadent ideas which contributed to the collapse of the relationship, still operate. We need to realize that progress will continue only if we cling to a selfless, careful, and unassuming attitude.

This line also refers to times when we allow resoluteness to become hardness. In this case we have observed only the amenities of doing what is right. A true sacrifice of self is needed. Maintaining a "relationship with those below" means that we maintain our humility. We resist seeking power and recognition, as in "see me, the tower on the hill." Every human being, in one way or another, is climbing the path of self-development. Some of us are ahead, some behind. We must neither be envious of those ahead, nor coldly disdainful of those behind. We do not give anyone up as hopeless.

Maintaining a relationship with those below can refer to matters of health. We must remain aware of the needs of our bodily inferiors, and not neglect to take care of them. Neglect would be a luxurious act.

Sixth Line: *He goes through the water....* Careless self-confidence and presumption cause us to plunge ahead to accomplish our task, no matter what happens. It is presumptuous to expect that we will be protected from the consequences of our mistakes by the Unknown. Instead of conscientiously allowing ourself to be guided by the moment, being alert to each change so that we do not lose our inner balance, we let everything go and say, "I need not concern myself with what is correct; whatever happens will be all right." It is essential to remain firm in what is essential and correct, to thus "attend scrupulously to everything." This is also to be responsible. To think "who cares," or "it doesn't matter what happens," needlessly causes the water to "go over our head."

If we have already behaved over-zealously, without first attaining the help of the Sage, it will be necessary to endure the dangerous results indicated by the image of the water going over our head. Even though we may have followed our principles, and remain free of blame, it is dangerous and useless to attempt to impose our will on others.

In addition to warning us against over-zealous or presumptuous behavior, this line confirms that some things are more important than life. Sometimes it is necessary, for the good of the whole, to give up something we value beyond almost everything else. This sacrifice is to have the water go over our head. Being responsible means that we are willing to endure it. Whatever happens, we strive only to keep ourself independent and balanced. Such conscientiousness and modesty meet the Creative halfway, and thereby engage its help to see us through the situation.

29.

K' an / The Abysmal (Water)

K'an ☵
K'an ☵

(Ambition and presumption always lead to danger.)

Danger, in the *I Ching*, refers to any emotion which leads to the thought of giving up, or to abandoning the steady, slow path of patient perseverance. Danger generally comes from restless discontent which leads to ambition and to a loss of our inner balance. On becoming too ambitious we then expect that our efforts should generate visible progress. We must be willing to see things through without looking for visible progress. Only a steady, persevering disengagement and inner independence, by which we remain true to our higher nature, will win in the end.

Whether we are trapped in an emotional abyss of despair, or in an abysmal situation, this hexagram counsels us to 'keep still,' for any effort to change the situation only makes it worse. For now it is useless to think of why we are in the situation, or of how to get out of it. All energy must be put toward relating properly and silencing inner conflict until we cease thinking of giving up, and until the correct remedy shows itself.

This hexagram confirms that in spite of appearances there is a way that leads out of danger and difficulty, but we may not find this way if we remain in an emotional state of mind. When our emotions rule, our reasoning powers are said to be enclosed in the dark. When the soul is "locked up within the body," we are not internally free.

Danger comes from wanting, from fearing, and from being ambitiously goal-oriented instead of perseveringly path-oriented. When we long for a particular solution, or for the comforts of another time, or simply for relief, we strive restlessly to bring the unpleasant situation to an end; we abandon the slow, step-by-step work that creates enduring change.

When we doubt that by working with the Creative, and by working with time, we will attain what we seek, desire to make swift progress is the culprit. Our inferiors resent having to follow what they see as a tedious, dubious process to correct matters. Another culprit, envy, occurs when we listen to our inferiors' resentment at having to be correct when others do wrong without penalty.

Desire and envy occur because at some time in our past we learned to doubt the healing power of truth; we also learned impatience, rejecting the way of the Creative to mend things through the vehicle of time. Such thoughts come from our childish inferiors who think only of their fears or desires. They secretly insinuate these fears because they have become convinced that without forcing matters, life will trick them out of happiness. By listening to these ideas we forget the obvious—that true and enduring happiness can be attained only by establishing the conditions which create it.

Because happiness depends, to a certain extent, on other people's spiritual development, we must give them the space they need to err, that they may gain the insights which lead to growth. So long as we desire personal comforts and are ambitious to make speedy progress, not only will we fail to arouse good in others, but our doubt, fear, and ambition will feed their distrust of us, and block the help of the Creative.

Pressing ahead is a mistake that engages our pride. Pride in turn makes it difficult for us to return to the path of humble and patient perseverance. It is important to relinquish hurt pride, and to disengage from looking at the situation, and from any feelings of concern, disappointment, or hopelessness that such looking creates.

Danger also refers to an inner pressure to do something simply to end the ambiguity of the situation. We should persevere in nonaction until this pressure is dispersed and we regain neutrality and clarity of mind.

The image of water falling into the abyss, filling the low places and passing on, symbolizes the Chinese doctrine of *wu wei,* which means to flow with events and allow time to work, rather than resisting it. Through nonresistance and acceptance we rely on the healing action of nature to resolve dangers.

The active water symbolized by *K' an* represents the most sincere, pure effort we can put forth to do what is right. We need to be aware, however, that when sincere effort fails to produce tangible results, our ego, which measures our effort and is always seeking rewards, enters to demand that we give up "fruitless" effort. This sort of thinking endangers perseverance, for danger is always incurred, from our ego's point of view, when we try to do the right thing and fail. If we can persevere through these dangers, we will fill up these holes in our character.

The *I Ching* approach to danger is to be sincere in trying to understand the situation from the Cosmic viewpoint. Attaining the Cosmic viewpoint corrects our inner attitude. In the Cosmic view, we should retreat when the dark force enters and advance when the light force returns. Keeping ourself detached we avoid throwing ourselves away or engaging our pride. We remain free to respond to the ebb and flow of the situation. Without predetermining what to do, we cling to what is relevant and essential; we do not allow ourself to be turned aside by pacts our ego has exacted—promises to "give this thing up if it doesn't work," or, to do thus and thus in "this case." Instead, we keep open and allow ourself to be guided by the requirements of inner truth, to which we keep assiduously tuned.

Another danger comes from expectation and presumption, as opposed to keeping an open mind. We are open-minded when we remember that everyone has the potential to succeed and to develop his higher nature. It is an arrogant presumption (playing God) to decide what the future holds, and whether people can, or will, grow. Perseverance is required if we are to keep our minds open in the face of obviously inferior behavior.

If, on the other hand, we expect or presume that a person's potential for good will come forward to right matters, we go too far. We can only cling to the idea that he is capable of pulling himself together. Whether or not he develops his Cosmic blueprint and fulfills his true nature is entirely up to him. Everyone must prove himself.

To be open-minded simply means to be unassuming, one way or another. It is one thing to "cling" to the idea that "somehow a person will come through," and another to assume it. Such assumption gives him the mistaken impression that he has no need to develop himself or to correct his mistakes.

To the alert person who is neutral in attitude, a difficult, obstreperous, unreasonable, or unjust person will betray himself, regardless of how he may attempt to disguise himself, or to flatter his way into acceptance. The alert one should be determined not to be manipulated.

Alertness means that we do not automatically assume good or bad things about people; instead, we listen to them. In doing so we feel their innocence, or lack of it. We should inwardly insist that they be trustworthy. If at some former time they have erred in dealing with us, we should be ready to return our trust to them, but only when we feel certain that they are firmly committed to doing what is correct. In doing this we should hesitantly feel our way, and restrict ourselves to problems that directly concern us; we do not interfere in other people's problems. This is the way the Cosmos deals with us. It is the way we are meant to deal with others. Whatever we may have done before, the Sage welcomes our choice to return to the correct path, yet he is unwavering in his demands for committed and reliable virtue.

Just as we should avoid expecting things of people, we should avoid expecting, in the sense of "relying on," the Creative to benefit us. Good luck is the result of a humble and unassuming attitude toward the Unknown. The minute we congratulate ourselves on having good luck, it disappears. We may not presume on God, so to speak. Presumption is similar to expecting a gift. Expectation deprives the giver of his joy and of the spontaneous appreciation that makes him wish to share his good fortune with us. When we depend on a situation in a presuming way, we may expect it to fail.

First Line: *In the abyss one falls into the pit.* Wanting a thing to happen before it is ready to happen exposes us to the danger of doubt. Even a small doubt may cause us to depart from our path. We should retreat and find peace in acceptance.

Second Line: *One should strive to attain small things only.* This is definitely not the time for big measures; we lack the strength and clarity to overcome the deficiencies of the time. Any effort to extricate ourself will not work; therefore we are counseled to "be content with small gains." We receive this line when we seek comprehensive answers in order to drive forward and make sizable gains. Our state of mind is such that even if we possessed such answers, we would not be able to implement them. Therefore, it is best to strive only to let go and allow ourself to be led. Even striving to let go, or to free ourself of emotions, entails considerable effort.

Third Line: *Abyss on abyss.* Every step leads to danger. Ambition, expectation, or feelings of negation have created troublesome responses in others. These troublesome responses cause us to doubt ourself and the path of docility, creating a pressure to act. This pressure to do something is dangerous. We should return to neutrality and disengagement until we have attained the correct perspective, and until the way out of the difficulty shows itself.

It is necessary to become accustomed to the dangers encountered in waiting, for all creative action is achieved through keeping our attitude correct and steady while the inner attitudes of others are being influenced to grow. Our inner independence and detachment must be maintained. When things get better, we must guard against becoming attached to the luxury of things being better. When things get worse, we must guard against wanting and its consequent pressures: ambition, striving, wondering, and wavering.

The chief means of making progress is keeping our heart constantly steady and our inner independence intact. This requires that we keep our inferiors strictly disciplined up to the very "cloud heights," as it is put in the sixth line of *Development* (Hex. 53). A willing submissiveness to the divine will and acceptance of the Unknown empowers inner truth.

Detachment requires having a goal, yet not being goal-oriented. Our general purpose remains that of rescuing all, as well as any particular ones. It is important to realize that we will waver, nevertheless, trying to keep steady will draw the help of the Creative. We can rely on the power generated from holding firmly to our principles. Such holding together (see Hex. 8) not only empowers truth, it brings the help of the Higher Power. This provides the chance happenings that point out the truth as obvious. We become ambitious only when we doubt that this help will come, and when fear invades our serenity. We need to realize that time is the vehicle of the Creative, and to reassure ourselves that we have the time to wait. Time is not of the essence, time is the essence.

Fourth Line: *Earthen vessels simply handed in through the window.* The Sage, knowing that we are endangered by doubt and misunderstanding, comes to our aid; consequently, we are enlightened by a breakthrough in our understanding.

Fifth Line: *The abyss is not filled to overflowing.* If the time is not ripe for a thing to happen, it will not happen. Wanting a thing to happen before its time brings the danger of frustration and doubt. Ambition leads to danger. The path of least resistance for now is to retreat from striving. This path is correct and in line with duty.

Sixth Line: *Bound with cords and ropes.* Even though we understand the correct way, we persist in doing things "our way." We allow our ego to lead, and thus maintain a wrong attitude. Misfortune comes because we press on, taking matters into our hands. This line warns of the failure we may expect in maintaining such obstinacy. The remedy is return to the path of perseverance.

Danger comes because we fail to understand the paradoxical way the Cosmos works. We become frustrated, throw up our hands, and cannot find the way out. We do not realize that life is meant to be a paradoxical, ironical puzzle that can only be solved by following the true and the good, and through being selfless and sincere.

30.

Li / The Clinging, Fire

Li
Li

(Through detachment and acceptance we acquire a moderate
and just view of things.)

This hexagram concerns disengaging, in order to attain clarity,
seeing things moderately, and clinging to the power of truth to
emerge, even if we do not yet perceive what the truth is.

The image of fire clinging to something in order to burn symbolizes the attitude we need if we are to attain and keep clarity of mind.
Clarity, like fire, can endure only if it clings to something that is not
easily exhausted. The inexhaustible is the universal truth we discover in our study of the *I Ching*.

When the dark power of doubt threatens, we should cling to what
we have learned, trusting it to prove reliable; we can wholeheartedly
rely on the power of truth to prevail. We turn everything over to the
Sage, and attend only to keeping doubt dispersed and our attitude
independent and balanced. It is important to persevere through
moments of potential wavering, when we might begin to doubt the
Sage's counsel, and what we have learned from our *I Ching* studies.
When events seem foreboding and people seem evil, we should
remember the good that was and that still has potential in them. The
more evil they seem to be, the more resolutely we must cling to that
potential. If we cling to the invisible sparks of light that are eclipsed
by their inferior natures, the power of clinging will enable the dark
force to be overcome.

We also need to keep our mind open by clinging to the potential
of the situation. Regardless of how impossible it seems that a
situation might improve, such an improvement can happen if we
remain firm and independent in attitude, and open its being possible.
It helps if we cling to the fact that the Creative follows an invisible,
zig-zag course; we need to be willing to endure ambiguous and dis-
ruptive times while the Creative resolves the problem its own way.

Care of the cow brings good fortune. The docility and acceptance of the cow epitomizes the attitude which leads to clarity. To become docile we let go of all resistance to, and rejection of, what is happening. We accept every twist and turn of events as something useful and essential to the creative process. We cling docilely to what is good in ourselves and others, even if this is the smallest of embers. Through docility we are able to keep disengaged from the inferior power. When others are sharp, we can be dull, able to maintain a moderate and just view of our own and of their mistakes. Docility thus allows clarity and inner independence to return.

The power of good lies in the consistency of our determination to serve the Higher Power. We take an active interest in rescuing others by giving them space to find their way; we give them space through clinging to their true natures, regardless of how much or how long this nature has been eclipsed. Clinging to these inner realities causes a breakthrough in the obdurate situation, and brings about a revolution in people's attitudes.

In maintaining docility it is important not to judge things solely by their external appearances, for in doing so we lose our sense of the inner truth of the matter. It helps if we cling to the view that "things are as they need to be" for purposes we are not able to see. If we are able to focus only on externals, either vanity, desire, or fear are the culprits. We want to know how the external circumstance makes us look, or we fear that others will misinterpret our failure to act—our not taking a stand. We should vigorously resist the considerations and demands of vanity, and the disruptions to our equilibrium caused by desire.

Often, those envious of our inner independence try to engage us in the king-of-the-heap game. They wish to know if our strength is real. If they can jar us off balance, they will remain content not to grow, stuck in their defensive rigidity. If they succeed in making us feel threatened, their ego will achieve a victory.

Perhaps it is more important that the challenges people present to us uncover doubts we still have about ourself, or our path. Through uncovering these doubts we are able to deal with them. Docility and detachment are the only correct responses to such challenges. Docility becomes easy, once we discard the vanity of being concerned with how others regard us. Docility enables us to understand and be patient with ourselves and others.

First Line: *The beginning holds the seed of all that is to follow.* This line indicates that through meditating on first awakening, we are able to intercept, examine, and discard inferior thoughts the instant they enter consciousness. If they are not intercepted at this point, when they are only faint moods, and when their energies are at their lowest ebb, they quickly increase in strength and are able to dominate our thoughts for the rest of the day. Then we are unable to prevent the frustrations that cause our personalities to disintegrate.

Second Line: *Yellow light. Supreme good fortune.* Yellow light refers to looking at things moderately. Receiving this line counsels us to follow the mean. Reading the hexagram *Peace*, for instance, should not cause undue enthusiasm, nor should *Darkening of the Light* make us feel depressed. Neither good nor bad times should cause us to lose our emotional equilibrium. If we regard such times as occasions for self-development, no shock will set us off-balance. When we understand correctly the meanings of the hexagrams, they bring a sense of enlightenment and release from the tensions of misunderstanding the truths of life. Truth is never a glaring harsh reality (white light); it is a moderate understanding (yellow light).

Also, we should not hold to bad experiences as reason for being hard and fast in our rules. If someone has failed to pay us the money he owes, we should not then be hard on others whom we know to be conscientious. We need to listen to our inner feelings and to our inner sense of truth.

Third Line: *In the light of the setting sun, men either beat the pot and sing or loudly bewail the approach of old age. Misfortune.* If we fear and worry about the time required to obtain recognizable progress, we put ourselves in the wrong balance. If, nobleheartedly, we can accept the fact that things will be fulfilled when they will, then we secure our fate by making them possible. So long as the ego stands by expectantly measuring and weighing progress, the dark force of doubt operates, making it impossible for the power of good to manifest itself. Receiving this line reminds us that adversity lasts only for a time; through it we shape our character. The fires of adversity clarify and purify our natures, as fat is rendered from bacon.

Fourth Line: *It flames up, dies down, is thrown away.* Worry is the fire that consumes. We know that perseverance over a period of time is necessary to accomplish our goals; nevertheless, our inferiors complain about the length of time this requires. Their complaints

143

cause us to doubt ourself, the great-man potential in others, and the Creative. We need to silence our complaining inferiors and stop their obsessive preoccupation with our difficulties. We can do this by refusing resolutely to listen further, and by refusing to allow them to "look" at the difficulties. We can also gain their cooperation by explaining to them that their activity only makes things worse. By such means we may overcome their resistance, and thereby restore clarity and steadfastness. As long as they doubt, there can be no success.

Fifth Line: *Tears in floods, sighing and lamenting. Good fortune.* The commentary to this line mentions that a "real change of heart has taken place," either in ourself or another.

We attain a clear view when, in going through difficulties, we acknowledge that adversity is necessary for growth, and when we humbly accept what is happening. This change of heart displaces the vain considerations that accompany change, such as the dread of growing older, of becoming less attractive, being alone, or of having to die. We undermine the power of the ego when we realize that despite its bravado, it has had nothing to do with our success, and is an obstruction to progress.

The change of heart also refers to having given up efforts to force conclusions to our situations through contrived means. Even though we have thought such means justifiable, sincerity has caused us to return to the correct way.

Sixth Line: *It is best to kill the leaders.* The most evil ringleaders of disorder in the personality are vanity and pride—the ego, whether it is self-depreciating, self-congratulating, or self-defending.

Vanity appears when our decisions and actions concern the way others see us. Our pride becomes wounded when we extend ourself more than halfway in meeting others; then we begin to construct defenses against them because we have foolishly thrown ourself away. When we fail in such an effort we engage vanity and pride. Both vanity and pride emanate from the spoiled child within, which is ever pushing to obtain fellowship with others whether or not the conditions for it are correct. This spoiled child disdains waiting, and puts out an either/or demand for measurable progress. It also distrusts help from the Cosmos, so it attempts to do everything by itself. A person with humility realizes that acquiring the help of the invisible Sage is essential to every undertaking; therefore, he is patient and persevering.

The childish self (ego) cannot be eradicated totally, but its worst aspects must be subdued. There is no way to fight vanity directly, because it is not visible as one entity. It is visible, however, in its many manifestations, and these may be combatted individually. Among these manifestations are desire and impatience, which have their origins in fear and doubt. Vanity is also present when we see ourselves as rejected, alone, abandoned. Vanity causes us to want "inside knowledge," to have a "handle" on things, and to seek assurances that things will work to our satisfaction. Vanity causes us enviously to compare our fate to others. It makes us think that everything in life is dependent on human decisions; it causes us to forget that the Cosmos is at work putting things to right, and that we are not required to accomplish everything by ourselves.

Pride, too, is elusive, manifesting as impatience, anger, giving up, and vindictiveness. The image is given in the *I Ching* that if the mountain (our character) is to stand for a long time, it should be broadly based (steady and tolerant), not narrow and steep (proud).

Simple self-acceptance is something luminous to which to cling. Otherwise, we tend to test and probe why we exist, or why we are affected by things which arouse our discontent (envy). We should be on guard against the slightest entrance of these, or any emotions which threaten our inner independence. In resolutely apprehending them at the beginning we are able to resist their pressures and block their negative energies.

Finally, having successfully resisted evil, we should avoid becoming the martyred good person—still another vanity.

31.

Hsien / Influence (Wooing)

$$\frac{\text{Tui}}{\text{Kên}}$$ ☱
☶

(An 'influence' is about to take place—an unexpected
event which will challenge our inner stability.)

This hexagram states that the steady, quiet influence exerted by a
strong, independent personality, involuntarily causes others to
"respond cheerfully and joyously." Because a steady, quiet attitude
attracts, the hexagram also concerns wooing and the courtship
between the sexes. The correct kind of attraction does not involve
seduction. The example given is the Sage, whose steady, quiet
influence "encourages people to approach him."

*The superior man encourages people to approach him by his
readiness to receive them.* First, this means receptivity to others. The
kind of receptivity needed is a willing suspension of disbelief.
Regardless of how a person may have presented himself to us before,
or how we may be inclined to regard him because of what others say
about him, we try to keep an open mind. Such readiness has a
creative effect. Even if we have momentarily become involved in a
negative exchange, restoring an open mind (an inner neutrality
achieved through dispersing or letting go of all opinions and feelings) can deprive a negative situation of its tension and even reverse
it. This allows another's higher nature to return.

The second meaning of readiness has to do with influencing
others. Before we can successfully influence others, we need to be
receptive to the suggestions of the Sage. These suggestions are
voiced quietly unless we are in imminent danger, in which case we
may hear a loud, warning voice. It is necessary, therefore, to keep our
inner ear receptively attuned, as if we were awaiting instructions
from the Cosmos.

Readiness also means that one's attitude is innocent and independent, free of self-importance and emotional pressure. Thus
balanced and alert, we automatically and without effort or intention
receive and transmit good influences to others, acting as a conduit

for the Cosmos to speak and act. Emotions such as desire, anxiety, feelings of negation, and alienation, not only block our ability to receive from the Cosmos; they also transmit our dependence and weakness with a destructive effect. A weak inner self that vacillates from desire to doubt, from hope to fear, and from like to dislike, is immediately perceived by others. Moreover, weakness and dependence make us objects of contempt, challenge, and aggression, invoking the king-of-the-heap game; in this weakened state we are more affected by others' positive or negative feelings. A correct inner attitude, in addition to making us a conduit for the Creative, holds other people's egos in check, cultivates the superior man within them, and frees us from being unconsciously affected by their inner feelings.

The essence of this hexagram is contained in the sum of its lines. The first line mentions an influence which originates in the toe; in the second, the influence originates in the calf of the leg; in the third it originates in the thighs. The toe, calf, and thigh represent impulses which are driven by emotions and the proddings of one's ego. In the fourth line the influence comes from the heart. If this influence is "constant and good," the "effects produced are right"; thus, keeping our heart steady and independent is our primary work. In the fifth line balance is lost: influence which originates in the neck means that although we seek to maintain the correct attitude, we are so intent on succeeding that we lose our receptivity. In the sixth line the influence comes from the mouth, meaning that an influence based solely on words or logic has little or no real influence, regardless of intent. Words have real meaning when they come from a heart steadily tuned to what is high and good.

Receiving this hexagram often indicates that "an influence" is about to take place in which we will be challenged to hold to the correct way of influencing others. We are counselled to monitor our inner feelings and maintain our inner independence, and not react to any elements which would stimulate desire, fear, anger, or a relaxation of inner discipline. If our attitude is perseveringly neutral, then the creative energies of the Cosmos will be aroused and our response will be correct; if not, the pressures of the moment will cause our ego to surface and spoil the good influence we would otherwise have. An innocent and independent attitude draws back those who are estranged, and keeps at a distance those who press themselves on us for personal and selfish reasons.

When we do have an opportunity to be helpful in a conversational way, we should take care not to go further than the moment allows. When reticence is lost we cease being a conduit for the Cosmos; we cannot hear within if we are infected with ambition, or attachment to "having an influence." When we fail to see that others' receptivity is waning, we throw ourself away.

Ambition is always driven by desire. Desire, in turn, is driven by the doubt that things will not succeed by simply allowing them to work out on their own, and by the arrogant presumption that people are unable to find the truth by themselves, or that they should not be allowed space and time in which to grow. Doubt, desire, ambition, and restless effort come from our childish ego. It distrusts the Unknown, and suspects that even if we were obedient to the Divine Will in allowing things to proceed through their changes, we would somehow be cheated of attaining happiness. As long as we allow the childish self and its rationales to hold sway without resistance and discipline, we cannot achieve the true humility and acceptance that leads to the help our inferiors so much want. In this way we perpetuate the vicious circle of no progress.

We should not consciously attempt to incite responses in others, or to push matters along. We should disengage from their efforts to incite responses in us, either through flattery, seduction, manipulation, or irritation. Conscious manipulation always springs from egotistical, selfish, and vain motives; it does not allow natural attraction to proceed along its own course. Attraction must be allowed to develop naturally. We allow ourself to be drawn along, while maintaining our innocence of mind and independence of spirit. This attitude, combined with willingness to wait through the changes, is consistently in harmony with the Creative; it automatically draws the affection and loyalty of others.

The hexagram also counsels us to keep joy within bounds; this means that we establish and keep the correct balance in our relationships. Happiness, without regard to this balance, cannot last, for happiness is always the happy consequence of something more fundamental. To seek joy without regard to what causes it is to misunderstand the truth. When joy (or gain) becomes an end in itself, we seek pleasure for its own sake (or profit and possessions as ends in themselves), and create all the conditions which cause suffering in life. True joy, in intimate relationships, arises from harmony between people's essential selves. A communion of spirits is the natural result of sincerity, truth, and a selfless devotion to the good and the great. When the joy experienced becomes something we strive to maintain, joy becomes an end in itself rather than the happy consequence of following the good. Pursuing joy, we only experience the discontent of striving; then envy and possessiveness grow to overshadow all.

The state of our mind and the attitude of our spirit affect the whole universe. Therefore, it is best to be conscientiously correct, even out of the sight and hearing of others. In Chinese philosophy it is said that the slightest wave of the hand moves molecules all the way to the end of the universe. It is also true that the slightest change in our inner attitude affects those to whom we are connected, however far away they may be. Should we not, then, be careful of our innermost thoughts?

First Line: *The influence shows itself in the big toe.* The big toe represents a small beginning that soon becomes a foothold—the proverbial toe in the door. The toe, therefore, is the first place that a deteriorating influence shows itself. Desire has its beginning in the mood of wondering, and thus wondering is the first seed of decay. We should check our inner attitude to see if we are wondering, or if there exists the slightest feeling of doubt, or discontent, or rising self-confidence. Such feelings invariably lead to wavering, because they are the beginning seeds of doubt. As soon as we give these seeds the slightest credence, then desire, ambition, impatience, presumption, arrogance, and other inferior emotions quickly follow to threaten our inner equilibrium. Once our inner equilibrium is disturbed, we communicate our uncertainty to others, and lose our ability to have a good influence. With the increase of any one of these emotions our relationship with others becomes more and more problematical.

Second Line: *Influence...in the calves of the leg.* We should not be influenced by an apparent change, for the better or worse in a person or in the general situation, by which we allow strong elements such as desire, anger, envy, or hardness to take control of our attitude. We should wait until others' innocence and sincerity are securely established before we relinquish our reserve, or give ourself wholeheartedly. In doing either of these things we throw ourself away. Meanwhile, we should not seek ways to influence, but remember that great changes in people take time; well-established trends may not be reversed in a wholesale manner, except superficially and temporarily.

Third Line: *Influence...in the thighs.* Through following desire we accept less than what is correct in people, or rush to believe in surface appearances, or accept flattery. Only through inhibiting the moods of our heart can we retain the inner freedom and dignity which is essential to influence them correctly.

Desire also causes us to wonder. Wondering is the beginning seed which brings about a loss of inner freedom and humility. In wondering we doubt the Creative.

Fourth Line: *If a man is agitated in mind...only those...on whom he fixes his conscious thoughts will follow.* Here, we are counseled against attempting to influence others by consciously projecting thoughts and images. Such efforts betray our suspicion that the Higher Power will not do what is needed, and our doubt that others are capable of finding their own way. A good effect may be achieved only by keeping our minds and hearts innocent and pure. In this way we 'hold together' with what is good and retreat from evil.

Fifth Line: *Influence in the back of the neck.* In spite of the pressure of negative influences, our will to discipline our inferiors remains firm.

Sometimes, however, our attention to being disciplined is so preoccupying that we are not able to hear suggestions from the Sage. We are too anxious to find the right answers: we try to figure things out rather than keeping empty, allowing the right things to come of themselves. We must not even allow the fear of doing wrong to cause us to lose our receptivity. In this case the "back of the neck" means we are reacting to events stiffly rather than receptively.

Sixth Line: *Influence in the jaws, cheeks, and tongue.* We recognize the folly of trying to influence others by words and logic. People can see only what they are ready to see. While we may help people who are receptive to us to understand concepts, we cannot help them skip steps in their self-development by trying to achieve intellectually what must be achieved in the heart. Each person must go through the experiences which make it possible for him to grow; each must proceed at his own pace, in his own way. Although we may help, the Sage is the Master, and the *I Ching* the lantern throughout the entire journey.

This line also means that if, in the pressure of the moment, we say something we don't mean, it will have no real effect; we can forget our mistake, but it is necessary to revitalize our attitude and regain our emotional independence.

32.

Hêng / Duration

$$\frac{\text{Chên}}{\text{Sun}} \quad \begin{array}{c} \equiv\equiv \\ \equiv\equiv \end{array}$$

(Go on, as before, without wavering, or changing direction.)

On one level this hexagram means to endure; on another, it means to remain the same. Here is described the *I Ching* principle that life is a 'going on.' While straying from our path invokes the *I Ching* counsel to 'return' to our true self, and to the correct way, we return to going on. In going on we are neutral in attitude; we detach from 'looking behind,' 'looking aside,' or 'looking ahead,' to turn our attention straight ahead. We pay attention only to that which is put directly before us to do, and concern ourselves only with what is essential and correct.

We get this hexagram when we wonder what state of mind we should have. Conditions have changed; we wonder whether we should be more open, or more reserved. Should we be glad, and more relaxed, or should we be more wary? The hexagram counsels that we should go on as if nothing has changed.

Often we hope that the change is for the better, or we dread that it may be for the worse. Involved in hoping or dreading, our ego insinuates that we should do something to aid, or block, or adapt, to what is happening.

If we have seen a situation improve, we should regard the improvement as only one of the many steps that must be taken in the right direction. We avoid becoming hopeful or enthusiastic; we go on as before. If we see the situation as worse, we remind ourselves that regressions are unavoidable. The situation will become irreversible only if we fix on it as "bad." If we relate properly, each new slide backwards will be less than the last one. The general direction will be towards improvement.

Improvements, we should remember, invite us to become self-ishly involved. We begin to see the improved situation as benefiting us, thus causing us to lose our inner independence. This, in turn, invites others to manipulate us. There is only one course—to go straight ahead without being impressed by signs of change. We should not change our way of relating, but continue on, "steady as she goes." The final victory will be so genuine that there will be no doubts to make us wonder.

The images of thunder and wind, as elements which always accompany each other, symbolize relationships which endure through times of challenge and change. The example given is that of marriage as a social institution which has endured through the ages. The hexagram also concerns the attitudes that are essential if marriage, and the sort of human relationships which provide a sound basis for society, are to endure.

Throughout the *I Ching* it is emphasized that a strong, orderly, peaceful society has its foundation in a strong, orderly, peaceful family. The strength and security of the family, in turn, has its roots in a strong and correct relationship between husband and wife. In *The Family* (Hex. 37) it is said that if the husband fulfills his duty and the wife fulfills hers, and if the relationships between the siblings are correct, the family becomes secure and has a good influence on society.

The hexagram notes that at the heart of the family is the persevering wife. Since either a man or woman may draw this hexagram, we must regard the wife as symbolizing the one (male or female) who, in the given relationship, or situation, must persevere. To have a beneficial effect and nourish everyone correctly, such a person must content himself to work in a background position; in this way he acts to keep the situation in order.

Duration refers to our spiritual development, reminding us to hold to our principles during times of challenge: "The superior man stands firm and does not change his direction." The ultimate constancy is exemplified by the holy man who, through remaining forever in his course, enables the world to reshape itself.

Steadiness requires that we prevent outer evils from affecting our spirit, and successes from making us arrogant. It means we remain modest and detached, listening to our sense of what is true, essential, and correct. Perseverance in the correct attitude leads to the firmness and unity of character needed to transform evil and create the willing assent of others to follow the good.

It furthers one to have somewhere to go. This refers to our path. If we keep our path in mind—the low road, as opposed to the high road—we will not so easily stray from it. The low road symbolizes serving the good through perseverance, patience, and restraint, and through being content to work through the invisible means of inner truth. The high road is that of self-assertion, the heavy-handed use of power, and the pursuit of self-interest by which we relax into indulgence, and act with abandon.

First Line: Seeking duration too hastily brings misfortune persistently. This line often has to do with expecting too much too soon. If we expect dependable, measurable results at times we specify, our ego leads. Then, when such results are not forthcoming, we forsake persevering. It is as if the ego, which has been displaced but not routed, stands aside putting forth doubts, saying "I told you so," in order to resume command. In listening to it we lose our inner independence. To keep on our path we should not allow our inner gaze to look toward the goal, but keep it attuned to the needs of the moment.

Second Line: *Remorse disappears* once we withdraw from our mistakes. We may be contending and striving, or wishing to give up or to relax in comfort and enjoyment. Or, our ego may be playing the king-of-the-heap game. In the pursuit of comfort and self-verification, the childish ego tries to undermine our perseverance and distract us from our path. Our mistake has been to listen to its complaints. If we could see such errors in time to prevent them, there would be no remorse, but that would be expecting too much of ourselves. It is enough that we have the strength to withdraw from our mistakes and return to acceptance and composure.

Reference to our inner strength as being greater than the external situation means that because we are now aware of our ego's deceptions, the power of inner truth will prevail to straighten matters out.

Third Line: *He who does not give duration to his character meets with disgrace.* If we look sideways at our teammates to measure their progress, we cannot walk straight ahead on our path. It is impossible to lead those we follow. Looking aside arouses hopes and fears which destabilize our character. Distressing experiences are also provoked; what we fear most seems to happen. In Chinese philosophy it is said that harm enters only where fear makes an opening.

Less obvious forms of looking aside include counting our good luck, or our money, or measuring our progress. If we are to give duration to our character we must look straight ahead at our path and stay free of the self-satisfaction or self-negation that comes from measuring our gains, or from comparing ourselves with others.

Fourth Line: *No game in the field. What is not sought in the right way is not found.* Trying to obtain the goal by frontal assault only leads to humiliation. Our eye is fastened on the result without regard to the means of obtaining it. In the Cosmic hierarchy of values, the path is more important than the goal, the way of making progress more important than the result. This means that we need to concentrate our energies on the path, on being consistent in character, innocent of mind, and humble of spirit. As for the future, we must let happen what will happen.

This line also refers to trying to impress others. Such efforts come from decadent family fears of others' presumed importance. We should be concerned only to see that what we have to say is sincere, modest, essential, and correct.

This line can also mean there is "no game" in the line of action we are tempted to follow to produce results. If we cease striving and let go, events will define the correct course of action.

Fifth Line: *Perseverance...is good fortune for a woman, misfortune for a man.* In this line the man symbolizes a person's tendency to go out and explore life. In doing so, he experiences life and learns. The woman symbolizes our duty to give others the space to learn, and to persevere in holding to our trust in their potential for good, and in their ability to find the correct way.

In the West we are expected to learn mostly through intellect. We take great pains, using threats and force, to get our children to accept what their teachers say without questioning. In the *I Ching* way, the student seeks the Sage of his own volition. Through being exposed to the dangers of his misconceptions he must do battle with his doubts and undertake the discipline of his own rescue. Thus, although he is helped by the Sage, his growth and self-discipline are his own achievements.

This line also deals with wondering if it is necessary for people to go through the risks of learning by experience; we wonder if it can be correct to stand by while others place themselves in what we perceive as jeopardy. The answer is Yes. If we are to attain self-mastery we must slay the false dragon of fear within ourselves. If we observe that someone is going on a false path, we should not despair.

Despair only indicates that we fear he won't succeed, a fear which hampers him, because we lock him into our doubt of him. If people are never exposed to risk, they are hampered in finding themselves. We need to let go of distrust and put our fears and worries in the hands of the Unknown. In this way we can endure what otherwise would greatly upset us.

It is also important not to strive to help others or supervise their development. We must follow our own path strictly. Only our inner independence and good example strengthens and aids others.

Sixth Line: *Restlessness as an enduring condition brings misfortune.* Restlessness invades our psyche when we think of the wrongs other people commit. Then, instead of persevering on the path of steady, correct waiting, we take the high road of aggression or self-defense to bring about change.

We may think we need to remind ourself that the other person has not yet corrected himself, in order to hold a firm attitude about him. This is not necessary, however, since events constantly reveal the true situation and we are not deceived.

Similarly, it is unnecessary to rehearse their wrongs mentally in order to remain reserved. In staying detached and dependent on the Cosmos, forces come to our defense. These forces cannot help us, however, if we are entangled in anger, fear, or desire.

33.

Tun / Retreat

Ch'ien
————
Kên

(Stop looking at the situation to figure it out.)

The situation indicated by this hexagram is that our ego, in the form of vanity, desire, or fear, is aroused either through observing a situation, or another's behavior. We may also be disconcerted by our weakness. It is important to disengage and cease going over the situation in our mind. This, in *I Ching* terms, is to retreat.

It is important to retreat (disengage) before we become further involved. If we retreat in time, we suffer no remorse because we will not yet have had an adverse effect on the situation. Now we may retreat with little effort, but once desire or fear is aroused, we become entangled. Pride may also be aroused, as when we throw ourselves away to someone who is not ready to hear what we have to say. Once aroused, the negative effects of wounded pride are difficult to disperse; pride makes it difficult to return to the path of humility and acceptance. If we allow our ego to dominate the situation, we invariably go on to act even more inappropriately. Involving ourself in this way causes reversals, humiliation, and remorse, which can be avoided if we retreat at the earliest stage of becoming involved.

The correct time to retreat comes when we begin to lose our inner equilibrium and serenity—when we begin to feel enthusiasm, desire, or ambition, or when others are no longer receptive, or when their delicacy of feeling wanes. Likewise, we retreat when we begin to be attacked by doubt and negation, or when our actions no longer yield progress. If we have enough humility we will be able to observe these times and withdraw, not in disappointment, but in the realization that times of influence are always brief.

We need to attune ourself to the wave-like manner in which people first become receptive, and then turn away. We should not hesitate to disengage the instant their receptivity falters. In retreating we cling to simplicity (recognition and acceptance of being powerless), sincerity, and serenity, and to the power of truth to correct the

157

situation. Thus, we retain our inner independence, preserve the power of our personality, and are able to go on our way without any loss of self.

Disengaging is also necessary when our ego awakens with enthusiasm, either on perceiving an improvement in the situation, or on perceiving new opportunities to influence; in its sudden interest the ego attempts to seize the moment of progress and push it still further, in order to dominate what otherwise would be a spontaneous and creative moment. If we remain aware that our ego is always waiting to interject itself, we will be able to keep it checked. When our ego does seize power in this manner, the other person's ego arises to defend itself. The person who succeeds in controlling his ego finds that the creative moments which allow him to have an influence continuously open up to him.

In all situations of retreat, we should prevent our ego from looking at the problem. Such looking causes us to feel a need to "straighten the matter out." So long as we strive, the situation will remain obdurate, energized by our involvement. By retreating, the obdurate elements become de-energized; then, new opportunities for influence become possible. Even though misunderstanding momentarily prevails, we must not abandon our position by saying to ourself, "Maybe I'm wrong and they're right." This is to abandon the field to the enemy. We need only maintain a dignified reserve which makes it difficult for other people's egos to advance and claim victory.

First Line: *At the tail in retreat.* We allow our ego to keep examining the issue. We may be considering a compromise with the evil element, or we may remain involved through desire, fear, anger, impatience, or anxiety. We must disengage and no longer focus on the situation.

Second Line: *He holds him fast with yellow oxhide.* Our inferiors want, and ultimately have a right, to justice. Justice, however, may not be procured simply because we want it, or because our ego demands it. Justice may be procured only through the firm leadership of our superior self. Through keeping aware of our ego, persevering, and keeping disengaged, we win the help of the Higher Power.

Third Line: *A halted retreat is nerve-wracking.* Our inferiors, which are composed of both good and evil elements, remain engaged with the problem. It is necessary to retreat as best we can, even though they argue on and on. This effort to do what is right gives us strength, because the good elements such as will power, dedication, devotion, and sincerity, here referred to as our servants, rally to fight off evil elements such as doubt, anxiety, fear, pride, and vanity.

Fourth Line: *Voluntary retreat...brings downfall to the inferior man.* In disengaging from conflict we preserve our personality from humiliation and find the correct defense against other people's envy, anger, or hatred. In abandoning the struggle their egos lose power. When we compete with other people's egos we only sharpen their weaponry and harden their resoluteness to continue. When we disengage, their resoluteness gives way.

Fifth Line: *Friendly retreat.* On perceiving the need for retreat it is necessary to be determined; otherwise, we will slip back into striving. We must retreat in friendliness, but also with absolute firmness. The other person may try to engage us further, but we must not allow ourself to be tempted. Yielding to ambition or impatience now will become the source of weakness later on.

In the king-of-the-heap game we may accede to the subtle flattery put forth by one who, in observing formal courtesy, invites us to explain our views, although he cares nothing about what we say. Once we have opened ourselves up to him, he suddenly attacks. We should retreat immediately from further discussion and refuse to participate in this game. While we may, without impunity, give expression to our views, we should never defend them, or rely on the bravado of logic, or wit. Through participation in such games we throw ourself away and jeopardize our inner independence, along with the power for good that such independence confers. In all discussions we should remember our responsibility to the Sage, whom we serve. We have a duty to respond sincerely only to sincerity. We should avoid promoting our point of view. The truth needs neither promotion nor defense; it is capable of standing on its own merits, and of enduring all assaults of the false dragon.

There is hardly anything so potentially deceptive as formal courtesy, or charm. Since much of the world conducts itself on this basis, we should not blame those who attempt to engage us, for the sake of being polite. Also, we should not blame ourselves if we occasionally get caught up in social games. Such games can only be eradicated through time, insight, and self-development.

Sixth Line: *Cheerful retreat.* In disengaging we are free to go on our way, no longer in the grip of negative elements.

34.

Ta Chuang / The Power of the Great

<table>
<tr><td>Chên</td><td rowspan="2">☳
☰</td></tr>
<tr><td>Ch'ien</td></tr>
</table>

(Great power lies in one's certain knowledge of the power of good.)

The Power of the Great. Perseverance furthers. Here, as in many other *I Ching* hexagrams, there are two meanings to consider. The first meaning is the true power which arises when we perceive the correct way to go. "The gates to success" begin to open, as it is put in the second line. The second meaning has to do with stolen, assumed, or intercepted power in which the ego seizes command by taking advantage of favorable situations.

Power is defined by the two trigrams as clarity (Ch'ien) which abruptly rises up as strength (Chên). A clear perception of a situation gives us the strength to deal with it. Insight opens the door. Perceiving the opening, we suddenly feel free to move ahead.

Ch'ien indicates the Cosmic idea; Chên indicates that movement is precipitated. However, Ch'ien also means perseverance. Whenever we perceive the correct way to go we must not become obsessively lost in the forward thrust so that we lose our inner composure, for our ego waits for just such an opportunity. The ego is like a wild card football player who, obsessed with ambition to attain to some sort of glory, is on nobody's side. Waiting on the sideline, it eagerly watches for an opportunity to jump out to intercept the ball (seize the power of insight). Needless to say, it often runs the wrong way. The ego can interject itself only if we become so absorbed in what we are doing that we lose touch with our inner being. (Our true self is always objective, reticent and reserved.) Awareness of this danger protects us from losing our inner balance, and from forgetting that right and justice must be accompanied by moderate thoughts and actions.

The idea of power combined with perseverance indicates a certain reticence. In possessing power (the consciousness that right is on our side) we must be cautious to use it, and we must certainly not glory in it. True greatness is the ability to possess power and not use it.

We often fail to realize that our inner thoughts communicate to others without any intention or effort on our part; we feel their inner attitudes as well. These are non-verbal perceptions which we are trained in childhood to distrust. All of us can remember when, as children, we reacted negatively to someone, only to be dissuaded from or cajoled into denying, and even suppressing our feelings. We harbored them, nonetheless, for they were to us an undeniable inner truth. This inner sense of truth, however suppressed, however denied, and however contrary to what we are "supposed" to think, is capable of emerging with great power under the right conditions. If we relate to it the way we are naturally meant to relate, inner truth can correct all wrongs.

On having either a positive or negative perception about something or someone, we should lift the perception to consciousness at once. Doing so enables us to understand fully the inner truth of the situation before our tainted habitual responses take hold. If we fail to do this, and leave the emerging perception in its semi-conscious state, the old reactive patterns will remain in effect simply through inertia. On lifting the new perception to full consciousness we preserve its integrity and empower it so that it automatically corrects the situation in question. We need do nothing at all.

The lines of the hexagram reveal many of the dangers inherent when the power of insight has been intercepted by the ego. As the first line states, power in the "lowest place" is "inclined to effect advance by force." On first perceiving an evil our ego interjects itself with the thought, "We must do something about this!" (This is an old reactive pattern based on doubt.) On perceiving an opportunity to advance (at the moment the door opens) the ego interjects with exuberant enthusiasm, "Now we can do something!" or worse, "The problem is over; we can relax and forget everything!" On perceiving that we have attained an influence, it says, self-importantly, "See me, I possess the answers; if you don't agree, I'll make things happen my way," or else we allow ourselves to indulge in the egotistical 'spiritual irritation' of being in the right.

On intercepting the ball, the ego always interferes with the natural direction of power; it either goes too far, or runs the wrong way. Pushing obstinately, it becomes entangled; once entangled, it adopts a belligerent pose. Only the fourth line of the hexagram describes the correct use of power: "a man goes on quietly and perseveringly working at the removal of resistances..." and, "such a man's power does not show externally, yet it can move heavy loads."

We receive this hexagram mostly when, if only in our thoughts, we have abused power. Power includes using leverage, as when we push (or nudge) people along, or when we keep pressure on them, or make them feel uncomfortable, or when we seek to manipulate them through flattery and the lure of comfort. Power abuse occurs when we hold grudges, or dismiss others as hopeless. Saying things in anger has an inner effect on others that is like an atom blast, the fallout of which may persist for years.

Persevering in the use of power means that we wait for the right time to speak or act—when we are free of the pressures and enthusiasms of the ego, and when we arc in full possession of the inner truth of the matter. Everything we say or do proceeds from a sense of what is fair, just, and essential, and we rely on the power of good in others, trusting that their sense of truth (however suppressed) will emerge to support what is right. We must be willing to trust that if we are sincere in trying to find the correct way, the power of good will come to our aid.

It is important when we are given the opportunity to express our point of view, that we go no further than the moment allows. To do so means that our ever-prowling ego has once more intercepted the truth and mixed it with its own purposes into half-truths. Then everything we say or do carries the taint that accompanies half-truths.

An incorrect use of power creates a bad reaction; this reaction can be undone if we return to sincerity and humility. We withdraw, not in anger or discouragement, but into neutrality. Being able to go on resolutely just when we are tempted to give up the struggle as hopeless creates great power. Firmness at the post of duty overcomes the evil force.

First Line: *Power in the toes. Continuing brings misfortune.* "Power in the toes" means that we try to win through persuasion, contending, or force. It also refers to inner pacts we have made that people must conform to what we want before we will have anything to do with them. It is egotistical to maintain any form of supervisory attitude. To correct people we must totally disengage. We will know when they have corrected themselves.

Power in the toes also means that we advance presumptuously. For example, we press ourselves on others who are not open to us.

Or, we fail to retreat and disengage in time—when others' receptivity peaks and begins to decline. We assume that even though we have been a little careless in such things, we will be protected. It is necessary, however, to be responsible in order to set the correct example, and to consider seriously the risks to which we expose ourselves. To presume on Fate is to court disaster. It is like buying an unknown stock on the Stock Market on the presumption that Fate will make it pay off.

Second Line: *Perseverance brings good fortune.* This line counsels perseverance because, once resistance gives way we tend to regress into the luxury of exuberant self-confidence. During such times we are self-assertive, expecting people to credit our inner worth and attainments, forgetting that it was through modesty and acceptance that the situation has improved. Now we feel liberated enough to abandon our limits and tell others what is wrong with them. To avoid such an abuse of power we should maintain a modest attitude.

Third Line: *The inferior man works through power. The superior man does not act thus. To continue is dangerous. A goat butts against a hedge and gets its horns entangled.* This line refers to times when we think or act as an adversary to others. We may have withdrawn with a hostile attitude to consider taking actions that would put them at a disadvantage. It is a mistake to think that through resistance and hardened attitudes we can force the great man in others to emerge; setting up an obstacle course only hardens what is inferior in them.

Fourth Line: *Perseverance brings good fortune. Remorse disappears. The hedge opens; there is no entanglement. Power depends upon the axle of a big cart.* We have made an external move which creates resistances in others. For example, we have priced our goods a little higher than we think will be accepted, even though our costs have required us to do so. When no one buys, we think it is due to the price. This is not so, however, for the buyers resist only because they intuitively perceive our doubts. Once we become firm that we have done what was necessary and correct, these resistances give way.

The axle symbolizes a persevering attitude. Through persevering (remaining firmly correct) we overcome adversity and danger.

It is also important that we do not destroy our inner power by indulging doubt about ourself when we have made mistakes. We should acknowledge our mistakes, correct them, and get on with life.

Fifth Line: *Loses the goat with ease. No remorse.* It is important not to make pacts with ourselves. When we decide that a particular person is not to be trusted, we erect an obstacle course over which he must climb to reach us. To persist in this is to punish him excessively. This line reassures us that we may safely give up defenses and pacts without coming to harm.

Sixth Line: *A goat butts against a hedge. It cannot go backward, it cannot go forward. Nothing serves to further. If one notes the difficulty, this brings good fortune.* The goat is entangled through using too much power. Obstinately pressing for results creates more rather than less resistances. We may have taken an action (or have thought of doing so) which would put someone either at a disadvantage, or at an unfair advantage. We may expect or demand someone to do a thing because he "ought to," even though it would be wrong for him to heel to our ego-demand, or we may have become too interested in what is going on. All such actions and attitudes create obstacles and resistances. We correct such errors by withdrawing from the obstinate use of power.

After using power wrongly we should be prepared to persevere while an eclipse in our relationship runs its course. Meanwhile, we should not stand in the crossroads, wondering what to do next. We should go on, keeping ourself perseveringly detached. Once we have corrected our attitude we should leave the matter behind, as if nothing had occurred.

35.

Chin / Progress

$$\frac{\text{Li}}{\text{K'un}}$$

(Brighten your bright virtue; the goal is to follow the path.)

The Superior man brightens his bright virtue. The image of the sun rising over the earth indicates a time of progress. Such a time also brings into the open careless habits or practices which impede or block progress, or which threaten our gains.

Receiving the hexagram affirms that we are making progress, even though it may elude our direct observation. Receiving it also reminds us of the basic principles on which progress is founded so that we can use the time of progress wisely. In particular, we should avoid sitting on our laurels and luxuriating in our achievements. Instead, it is a time to "brighten our bright virtue."

Progress is not the result of working for progress as a goal in itself, or toward comfortable and personally desirable objectives, rather, it is the result of working on being consistent and true to one's principles, and of serving that which is higher. We cultivate an attitude of inner independence by focussing only on what is essential and correct. We fail to serve the good when, on achieving some small progress, we forget about continuing humbly on our path, and only indulge ourselves in the comfort of the moment.

Receiving individual lines of the hexagram tells us to search for specific attitudes which block progress, or which threaten the progress already gained. Progress is blocked when we harbor viewpoints contrary to those of the Sage.

An enlightened ruler and an obedient servant.... This line reminds us that progress is the consequence of serving the Higher Power "obediently," and of following the true and the good selflessly, without thought of reward. This means that we must take care not to luxuriate in "having an influence," or to use the affection and respect we have gained to indulge in desires. To truly help others, and to solidify our gains, we must remain selfless. Thus, our work remains "at the disposal of the ruler."

Among the more subtly decadent attitudes is our tendency to be goal-oriented. For example, we focus on our goal to rescue or to reunite with someone. Then we fasten on any idea which seems to advance progress in some measurable or dramatic way. Once we become goal-oriented, we tend to intervene in affairs to make sure they are moving in the direction and with the momentum we desire. Or, we intervene to prevent others from proceeding in what we perceive as the wrong direction. A goal-oriented person is like a particular type of horse known as a "barn rat." This horse is so emotionally attached to the barn that when its rider points it in any other direction it walks slower and slower, and when it is turned back towards the barn, it can hardly be restrained from running. When we are goal-oriented, we distrust the willingness or ability of the Sage to use diverse circumstances creatively. Just as in a sailboat one tacks along different angles to make progress against the wind, the Creative uses all events and directions to make things work.

We slip into goal-oriented habits whenever we allow our ego to engage in any kind of measuring to see how far we have progressed (or have failed to progress). This, in turn, initiates doubt and effort by which we lose our center of gravity and the inner independence which brings about progress.

Time is the vehicle of the Creative power. Time alone heals. When we allow our ego to resist the time required to make progress, because of its fears and doubts, we become locked in the vortex of the dark force and we lose the power for good which accompanies an open mind.

The dark force is potent and dynamic. When we see someone's attitude as hopelessly stuck, we "darken their light" and lock them into a negative pattern of resistance. Similarly, we block ourself when we doubt that we are able to do something. Doubt disables our ability to mobilize the Unknown to help us, and blinds us to our hidden abilities.

We allow the Cosmic outcome to emerge when we cease striving to shape the direction of change through conflict and leverage. When we trust that the correct way will show itself, we experience a dramatic change in the circumstances. This change is described in the fifth line of *Splitting Apart* (Hex. 21) as a "shoal of fishes." The moment we relate correctly, splitting apart ends; the entire school of fishes wheels and changes direction simultaneously.

167

First Line: *Progressing, but turned back.* We have done what was right and necessary but it seems there is no progress. We should not allow ourselves to be roused to anger but simply continue to do what is right in a calm and cheerful manner. Thus we will "bite through" the obstacles to achieving justice and equality in our relationships.

Second Line: *Progressing, but in sorrow.* It is better to endure suffering and loneliness than to be in someone's company if it means we compromise our principles, or if the time has not yet been fulfilled. Only when the fundamentals of human unity are correct can we find happiness. If others do not follow our way, we should allow them to go their way without trying to influence them. To accept humbly going on alone brings happiness because it is the correct thing to do.

Third Line: *All are in accord. Remorse disappears.* Although we are grieved at not having had the strength and self-discipline to follow our path with total steadiness, this regret will be dispelled. In returning to our path we are aided by all who love good.

Fourth Line: *Progress like a hamster.* Wrong possessions refer to luxuries of attitude such as the following: when we expect or demand things of people; when we demand rewards (of the Sage) for our good work; when we use the time of progress to amass power and influence for ourselves; when we indulge in the comforts of the situation rather than doing what is right; when we justify our caprice by putting responsibility for it on the *I Ching*; when we look for ways to turn over to others our responsibility to decide things for ourself; when we indulge feelings of anger or frustration. The ego is on hand in every situation, searching for glory, comfort, and for a reason to exist, or for a reason to abandon the path. We must constantly guard against its secretly amassing such possessions for itself.

The "dubious procedure" mentioned generally refers to over-energetic behavior that might be called the "white-knight-in-shining-armour" syndrome. In close proximity to evil, our inferiors, thinking that truth needs defending, crystallize themselves into a knight in shining armour to do battle with the evil thing. Truth, however, needs no defense. It has the ultimate power and is bound to prevail in the end.

Fifth Line: *Take not gain and loss to heart.* Although it seems that we have failed to take advantage of a good opportunity to influence the situation, we should not mind this. Although it is not obvious, progress has been made by keeping ourself detached and free. If we view each moment as an opportunity to influence, we become too ambitious and goal-oriented. We should let the moments flow and keep alert; then, everything will happen as it should.

Sixth Line: *Making progress with the horns....* We cannot teach a person a lesson or bring him to his senses by being openly offensive, alienated, or hostile, all of which represents the over-energetic behavior mentioned in the fourth line. Aggression is justified only against our inferior self ("our own people").

This line also refers to the negative effects that come of harboring feelings of blame and anger instead of disengaging from them.

36.

Ming I / Darkening of the Light

$$\frac{\text{K'un}}{\text{Li}}$$

(Discontent with slow progress, we lose our inner independence.)

The light has sunk into the earth. This image refers to adverse circumstances which make it difficult to maintain our will to stay on our path. It would appear that no progress has been made, and therefore our balance and inner independence are threatened. Because the situation seems difficult and immovable, we despair, fearing we will never find a solution.

Our inner light is always threatened when we engage in looking at a difficult situation from the viewpoint of our ego, or childish heart. It is as if we have on dark glasses, and everything we see is sorted out under headings of "no better," or "worse." People's habits of mind seem so defective that we cannot imagine any possibility of their changing. Nor can we conceive that following our path will make any difference during the time frame in which we feel they need to change.

In this clouded view we forget that all changes are like streams which travel a long way underground before they come to the surface. We need to remember that we cannot attain a clear view if we confine ourselves to observing the external situation; similarly, we cannot see with clarity if we fail to quiet the clamoring inner voices. We need to disengage from looking at the situation. Disengagement is made difficult if we fail to give up feelings of resentment, hostility, or frustration. For the time being we need to accept the situation humbly, as it is.

We should not be concerned about the way others see our disengagement; vanity, in the form of wounded pride, acts to mobilize our inferiors to anger, hatred, and self-defense. Our ego (in the form of vanity) is involved whenever we have an emotional dependence on making visible, measurable progress. Its continued leadership perpetuates the endless cycle of "no progress," for as long as it rules we cannot engage the power of the Creative, which responds only to selflessness.

To escape the ego's domination we need to reaffirm that the Creative (nature) works slowly and imperceptibly until one day it rains, the blossom appears, and the fruit ripens. The dénouement in the drama of life brings all diverse elements into alignment; then the impossible happens. We need to keep in mind that the miracle of the blossom, the rain, and the fruit, is nature's business.

Because looking aside darkens our inner light, we should avoid dwelling on, or discussing, either our own or other people's incorrect behavior. Focussing on negatives has a bad effect.

First Line: *Darkening of the light during flight.* Because we have made a great effort to follow our path, to discipline our inferiors, and to be modest and sincere, and because we keep thinking about the effort and time we have put in, we are disappointed to see that no great visible progress has been made.

All such beginning seeds of doubt give rise to desire, and in turn, to striving; when we do not succeed, we feel embittered, so that in self-defense we adopt a hardened and hopeless attitude towards everyone in the situation—the other people, the *I Ching*, life itself. All along, the ego has been on the side, testing and measuring, agreeing to be subdued only in return for visible gains.

The remedy is to cease looking sideways. This is possible if we hold to our inner light, and cling to what is good in ourself and others. In a more objective mood we are able to see that Fate has not led us to an ugly and repulsive end, but to a greater, enduring harmony between ourselves and others. We are able to see that our adversities have brought about new growth and understanding. We also see that as long as our ego is still able to dominate, even if only for short periods of time, we have more work to do before our problems can be resolved and our goals attained.

Second Line: *Darkening...injures him in the left thigh.* Because we have failed to overcome all the difficulties in one great sweep of effort we are tempted to give up. However, something within hangs on and helps us cling to our path. We need only trust the Higher Power to lead us past the difficulties. We need not know the answers in advance.

171

Third Line: *Their great leader is captured.* This means that we recognize the source of the problem, either within ourself or within another person. It is usually some habit of mind that is difficult to break; therefore, the line says, "one must not expect perseverance too soon." Expecting to overcome a faulty attitude all at once leads to disappointment and splitting apart. It is important to be tolerant of ourselves and others. Only perseverance, sustained over a period of time, enables us to dissipate the power of the ego. When it sees that we are determined, it relinquishes control. It is as if our faults have an existence independent of us; they can be defeated only if we repeatedly hunt them down and deal with them. We must get used to the danger and difficulty this effort entails.

Fourth Line: *One gets at the very heart of the darkening....* We leave the wrong path behind when we realize that there can be no improvement in following it. The heart of this matter may be impatience, or righteous indignation (pride) toward others' inferiors.

Fifth Line: *Darkening...as with Prince Chi.* As this line advises, we "need invincible perseverance of spirit and redoubled caution" in our "dealings with the world," for surely, as with Prince Chi, our virtues will be tested. If we persevere, our current trials will end in success. Our current troubles will be seen only as necessary difficulties that precede great and enduring changes.

Sixth Line: *Not light but darkness.* The climax of the darkening is reached. It would seem that all efforts and trials were in vain. Precisely now, however, the tension of the "false dragon" has been stretched to its limits. It cannot harm us if we stand fast and renew our resolve to go on. Through not falling victim to alienation and negation the evil element fails. Our will to continue, to follow sincerely and modestly the good and the beautiful, is all that remains, and it does so victoriously.

37.

Chia Jên / The Family [The Clan]

Sun
Li ䷤

(Working in a background position, and relying on the power of inner truth.)

This hexagram defines correct relationships between people within the family unit. This may also mean the spiritual family (oneself in relation to the Sage), or the human family. An old Chinese proverb says that if you want to correct the world, you must first correct the state; if you want to correct the state, you must first correct the family; if you want to correct the family, you must first correct yourself. Working at self-correction is of the first and perhaps only importance. By making one's attitude correct, great changes in others' attitudes are made possible.

As the sixth line indicates, we influence others through the force of inner truth rather than through the exercise of physical or verbal power. *Perseverance of the woman* means that we cultivate the receptive and persevering components of our nature, for these activate the power of the Creative. This means that we must often work in a seemingly insignificant position (as seen by our ego) in which we forego striving and self-assertion. While we are always firm in our values, we remain gentle in dealing with others. Another proberb says, "Be like water. Water is soft, but its force is irresistible." True leadership, from the *I Ching* point of view, is not standing out in front, or on top. We support from beneath, through patience, inner firmness about what is right, and inner independence. We are always ready to withdraw when the moment requires it, to go our way alone. This is truly to love.

Instead of acting overtly, we allow the power of just and correct thoughts to penetrate to others. By keeping neutral in attitude, we allow ourself to be called into action spontaneously, as the moment demands. The inner truth we convey to others is the essence of the matter—what is universally true. We need only recognize this truth

173

for it to penetrate to others. We neither project our thoughts, exercise our will, nor say or do, anything.

Inner truth is also the higher truth we do not yet perceive. We can put our trust in this higher truth to show itself at the right time, and to have the correct effect. We need only trust that it exists. To trust means simply that we suspend disbelief. Until inner truth shows itself we respect only greatness of soul (humility, sincerity, and constancy), otherwise we remain patient and firm in dealing with people's faults.

First Line: *Firm seclusion within the family.* Our work is straight before us and concerns the way we relate, in our inner attitude, to the people with whom we have a direct relationship. Our job is not to preoccupy ourselves luxuriously and magnificently with remote or abstract issues, but to confine ourselves to the problems put directly to us to solve.

This means that while we should not become preoccupied with events outside our immediate sphere, we should, nevertheless, develop a correct attitude toward them, for in attaining a Cosmic perspective, we activate the power of truth to rectify them. If we hear reports of injustice, catastrophe, famine, or misery, we should not bemoan them, or chastise the Cosmos, or indulge outrage and blame against the cruel and the unjust; in doing so we galvanize the causes of injustice. We should not distrust the power of the Creative to correct decadent situations, or doubt its inclination to come to the aid of the miserable and defenseless. If decadence has been brought to light, it means that the Creative is actively at work putting the situation before the human conscience. This gives us the opportunity to exercise a creative attitude. The conscience of humanity bears heavily on those who, up to now, under the cover of anonymity and obscurity, have indulged their indifference and cruelty. However, in regarding their offenses we must not see them as outside the human family. We must endeavor to discover, as sincerely and deeply as if the person were our own child gone astray, why the offender does what he does. If we have dealt sincerely with our own bad habits of mind, we will understand that others have merely carried some of our seemingly harmless attitudes many steps further. We should regard offenders as the Sage has regarded us and our offenses. This attitude is never to give up on anyone's ability to return to his better nature.

Correcting others requires that we be consistently correct within ourselves. We respond affirmatively when others are correct; we withdraw within when they indulge in temper tantrums, spoiled demands, or negative attitudes. If on one occasion we are lenient with the child who marks the furniture, can we blame him if he marks it at a later time? If we have spoiled someone by yielding to his wrong attitudes, we can only break his childish will through correcting our lack of self-discipline. We are not allowed the luxury of supporting people's egos.

Second Line: *She should not follow her whims....* We follow our whims if we depart from self-discipline by striving to influence and force results. Each person must have space to find his own way and freedom to learn through his own efforts. This means we must often stand aside in what seems to be an unimportant or unnoticed position. Adherence to this duty has creative results far beyond casual observation, and beyond the immediate time and place.

This line also indicates that we have stopped attending to our inner thoughts to concentrate on what others should or should not do; or we have stopped attending to those in our immediate circle to romantically "save the world," or "conquer" outer space. This is not to say we should not go into outer space; it is simply that we should not be so ambitious as to compromise what is truly important. When we forget our life of the moment to dwell on the past, or to fantasize about controlling the future, we "follow our whims."

Third Line: *When tempers flare up* refers to times when another person's ego asserts itself forcefully; this calls for maintaining reserve; we do not "dally and laugh" with him. Duty requires that we remain withdrawn and reserved until his Inferior Man is displaced by renewed modesty. In this case it is better to be too severe than too weak.

Sometimes this line refers to the flareup of our temper, especially our impatience with the length of time it takes to correct the situation, and to being angry at how much we must endure. If we busy ourselves with such feelings, the Sage withdraws, so that in addition to all else we feel abandoned.

Fourth Line: *She is the treasure of the house. Great good fortune.* The welfare of those around us depends on our right actions. We further the general welfare when we resist getting swept away by considerations of self-interest. This line calls us to reflect on whether we are doing things for the right reasons. Checking ourselves for hidden motives helps us keep in balance. The conscientious person cares to do things for right reasons, therefore he produces great good fortune for all.

Fifth Line: *As a king he approaches his family.* The king symbolizes the way the Sage relates to us, his family. Love, not fear, is the basis of this relationship, and therefore it can be trusted. The love that the Sage bears us, by his ceaseless caring and trust in our superior potential, provides example of the selfless loyalty we are meant to develop for those in our charge. Although we often must disengage and let people go, we do so not because we are indifferent, but because we care, and because we cannot give up on the smallest remnant of what is good in them, or on their potential to return to their true selves.

Sixth Line: *His work commands respect.* Only through developing our highest nature can we influence others correctly and create order in life. This means that we develop a firm sense of values we are unwilling to compromise. This sense of values acts as a storehouse of inner truth. Through all difficulties we cling to it to provide the solutions and point the correct way to proceed. We firmly and resolutely follow our own path. We are glad when others walk with us (going toward the good in themselves) and we freely leave behind those who take different directions. When we succeed, we go forward without hesitation, not dwelling on our accomplishments. When we fail, we go forward without hesitation, without recrimination, without useless self-flagellation. Thus, our work commands respect.

38.

K'uei / Opposition

$$\frac{\text{Li}}{\text{Tui}} \quad \overline{\overline{}}$$

(Misunderstanding)

Opposition describes a situation in which people go in opposite directions due to misunderstanding. Either we misunderstand the Sage, Fate, the meaning of life, the Cosmic order of values, ourselves and others, or others misunderstand us.

In *I Ching* terms, people follow false paths and oppose the truth not because they are contrary or bad, but because they misunderstand the truth. They perceive that following the truth will lead them to difficulties, so they adopt a hopeless attitude about following the good; they do not perceive that only by following the path of the true and the good can they achieve what they really seek.

Such misunderstandings occur when we focus only on the external factors in a situation. We may imagine all sorts of reasons why a thing "can't work" without realizing that our negative thoughts block the success we seek. Simply by freeing ourselves from these moods, we reopen the door to success.

We often receive this hexagram when we begin to suspect that everything is going against us, or that we must meet life's challenges without help from any source, or that there is no purpose to life, or that hostile events have no meaning. This hexagram tells us that although we fail to realize it, we are being helped. We should not allow ourself to become isolated by mistrusting the life process. Events have meanings we are not meant fully to comprehend; our life has higher purposes we are meant to fulfill. Adversity is necessary to growth and to the fulfillment of our higher nature.

The primary reason we misunderstand is that we fail to take into account the presence of the Higher Power in all our activities. Hostile events occur when we obstinately refuse to consider its reality. The degree to which we disregard the Higher Power is the extent to which it resists aiding us; the extent of our obstinacy is the extent to which the Higher Power must shock us to make us aware of its presence. When we experience shock, the Higher Power is simply knocking at the door of our consciousness to say, "See, I am here too, and you cannot disregard me in this situation." Once we become aware of the hidden force present in every situation, we are aided in everything we set out to do. Events need not be hostile; like a river, the Cosmos flows along a certain course; when we paddle our boat sideways, we hit the bank; when we paddle upstream, we become exhausted and give up; when we go with the Cosmos, all goes well.

We often receive this hexagram because we distrust the Sage, our teacher. We think he is indifferent, or "out to get us" in some way, or that he is, perhaps, a trickster. We are simply misunderstanding the way things work. Our ego, for instance, always wants to see a straight line to success. The way of the Sage, however, is the way of nature, diverse and roundabout. Everything is achieved by hidden means which work matters out as a whole, just as the power of the sun, the earth, the wind, and the water all contribute to the growing and maturing of things. The path meanders out of the sight and measurement of our ego. We must learn to trust this hidden process and cling to it, for it is the inner truth which carries on when everything seems impossible. It is the Tao which can be realized, but which cannot be known. It has no rules which can be memorized, yet when we perceive it, all opposition melts away; we are in harmony with it and are nourished by it.

Fire and water never mingle. It is the same with enlightenment and worry. We cannot see with clarity, attain the Cosmic view, as long as we are subject to restless fears. Opposition (misunderstanding) occurs because of mistrust, doubt, fear, or anxiety. While we are captivated by these emotions we are unable to see that events which appear evil are often the only means by which matters may be clarified and corrected. It is essential to hold our minds open and eliminate mistrust by refusing to listen to our arguing ego.

In times of opposition, situations cannot be rectified by frontal attacks, brusqueness, wooing, or persuasion. Effort only intensifies mistrust. We must truly disengage, go our way with dignity, and depend on the power of truth to penetrate through gently.

Finally, we should not chastise ourself for misunderstanding. Through being confronted by our ignorance and arrogance we are able to become humble and attain true understanding. Misunderstanding is the necessary prelude to understanding. Just as the Sage gives us the space to misunderstand, we need to give ourselves, and others, the space to err. Then, when the light of truth finally breaks through, understanding and enlightenment follow.

First Line: *If you lose your horse do not run after it.* It is not necessary to strive or struggle. We may safely flow with events. If two people who are meant to be together become estranged, one need only let the other go for him to return of his own accord. We should not go more than halfway in trying to make anything work. Indeed, we must only come to meet others halfway—when they, as well as ourselves, make the effort to do the right thing. Until they do wc must disengage and go on. This is true of all situations, and is the correct 'waiting attitude' (see *Waiting*, Hex. 5).

Second Line: *One meets his lord in a narrow street.* This means that opposition and misunderstanding break through momentarily because we disperse mistrust. An open attitude leads to a break-through in which we understand a general principle in the particular circumstance of the moment.

Third Line: *A man's hair and nose cut off.* We should not be influenced by the negative appearance of things, but stick to our path. True joy is founded on inner stability. We are being tested and tried.

Fourth Line: *Isolated through opposition.* We should not regard Fate as hostile. Through such distrust and lack of steadiness in our way of life, we become isolated. Because we hold with wrong ideas and are not yet trustworthy in the Cosmic sense, we become isolated from the Sage, who retreats from cooperating closely with us. If we realize this and rejoin the correct path, we will become free of faults and be in harmony with ourself. In dispersing distrust and trying to do what is right, we will find the help we need.

Fifth Line: *The companion bites his way through the wrappings.* The "wrappings" symbolize misunderstanding something. Here, we 'bite through' the misunderstanding, thus begin to understand correctly. For example, we misunderstand the Sage's beneficial action and interpret events as Fate being against us, or we don't perceive that another person is really sincere. Through this distrust we have become isolated. In perceiving our error and discarding mistrust, we "bite through the wrappings," thus regain our inner balance and independence.

This line also means that others are gaining the insight needed to cease misunderstanding us.

Sixth Line: *He is not a robber....* Despite appearances, other people or the Sage, do not seek to harm us. Life, or Fate, is not against us. An unpleasant situation is always compounded by mistrust and misunderstanding. When we let go of our inner defenses and return to an open-minded readiness to see events as instructive of higher meanings, the situation will right itself. We always need to be aware of the emotional perceptions urged on us by our childish heart.

39.

Chien / Obstruction

K'an ☵
Kên ☶

(We suffer from an exaggerated perception. By a change
of attitude the obstruction will melt away.)

We become obstructed when we fail to do the right thing for its own
sake, as when we do things to have a desired effect on our situation.
When we see the obstructing attitude and change it, the obstruction
melts away.

It furthers one to see the great man. Chief among obstructing
attitudes is the tendency to regard other people or situations as
"hopeless," or a given situation as dangerous, hence requiring
vigorous action. Such exaggerated perceptions develop when we
dwell on others' mistakes and injustices.

Being fixed on watching what others do, we seem to be compelled
by all their acts to such logical conclusions as: "If I don't act now
irreparable harm will be done," or, "Even if they did change it would
not be in time to make any difference," or, "It is already too late for
things to work out correctly." Such images and thoughts accompany, and are part of, desire and fear. When desire and fear dominate
our thinking, we cannot see with clarity. Moreover, the power of
desire and fear guarantee a negative outcome.

If we are to have a beneficial effect, we must hold to the suppressed great-man potential in those who err, and keep a "just and
moderate" view of their transgressions. At the same time we let them
go and pursue our own path. By keeping our mind open we give them
space to awaken this potential in themselves, in their own time. By
persevering through bad times, we give them the time they need to
understand their actions. We recognize the evil of the situation, yet
turn it over to the Cosmos to solve. In this way we maintain a neutral
attitude which reflects, as a mirror, the inner truth of the situation.
We do this in spite of vain or personal demands that we act
forcefully, because it is in harmony with the Creative, and with the
true needs of the moment.

Receiving this hexagram acknowledges that a cloud consisting of

181

one or more hidden emotions obstructs our view, and consequently everything is just short of working. It is the sort of obstruction from which we cannot extricate ourself without help. To "see the great man" means that we need to realize that the situation is beyond our best capabilities, and that we need help from the Sage to find and correct the obstructing element in our attitude. With this humility we will attract help from the Cosmos to meet the needs of the situation.

First Line: *Retreat and await the right moment for action.* This means we must retreat from feelings of resistance because of having met an obstruction. The obstruction has a good purpose. If we gain a correct perspective, and hold our minds open to what we are meant to learn from it, we will find that it is ultimately to our benefit. Striving blindly ahead refers to trying to figure things out, and to taking defensive actions. We need, instead, to allow the difficulty to work itself out. If we are patient and persevering, the opportunity to move ahead will occur of itself. This is what it means to be activated by the light force to move ahead, and by the dark force to retreat. Here, retreat is correct.

Second Line: *...obstruction upon obstruction, but it is not his own fault.* This line reassures us that the obstructions which have occurred are not our fault. All adversity, however, gives us opportunities to enlarge and develop our attitudes, and to acquire the Cosmic viewpoint.

Situations often force us to make judgments. It is correct and necessary to judge the matter for what it is—an error, for instance. Then we let go of it. But if we allow our ego to watch for signs of change, or if we mentally supervise and measure others' progress, or if we act to make them do what they "ought to do," we prevent them from changing. We trespass against their dignity to choose the correct path of their own volition. People can do what they "ought to do" only if we truly leave it to them to find the correct way.

We need to be aware that in disengaging, we should not go from the extreme of discarding the person to the extreme of excusing him. Such decisions and feelings vindicate and reinforce their inferiors, enabling them to crush any efforts of their Superior Man within. Their inferiors hasten to point out how useless it is to attempt to regain our trust and goodwill, something their Superior Man would want to do. Moreover, such decisions create what the *I Ching* refers to in *The Wanderer* (Hex. 56) as "lawsuits." Their inferiors argue correctly, "Who are you to cast us off as hopeless?" When we initiate these subconscious wars, those we cast in the position of being an adversary begin to perform competitive and hostile acts to pay us back for our arrogance. These wars often continue for years. To everyone except those who admit that they have brought them about, they seem to have no justifiable reason to exist. Because our inmost thoughts have the power to create such "lawsuits" and "wars," we must control them. In letting others go, we must truly forgive them, and keep a just and moderate view of their transgressions.

Sometimes we become afraid that the situation will work out. It is important not to allow our ego to imagine an unpleasant outcome. We should not adopt any view that might cause us to give up our goal. We need to allow the Sage, who knows how to make the impossible succeed, to be the playwright.

Third Line: *Going leads to obstructions; hence he comes back.* This line, related to the first line, notes an obstruction in our attitude which needs to be recognized. We are warned against telling others what to do. People must be free to return to the correct path of their own insight and volition. When we expect, demand, or pressure them to do the right thing, a free and spontaneous action becomes impossible. We must truly let people go.

Fourth Line: *Going leads to obstructions, coming leads to union.* Even though our cause may be just, it would be a mistake to depend on logic, for here our logic is the product of inner conflict. Trustworthy companions (help from the inner world) can be found by holding back, keeping still, and persevering until the way out shows itself. Time is the vehicle, perseverance the precipitating force that will dissolve the obstruction. Clarity can be attained only if we withdraw from inner conflict ("come back," or disengage).

Fifth Line: *In the midst of the greatest obstructions, friends come.* The Sage comes to our aid when we persevere past all obstacles, clinging to what is right, making no defense of our own. When we are helped to say the right things without having pre-thought them, sensitivity and clarity are awakened in those who, until now, have seemed hopelessly obdurate.

The "friends" are those intrinsically good elements within others which up to now have been shut off by fear or distrust; without their cooperation and trust, the obstructions cannot be overcome.

Sixth Line: *It furthers one to see the great man.* The great man within us has turned his back on the struggle, leaving matters to our inferiors. Detachment has turned to indifference on the assumption that we are not meant to attend to the rescue. Thinking there is nothing we can do, we doubt the power of inner truth. In fact, though, the matter is not out of our hands. We must return to seek the help of the Sage, with whom we can deal with the matter resolutely and completely. The effort to return must be put forth even though it seems extremely difficult. The great man within us is capable not only of rescuing himself, but also of rescuing the others who depend on him.

40.

Hsieh / Deliverance

$$\frac{\text{Chên}}{\text{K'an}}$$ ☰☰

(On being delivered from obstructions.)

The superior man pardons mistakes and forgives misdeeds. The movement in this hexagram is upward, away from danger. The danger mentioned either involves an outer or an inner situation, one which has been, or could be, resolved by a change in our attitude.

Receiving the hexagram without lines either means that the situation is changing for the better and that we need to "keep still within" so as not to renew the danger, or that we should contemplate any changes we need to make in our attitude to bring about deliverance.

The changing lines indicate specific problems in our attitude. For example, the first line counsels us to relinquish any hard feelings we may have, and to forgive misdeeds and pardon mistakes.

First Line: *Without blame.* Through attaining the correct point of view we have overcome the obstacle before us, and resolved the inner conflict. We must keep still within so that the conflict is not renewed.

If the problem with another person has eased, we should not linger in the crossroads, asking, "Should this be happening? Did I take the correct road?" We should keep moving steadily forward on our path.

Second Line: *One kills three foxes in the field.* The foxes symbolize ideas which flatter our self-image. They cleverly keep us under their spell because they seem so logical, practical, and well-balanced. If we are devoted to delivering ourself (or others) from false ideas, our sincerity will cause the flattering and false nature of the ideas to become visible, and we will no longer be subject to their hidden influence.

Third Line: *If a man carries a burden on his back and nonetheless rides in a carriage....* It is arrogant to be hard, and to lay either/or demands on people. When we are right and proud of it, we lose our modesty and "ride in a carriage." If, after being helped by the Sage, we feel confident enough to take our ease in such luxurious attitudes, we attract "robbers"—disagreeable experiences and hardships which will remind us of our dependence on the Higher Power. Through abandoning the path of docility and acceptance we lose the benevolent protection of the Higher Power, and thereby subject ourselves to the whims of chance.

It is important for us to determine whether we have lost our sympathy for those less fortunate than ourselves, or whether we now feel we can't be bothered with others—attitudes which are symbolized by the expression, "to ride in a carriage." Rigidity is no fit substitute for firmness. Firmness does not mean that we barricade ourselves with pacts, or arm ourselves with rigid vows.

After things get better it is time to work, not relax and enjoy ourselves. We should keep alert and firm in inner independence so that we continue to have the correct effect.

Riding in a carriage also refers to choosing a point of view with which we can live more easily—one that better suits our ego.

Fourth Line: *Deliver yourself from your great toe.* Dependence on the big toe symbolizes clinging to the way we solved problems before we began studying with the Sage of the *I Ching*. For instance, we take matters into our own hands in an effort to achieve results or to block events because we still distrust being led. This distrust prevents deliverance. A similar habit of mind is demonstrated by accepting evil: "Well, whatever happens will be okay." If we are firm in our quest for what is right, "the companion comes whom you can trust."

Other habits of mind on which we lean (as we lean on the great toe in walking) include looking at a situation, deciding what it is on the basis of its appearance, and then choosing a way of relating to it. The problem is never definable on the basis of its appearances. There are always hidden things we can see only after the fact, and still more we can never see. Problems can be resolved only if we remain detached and follow the truth as we clearly see it.

Another aspect of the "big toe" we often overlook is that we may be using the *I Ching* only to solve our relationship with a particular person; although we correct our way of relating to him, we fail to apply its principles to other situations. Thus, we use the *I Ching* to gain selfish ends instead of correcting our way of life. Others cannot follow such partial values, and they will always be confused by our hypocrisies and inconsistencies.

Fifth Line: *If only the superior man can deliver himself....* The only way that entrenched habits of mind can be overcome is through firm determination to resist them. It is important not to listen to their persuasive arguments. At times they seem almost invincible or demonic in their insistence, but this false strength quickly dissipates when we decisively reject them and refuse to listen to them. In an external situation it is important to become firm in one's mind, disengage from our emotions, and then, with few words, say what must be said, or do what must be done. One must be totally firm about what is correct so that there is no argument.

Sixth Line: *The prince shoots at a hawk on a high wall. He kills it.* A remnant of our ego prevents deliverance. It still attempts to lead by becoming involved in searching for the obstructing element— itself. This happens when some small bit of pride remains, keeping us from humbly asking the Sage for help. When we put aside this bit of pride, we kill the hawk on the high wall and are free.

This line also refers to having the wrong viewpoint. If we want to unite with someone we must first let him go. When we cease inner resistance to what we perceive as a negative situation, or hostile fate, the obstructing element will disappear.

41.

Sun / Decrease

Kên
───
Tui

(Sacrifice feelings to which we are attached, such as desire, affection, repulsion, negation, alienation, or irritation, for the good of the whole.)

Decrease combined with sincerity.... Decrease, on the whole, is a call to sacrifice all forms of self-importance, including feelings of anger and retribution which occur when we feel forced into a seemingly impossible situation. Such emotions cloud our perception, and even though they may be justified, harboring them prevents our attaining a correct point of view.

Decrease also refers to the moment when we recognize that we are powerless to achieve our goals. The moment of decrease is the all-important point of beginning, for it is the point when we become aware of our poverty and defenselessness. Recognizing that we are helpless means that we also perceive the impotence of the ego. This recognition displaces the ego as leader of our consciousness, if only momentarily. During moments of decrease we are able to see that we need help, and we have the humility to ask for help. If, however, we are still looking to anything other than the Higher Power for help, our ego is trying to retain control.

Decrease also refers to the sense of dismay we feel when we realize that our ego must relinquish leadership of our personality. This dismay is similar to how we might feel on giving up a crutch that we have thought was indispensable for walking. Moreover, on perceiving that it must be decreased, our ego often reacts with alarm, anger, or frustration. If it is not met with firm resistance at this point, when it is weak, it swiftly regains strength, throws up defenses, and begins to strive and resist Fate. To decrease the ego, by letting go of such feelings, is to "express the true sentiments of the heart." By decreasing our ego, the correct messages are transmitted to others and the Higher Power is able to help and defend us.

Our ego continues to lead so long as we seek to be understood, to gain recognition for our views, or attempt to vindicate ourselves. It also remains in control if we defend ourselves, make pacts, or steel ourselves against what might or might not happen. In doing these things we hedge, doubting that the Creative will come to our defense. Even though others may wish to change, or relate to us in a better way, they remain resistant because they sense our doubt and defensiveness. So long as our ego is able to control us, we remain unreliable. To accept our need for help, and to call for help, is to gain the help of the Higher Power.

First Line: *Going quickly when one's tasks are finished....* The way the Sage relates to us shows us the way we should relate to others. Going quickly quite literally means to go quickly when one's tasks are finished. The performer, on ending his performance, leaves the stage without further ado. He does not stand waiting beyond the time the audience demands his presence. He retreats, detaching from what he has accomplished. This selflessness prohibits the ego from assuming power; it keeps one's inner equilibrium, and enables inner truth to prevail. We may trust this.

Being defenseless, we must take care not to jeopardize our personalities. Since our means of influencing others is limited to our good example and the power of inner truth, we must take care to keep our thoughts correct and our attitude detached and neutral. The Sage does not throw himself away by chasing our approval. He does not cater to the demands of logic, or intellect. Although he withdraws in the presence of arrogance, he tolerates our mistakes. Thus, if a person is not receptive, or if he is dubious about us, we should reserve ourself until delicacy of feeling is sufficient for open communication. When a person's ego leads, we throw ourself away if we confide in him or try to convince him of anything.

This line may also concern our relationship with the Sage. We should ask ourself, therefore, if we have delicacy of feeling toward the Sage. Do we take what we want from his advice and reject what is unpleasant? Do we treat him as a helpful friend?

Second Line: *Without decreasing oneself one is able to bring increase to others.* This line confirms that it is correct to be paid for one's services. It is is not necessarily a good thing to serve another if, in doing so, we teach him to be self-centered and spoiled. We should not cultivate the idea that we can receive without being sensitive to the needs of those who serve us. In the *I Ching* view it is wrong to serve another if it means we cater to his ego, or to unreasonable expectations, or if such service entails compromising our principles. (See *Coming to Meet*, Hex. 44, for an explanation of the *I Ching* principle of 'coming to meet halfway.')

This line also means that even though we have experienced a decrease of self, we must not lose our dignity by bringing our deficiencies to others' attention, or make a practice of confessing. Everyone is similarly deficient. It is false humility to make something of it.

To help others it is never necessary to put oneself in a dubious or humiliating position. To help them requires only that we adhere strictly to the limits of modesty and patience; the right moment to say or do something will arrive by itself, without our intervention. We need only wait in a state of conscious innocence—free of forethought or fixed ideas about what the situation 'is,' and what to do about it. When we wait with a pre-structured idea, we wait in ambush. Being on the lookout for opportunities to explain, confide, or lash out angrily, we throw ourself away, and thus incur an unnecessary decrease through being humiliated.

If we are self-contained, self-reliant, and careful to adhere to the limits imposed by the principle of 'coming to meet others halfway' (see *Coming to Meet*, Hex. 44), we will be called into action by events; then, everything we say or do will be appropriate, and will meet with no resistance. At a degree below freezing ice clings stubbornly to surfaces, whereas at a degree above, it is easily dislodged. This is the importance of working with the situation (see *Limitation*, Hex. 60), and of following the path of least resistance (see *Enthusiasm*, Hex. 16).

This line may also mean that if, in our inner attitude, we are willing to risk misunderstanding and disfavor by adhering to our principles, we will bring increase to others. Ironically, our willingness to be firm and correct protects us from any decrease of self.

Third Line: *When three people journey together their number decreases by one.* By giving up wrong elements in ourself we open the door for good elements to enter. The Sage cannot be associated with evil. We may be adhering to something other than the Sage for guidance (such as a defective idea); thus, "three's a crowd."

We also receive this line when we have plunged ahead without waiting to acquire the Sage's help. Here, the third person is our ego, manifested as fear and as contrived solutions to problems. We need only let go and wait for help to show itself.

Fourth Line: *If a man decreases his faults, the other comes.* Here we are counseled to review our attitude to find the specific fault that obstructs progress.

The root of many faults is "looking behind," "looking aside," or "looking ahead." This means we focus on what others have done, are doing, or might do. Such focussing causes us to attempt to change things. Becoming emotionally entangled in this way disturbs our equilibrium.

Another form of emotional entanglement occurs when things have been going well and we begin to depend on good times continuing; we are then not prepared when things change for the worse. Similarly, during bad times we assume that negative situations will continue indefinitely, hence we adopt an oppressed and hopeless view. We should not depend on affairs either to be stable or unstable; change is the rule of life. Such dependencies cause us to lose our sense of caution during good times, and to rely on contrived solutions during bad times. We become so careless or preoccupied with our problems that we are not open to suggestions from the Sage.

External observations of a situation are incomplete. It is important to come to the 'inner truth' of the matter, which may be simply that there is nothing to do now but disengage until a greater understanding becomes possible. Once we think we have identified the problem, we tend to set ourselves on a course to "correct" it, even though our scenario is incomplete. We must allow the correct perception to come through. This is possible only if, for the time being, we resist defining the problem or contriving any solutions. If we will persevere through what might be called the "moment of ambiguity," we will create an opening for the Sage to help. This help will come at the moment we need it. Meanwhile, we must resist the fear that the Sage will not help, or that the time will run out, or that we must somehow come to a conclusion.

Finally, in doing what is correct we must stop looking to the Sage for vain approval or disapproval. We know whether or not we have done the best we can at a particular time. We must let go of effort and of any mistakes we have made.

Fifth Line: *Someone does indeed increase him.* Our effort to follow the path of the good and the beautiful will lead to success, and to the rescue of those to whom we are tied by inner ties.

Sixth Line: *If one is increased without depriving others....*
Through withdrawal and self-discipline our situation improves, and
we experience an increase in self-reliance and inner independence.
This should not, however, become a justification to look down on
others, discard them, wish them ill, tell them about their faults, or be
hard or brusque. If we remain modest and sincere, we will win the
help needed to rescue them. The perseverance and zealous work
mentioned refers to restraining one's inferiors.

This line also means that while it is correct to be paid for one's
services (see Line 2), the payment we require must not be exorbitant.
It also means we should expect to pay a just amount for others'
services.

42.

I / Increase

Sun
―――
Chên

(We are being helped; therefore, we should keep our heart steady (free of desire).

Increase means that we are now in a time of powerful movement towards improvement. We are being helped by the Higher Power. This help puts us in a position of strength and gives us the feeling of inner and outer independence. In following our path we find a measure of self-assurance and peace. Progress is easy compared to former times of obstruction and decrease. Now, however, we need to be even more conscientious, for the time is similar to 'after completion' (see Hex. 63), when carelessness, lassitude, and indifference encroach into our attitude. We are reminded that the time of increase does not endure, and we must therefore keep our attitude steady in going forward and strong in inner independence. During the time of increase we are able to influence others, provided our attitude remains correct. We "utilize" this time when we renew our humility, remain conscientious, and keep 'going on.'

This hexagram also states that sacrifice on the part of "those above" yields benefits to those below. When we feel freed of inner pressures, we tend to become intolerant of others, and to measure their progress impatiently. No matter how independent we feel, we must not forget to rescue those for whom we are responsible. Although rescuing them means that we let them go their own way, we continue to hold an open mind and sacrifice any temptation to execute them mentally as hopeless. To help others we must sacrifice any feelings of alienation, or grievances, however badly they behave. During such times we need to remember how far along our path we could have come without the help, fidelity, and open mind of the Sage.

First Line: *It furthers one to accomplish great deeds.* We have not

193

been helped merely to sink back into luxurious and indifferent attitudes, or to otherwise abandon our path. If we use our power and position to put others at a disadvantage, we cannot achieve anything great, or remain free of reproach. Great power is exercised when we find ways of not using it. We remain humble and blameless by holding to what is universally true, and by negotiating from this basis. We should not focus on what other people do or fail to do, or give them up as hopeless because of appearances; we need to hold our minds open to what they can yet become, once they discover how and why they need to be true to themselves.

This line also reminds us that because it is a general time of increase, no harm will come of our mistakes if we correct ourselves.

Second Line: *Constant perseverance brings good fortune. The King presents him before God.* If we have contracted a hostile fate, it is not enough to work only to be released from its oppressions; this fate will change only when we come to love and follow the path of the good for its own sake. When we achieve harmony with the Creative, we are no longer subjected to the voices of doubt and fear, and our life takes on strength. It is in accordance with Cosmic law that what we have lost will be restored to us. If we can persevere constantly in keeping our heart steady, the Sage (king) will argue our case, as it were, before God.

Third Line: *One is enriched through unfortunate events.* This line means that because it is a general time of increase and self-correction, we have made progress in spite of our mistakes and incorrect attitudes.

Fourth Line: *If you walk in the middle....* We embody the example of the Sage (serve as an intermediary) through being dedicated, responsible, sincere, and perseveringly disengaged. We shirk this responsibility if we do what we want instead.

Fifth Line: *If in truth you have a kind heart....* True kindness arises from inner necessity, involves no forethought, and is purely spontaneous, because it accords with our true nature. In the war against vanity we must consider whether we are acting from innocence, or whether we are acting to gain recognition. Often, the greatest kindness occurs when we forego pleasures to achieve a more correct relationship. We need not worry that our point of view will not be recognized since anyone who remains true to himself and pure in heart will be recognized.

If we make a point of demonstrating our feelings in order to influence others or to give others pleasure in being recognized, we make the mistake of regarding our caring as a prize. In prizing the way we feel, we are under the influence of vanity. If we state our feelings because we fear others need proof that we care, we cater to their egos. Whenever we allow ourselves to be driven by desire or fear to demonstrate our views or our feelings, or to defend our acts, we throw ourself away. If we are conscientious to be correct in our motives and firm in our principles, what we say spontaneously will be correct.

True kindness, ultimately, lies in caring conscientiously to do what is correct out of the sight and hearing of others. When we decide, "I like that person," we risk the danger of forming a faction with him, especially if we say, in effect, that henceforth we will overlook wrongs he may do. True loyalty, like true kindness, is to hold to what is correct in ourself; from this basis we relate to people as they come and go. When they deviate from the good, we withdraw and remain faithful to their Superior Man. This is to be a true friend.

Finally, kindness means to be patient when mistakes are made, either by ourselves or by others. Forgiveness is to require neither an act of penitence nor an apology. We require only that we ourselves be patient, moderate, and just in our attitude towards them.

Sixth Line: *He brings increase to no one.* This line warns that in using power wrongly we lose the help of the Creative and invite the attack of hostile forces. In losing modesty, we lose both our shield and our sword. Above all, we lose the benefits of the time of increase if we fail to keep our hearts steady, as when we waver about our values and reconsider whether our path is the correct one. It is important to maintain our modesty, and the inner independence to maintain our forward direction.

43.

Kuei / Breakthrough (Resoluteness)

$$\frac{\text{Tui}}{\text{Ch'ien}}$$

(Be resolute to keep within the correct limits.)

Breakthrough refers to two points of change: when yin flows into the space left behind by yang, and when yang flows into the space left behind by yin. One form of breakthrough follows the other. Through following the correct path resolutely, we find that obstructions give way, or "break through." If we then exceed the mean by becoming hard and proud, or if we give up perseverance to luxuriate in the improved situation, breakthrough occurs again as a breakdown in relationships.

We achieve the first kind of breakthrough (removing obstructions) by persevering resolutely in the correct attitude. This means we keep emotionally disengaged from situations which tempt us to react in an emotional way. As each emotion approaches we defuse its energy by recognizing it and resolutely resisting it. We forego striving, sacrifice grievances, disperse anger and frustration, resist desire, dismantle overconfidence, and sacrifice feelings of rights and expectations. In such ways we deprive our ego of energy, thus give other people's egos nothing to compete with. By such resolute inner firmness we strengthen other people's superior natures, and the situation breaks through. By remaining determined to follow this discipline we invoke the power of the Creative, which always acts to help those who unselfishly follow the good.

When our situation improves, a new sort of resoluteness must be undertaken. Now we must guard against intervening in others' affairs to tell them what to think. We must not allow ourself to slide back into the habits of mind which led to our problems. When success comes we should not allow ourself to be hard or proud, nor should we congratulate ourself for being in the right. We neither rest on our virtue, nor measure our progress. Resoluteness means that we continue humbly forward, determined to stay balanced and on course.

Resoluteness, then, entails being decisive against the passions and fears that take hold in our minds, causing us to lose our sense of limits, as when we depart from acceptance and non-action, or when we allow self-importance to return. Every day we encounter all sorts of ideas. Those we clearly recognize as absurd or unworthy we immediately discard. Ideas less easily defined tend to linger in our minds until they achieve credibility simply because we haven't decided what sort of ideas they are. In this manner they become accepted by default. By default they slide down into our unconscious, where they continue to influence our thinking and behavior. It is necessary to bring these ideas to the surface to see what they really are. When we discover that they are seductive half-truths, we are able to discard them.

If unworthy ideas have become habitual responses to situations, we must guard against their return. Once we have withstood the compulsive appeal (or threat) that such habits put forth, as many as three times, the habits will have been greatly weakened, or even totally overcome. (This is the meaning of the "three times" mentioned in *Revolution* (Hex. 49)).

It is important to note that the different hexagrams give us different ways of approaching negative influences. For example, *Dispersion* (Hex. 59) refers to a specific technique of "dispersing" feelings of anger and alienation. By choosing to give them up, we allow them to "float away." We free them mentally, as one would let a bird out of a cage. Through employing such images we gain power over the negative influences. Until we try this imaging technique, we are unaware that such a simple means can free us from something which has heretofore controlled us with an iron grip.

When we receive lines in *Deliverance* (Hex. 40), it usually means that we are under the influence of subtle and intransigent emotions such as vanity. These emotions are referred to in one line as "three flattering foxes," and in another as a "hawk on a high wall." The hexagram indicates that these emotions must be "killed." The act of killing an evil motive requires first that we see it as standing between us and deliverance from obstructions; then we must conquer it through resoluteness against its influence. We are so sincere in our effort that it is "killed." It also helps if we mentally imagine ourself as killing the evil ideas, as in shooting them with arrows. This inner act is successful only if we sincerely want to free ourself from the habit of mind.

Sometimes an evil impulse is so ill-defined that we can perceive

197

it only as a general mood, corrupting our attitude. The technique for dealing with this sort of situation is described in *Coming to Meet* (Hex. 44). We remain gently aware that the mood is there; we watch it as one might watch a "fish in the tank." While we are not able to get rid of it immediately, such means enable us to keep it from getting out of hand during critical moments.

For each situation confronting us the appropriate technique is given in the daily *I Ching* reading. Each technique requires a certain type of resoluteness. Only resoluteness breaks through the problem. Gradually, through practice we develop the ability to recognize the appropriate technique for any given situation.

First Line: *Mighty in the forward-striding toes. Mistake.* Here danger comes from overconfidence and exuberant enthusiasm. We see that we must be resolute in withdrawing from others to "bite through" the obstacles. Our ego, however, would have us go past the point intended, to withdraw enthusiastically. Or, we see that we must disperse alienation, but we go past dignified reserve to be too lenient. This dominance of our ego is intuitively perceived by the other person, therefore he returns to defending himself, defeating our purpose.

Second Line: *A cry of alarm. Fear nothing.* Events or images approach which might press us into action. We should not allow self-confidence to cause us to step outside our limits. If we remain aware that we are not yet in a state of balance, we can avoid making such mistakes.

Third Line: *The superior man is firmly resolved. No blame.* The ambiguous situation seems to compel action, such as turning against someone to bring his wrongs out into the open for redress or, because things seem better, re-entering a close relationship with him. Non-action is called for, however, because he has not corrected his attitude of careless indifference. We do nothing, even though no one will understand why we do not take a stand to conclude matters. "No one" includes our own inferiors.

This line can also refer to thinking it impossible to follow the path. We should not give up on ourself. We need to be firmly resolved to try to continue on the path, to remain conscientious, and to ask for help.

Fourth Line: *If a man were to let himself be led like a sheep, remorse would disappear.* Here we encounter the dangers of being resolute. When resoluteness goes to the extreme of being hard, or when, in ridding ourself of alienation, we become too soft, we depart from the path and are no longer able to hear within. Our feelings harden when we listen to our sense of pride and humiliation, or they soften when we listen to desire. We must sacrifice hardness and resist desire if we are to return to modesty and simplicity, and to reserve and inner balance.

To be led like a sheep means that we depend on inner truth. We do not memorize what to say, but allow the right thing to come of itself, at the right time. This is possible only if we maintain inner emptiness: we neither listen to the clamoring of our emotions, nor pretend to know the right answer in advance.

Fifth Line: *In dealing with weeds, firm resolution is necessary. Walking in the middle remains free of blame.* Habit, symbolized by weeds, is strong. We must be resolute against losing inner independence and balance, and against allowing others to cause us to want, worry, or wonder. We must keep our serenity. It is necessary to let people who wish to err go on their way, while we remain firmly resolved not to give them up as hopeless. We should not give up on ourselves, either—on our ability to persevere and endure others, and to endure the general situation.

Sixth Line: *No cry. In the end misfortune comes.* Breakthrough has occurred. Things appear much better, but the matter is not entirely resolved. We must guard against losing our reserve, becoming too lenient, or compromising in order to accommodate incorrect behavior. If we re-enter fellowship with someone while problems remain unresolved, we throw ourselves away. The conditions of equality and justice must be firmly established, not by what is said, but by all the essentials of a person's way of life.

We need not harbor anger or hold to bad memories to remind ourselves that the situation is not ready to be resolved. Reminders occur of themselves. We must leave correction or punishment of the evil inferiors to the Sage, as this is not our province of action. So long as we hold to any particular grievance, we prevent its correction. The force that heals and corrects cannot respond if our ego stands by, demanding results.

If we have stabilized ourself and become freed from pressures to act, we should remain on guard against the resurgence of these pressures until all habitual responses are completely conquered.

44.

Kou / Coming to Meet

Ch'ien	☰
Sun	☴

(Do not respond to seduction, especially the seduction of power.)

On one level 'coming to meet' means to be open-minded, patient, and tolerant toward that which approaches us, the way the Sage of the *I Ching* is open-minded, patient, and tolerant toward those of us who consult him. But, as the hexagram mentions, we are only meant to "come halfway," or go only so far. When any person, situation, or idea requires that we sacrifice our higher nature or compromise our inner dignity, that is going too far. We are not meant to go beyond the limits of dignity and correct behavior.

The commentary notes that the "inferior man rises only because the superior man does not regard him as dangerous and so lends him power." This means that we allow evil ideas and situations through dismissing the warning flashes of intuition. Thus, we go to meet them halfway. On the approach of any situation or idea, we are meant to ask whether becoming involved will take us beyond the limits of correct behavior. We should certainly not entertain any idea, or become involved in any situation which contains the element of seduction. Receiving this hexagram often indicates that we are entertaining ideas which are incorrect, seductive, or flattering.

The easy, seductive, or flattering thing is pictured as a "bold girl who lightly surrenders herself and thus seizes power." Whether it be a flattering or comforting person, situation, or idea, the fact that it comes boldly and easily should be warning enough to stand by our inner guidelines of what is correct and essential.

The principle of darkness, after having been eliminated, furtively...obtrudes from within and below. Just when we have become detached, new inner complaints begin in a subtle, seemingly innocent way. Once we listen to them we become dissatisfied; then we are presented with a tempting solution in the form of a person, idea, or desirable objective. While the temptation may seem harm-

201

less enough, once we seriously consider it, it takes over completely and plays itself out with force. All this happens because, through "listening to it," or going to meet it halfway, we have allowed the ego (our spoiled child within) to gain power.

A similar situation occurs when we perceive that the inferior element in others approaches, seeking to manipulate or unbalance us. To respond correctly to others' inferiors, we need first to recognize any tendency of our inferiors to go and meet the others halfway. Observing evil in others invariably arouses our ego, which wants to pay back insult with insult and blow with blow. (It self-righteously thinks that because it has had to accept discipline, others must be punished and restricted too.) Once we allow our ego to be brusque and intolerant, it develops a demonic power. To undermine its power we need to return to humility. This may require that we remember how we have been helped to overcome some of our weaknesses. We may need to recall the power that our fears and misconceptions have had over us, and our difficulty in becoming free of them, for these are the same fears and misconceptions that give rise to the evil we observe in others.

All the changing lines of the hexagram have to do with keeping our ego disarmed in the presence of others' egos, or their undisciplined inferiors. When they are insincere, we should not throw ourself away through angry and frustrated responses by which we lose our inner independence. Nor should we seek to resolve problems through conflict and striving, or through wooing and seduction. Instead, we should allow the way by which problems can naturally be resolved, to open. This becomes possible when we give others space, and when we retain our inner independence and dignity.

To control our ego and inferiors, it is essential that we do not feed them by listening to their whining complaints. We empower evil thoughts when we give them serious consideration. To cease listening to them, once they have begun, requires persistence and firmness. It is easier to curb them in the beginning; the more we entertain them, the more completely they persuade us to their viewpoint. When evil shows itself in others we must monitor and curb our reaction immediately so that we neither acquiesce in what they do, nor react in a combative way. We turn the matter over to the Cosmos, and cling to a just and moderate view of everything that happens.

In controlling our inferiors, it is necessary to recognize our emotional status. Are we impatient, angry, or frustrated? Do we desire something? Are we thinking of wrongs other people do, or do we consider giving them up as hopeless? These ego-voices endanger perseverance; if they go unchecked, they will soon destroy the inner independence which has true power to overcome evil.

To control others' inferiors, we endure them so that the opportunity for a good influence will remain possible. At the same time, we neither cater to them nor heed any demands they may make. We do not explain or defend our position. To confide our way of life to someone who is not receptive is to throw ourself away.

We should also realize that we cannot overcome evil. We can only undermine it through modesty (being conscientiously correct), reticence, and the power of inner independence (inner truth). We may recognize evil, but we must not allow it to draw us into its vortex. We succeed in this battle when, in spite of everything, we retain (or regain) our compassion for those who err. We remember that they err because they misunderstand the truths of life that would liberate them from the dark force.

When we succeed in maintaining discipline during such challenging situations we come to meet the Creative halfway, and thus attain the help we need to complete our task.

First Line: *It must be checked with a brake of bronze....*Even a lean pig has it in him to rage around. Our ego often begins in a plaintive, helpless, self-pitying voice. Once we listen to it, it suddenly gains power, ranting, raving, and demanding action. It is easiest to check at the beginning. The "brake of bronze" refers to the stern act of will power required to bring it under control. The ego's power arises in the emotions of fear, vanity, desire, enthusiasm, alienation, anger, impatience, restlessness, dissatisfaction, anxiety, doubt, and righteous indignation. These emotions undermine our good servants: will-power, dedication to good, kindness, and our inclination towards moderation and justice.

Negative emotions first show themselves as a vague mood, the merest ripple on the shining lake. Since it is only when they are first arising that we can gain power over them, we are advised to check their advance consistently. (This is why, in the first line of *The Clinging*, Hex. 30, we are counselled to deal with the first thoughts we have on awaking, because these are the thoughts which control the remainder of the day.)

Second Line: *A fish in the tank...keep under gentle control.*
Sometimes we seem unable to free ourself from an evil impulse, or
from restlessness or desire. Instead of resisting it violently—which
means that our ego is trying to control itself—we should persevere
in gentle but firm resistance to any impulse to do anything. Gradually this resistance gives us strength over it. Meanwhile we should
take care not to allow the evil impulse to show in our actions. By
concentrating our attention on looking inward, we cease looking
outward at whatever disturbs our inner independence.

This line also refers to our tendency to be brusque towards other
people's inferiors. Feelings of disdain come from our ego. Indulging
them certainly causes trouble.

Third Line: *Walking comes hard.* We are tempted to contend with
others to make points, or to make ourselves felt, or understood. This
heightens the self-conflict already present. Hopefully, we will avoid
abandoning our path because of such ambition, desire, or other
emotion which comes from our ego. To do anything to impress
others, either through desire or anger, comes from attachment and
perpetuates the vortex which begins when we throw ourselves away.

Fourth Line: *No fish in the tank.* The tendency to be brusque in
response to others' inferiors comes from our inferiors. In learning
from the *I Ching*, our inferiors, which have had to be disciplined,
now become intolerant of others' undisciplined inferiors. Harshness
is not a fit servant of the good. Even though there is no blame in
finding evil repugnant, we should correct a discontented, righteous,
envious, or superior mood, and not allow it to continue to ferment.
If, in having this attitude, we have already alienated people, we
should bear their dislike with composure.

Fifth Line: *A melon covered with willow leaves.* We should not try
to convince people of what is right. Instead, we should place our trust
in being a good example; this alone has the power to convince people
of what is good.

The more we depend on logic, intellect, and "formulas of success"
to influence others, the more doubt and conflict we arouse. Reliance
on logic indicates that we doubt that the truth will reveal itself, or that
people will be able to see it in their own way, in their own time. If
we disengage and go on our way, the eclipsing power of argument
and the doubt initiated through persuasion will wither away.

Sixth Line: *He comes to meet with his horns.* When the inferior elements in others approach to challenge us, it is necessary to withdraw and keep disengaged from their distrust or hostility. This may seem brusque and unreasonable to them, but it is the right thing to do. We can bear their dislike with composure.

This line also refers to times when our inferiors clamor for logical explanations and "reasonable" answers. Such a logical, intellectual approach to the inner life, or to the *I Ching*, or to our path, does not work. Here, we must bear the dislike of our inferiors.

45.

Ts'ui / Gathering Together (Massing)

$$\frac{\text{Tui}}{\text{K'un}} \quad \equiv\!\equiv$$

(We must not engage in self-doubt, nor in doubt of our principles.)

The judgment in this hexagram warns us to be prepared for discord when people congregate in groups, and to "renew our weapons to meet the unforeseen." Its message is not to gather people into groups, but to develop the firmness of character needed for times when we are in positions of leadership.

In following the way of the Sage we are always leader of some group. Our responsibility is not to mother or father that group, or to supervise others' behavior or their learning process, but simply to follow what is high and good in ourself. This communicates to others through the power of inner truth and a good example.

While groups may have assigned leaders, the true (subconscious) leadership of any group is the person who connects with others through firmness in his inner sense of truth. Such a person may be young or old, male or female. Through learning the way of the Sage and receiving his help, we develop a responsibility to lead others. This requires that we accumulate (gather together, or amass) a knowledge of the Cosmic principles that govern life, the firmness of character to uphold them, and the ability to wait without wavering in our essential direction. By "amassing" these qualities of character, we accumulate the power that automatically accompanies them.

We frequently receive this hexagram as a reminder that great things cannot be accomplished until we have achieved inner stability not disturbed by ambiguous situations. Outside events no longer jar us off course, making us waver in our sense of inner truth, pause in our forward direction, or doubt the power of truth to resolve problems.

We can also receive this hexagram when we feel disappointed because we have not yet achieved visible progress in our situation. We need to realize that before obvious changes can occur, invisible changes in people's psyches must take place. All things come in due time. It is the way of the Sage to achieve progress only by tiny steps which cannot be measured or observed by our ego. Meanwhile, we must keep our will directed forward. This is to have a correct 'waiting attitude' (see *Waiting*, Hex. 5) and it fulfills the counsel of the first line, to "be sincere to the end."

In situations of gathering together we are meant to bring our accumulated knowledge of inner truth to work; this happens when we remain firmly resolved during challenges and difficulties. We control inferior nourishment—ideas which weaken our will and make us vacillate, losing our inner balance and doubting our inner sense of what is correct. Vacillation in our inner balance, and in holding to our principles, causes those who follow us with their inner eye to hesitate.

Through having a correct attitude and conducting ourselves accordingly, we acquire the help we need from the Higher Power to complete our task. Asking for, receiving, and remembering this help is essential. No great task can be completed without it.

After every step of progress, however small, we must renew our inner discipline, otherwise, a growing sense of power will turn into expansive over-confidence and carelessness. We should also return to reticence and simplicity. Simplicity is the attribute which enables the leader's vision and awareness to become manifested as the people's achievements.

Every step of progress leads not only to our own success, but to a better world and heightened spirituality in all beings. Our smallest self-improvement is of the greatest importance to ending suffering in the world, and to bettering the human condition, for how things are in the world is a reflection of the accumulated effort of human beings to follow the good within themselves.

First Line: *If you are sincere, but not to the end....* Our goals must be the highest. We must be absolutely firm as to what is right and correct, and we must not vacillate. Lack of firmness causes others who would gather around us to waver. Similarly, if we look back to see if others are following us, we hold a secret doubt that following the true and the good will achieve their rescue. People will follow us only if we are free of doubt and hesitation about what is good and true, and if we continue on our path regardless of what they do.

In following our path it is inevitable that we shall be challenged by other people's egos. While our inner independence draws others to us, and invigorates their spiritual potential, it also threatens their egos, making them feel unsettled about the wrong paths they have been pursuing. They also feel envious, for they sense the power of inner independence, and would like such power for themselves. Their egos seek our "formula" or "secret," believing our inner independence to be some sort of trick which can easily be emulated.

They also wonder whether we can be thrown off-balance, and whether we can be made to doubt what we know, for if their egos can prove to their real selves that we are false, their egos will remain firmly in control. Thus they test us, either by flattery, or by seduction, or by imposing themselves as a problem for us to solve, or by being aggressive. Often, during these tests, we are pitted against something we do not understand. The first impulse put forward by our inferiors is to waver, questioning all we have learned. Through listening to the doubts thus aroused our ego resumes control, returning us to old habits of contending, jumping to solutions, and pressing forward to create changes. We can avoid this if we recognize that we are being tested, and if we cease doubting what we have learned. Instead, we fall back on what we know to be true and depend on it to show the way past the difficulties.

Realizing that we will be tested in this manner helps us remain resolute and firm. We accept apparent reversals and guard against allowing resoluteness to degenerate into brusqueness or intolerance. While we gently endure other people's inferiors, we in no way play any games they set in motion for the purpose of unbalancing us. If they have imposed themselves as a problem, we simply ignore the problem. We are obligated neither to play the game nor to solve the problem.

Second Line: *Letting oneself be drawn.* This means that we should not adopt any contrived attitudes which we think will keep things in balance, or which will move things along more quickly. We should not even try to keep things in balance, or be afraid of any existing imbalance. We need only keep ourself open and free to allow things to happen as they will. We neither resist attraction, nor read more into it than it contains. We remain simple and innocent, and thus retain our inner balance.

While relationships are mending we should not allow pride, self-pity, or other emotions from the past to cause us to structure how things should work out. We neither plot how we are to get back together, nor erect arbitrary obstacle courses which require them to "do this" or "agree to that." We allow the Creative to do the mending. Meanwhile, we keep ourself firm in our values, independent and self-sufficient, careful to accept nothing false, and careful not to participate in any seduction.

Third Line: *Slight humiliation.* This line indicates that a person (either ourself, or another) would like to reunite with us (or the Sage) and follow the path of the good. However, because he feels isolated and humiliated, the situation proves untenable. For the time being, therefore, it is better that he proceed with his development outside the group. In spite of being separated from those with whom he belongs, he will make satisfactory progress so long as he steadfastly allies himself with his higher nature, and follows the way of the Sage.

While we must let him find his own way, we should not regard him as a tiresome bother because of his mistakes as a beginner; we must remain open-minded and patient.

When anyone seeks to join the unity of the good he must accept the humility of starting from a decreased position. True humility is the beginning of enduring change. Since he is a stranger in a strange country, so to speak, it is necessary for him to ally himself with the Sage, the invisible universal teacher who teaches through dreams, meditations, one's inner sense of truth, and the *I Ching.* The Sage, accessible through these resources, is the center of all spiritual fellowship. If the beginner will submit himself sincerely to the Sage's guidance (by trusting the Unknown and not pretending he already knows the way), this subjugation of his ego will guarantee his progress. It is not enough to "sigh," or simply to want to be part of the unity of good, or to want to make progress. We can attain goodness and progress only by submitting ourself to being taught by the Sage, and by sincerely working at self-correction.

Fourth Line: *Great good fortune.* Because we are willing to put aside the sighing of the third line and work unselfishly for the good, our work is successful in bringing about human unity.

This is true even though we must often proceed alone, our thoughts and actions misunderstood, there being no opening to have an influence. Because we are truly unselfish and persevering in seeking the general welfare, and undisturbed by how others view us, our work becomes "crowned with success," with all obstructions re-

209

moved.

Fifth Line: *If there are some who are not yet sincerely in the work....* The only means of dealing with people who secretly mistrust us is to maintain our inner independence. This does not mean that we should avoid, for comfort's sake, our responsibility by discarding the situation or by taking action to change it. We need only be willing to go on alone, without contrived or forced attempts to persuade others of our point of view. It is natural that they be suspicious of our influence. A position of influence and inner independence always arouses envy. Envy, manifested as distrust, can be dismissed only through our becoming more conscientious. In time, and in the face of our consistency of character, this resistance will melt away.

Sometimes this line refers to our mistrust of and resistance to the Sage. We are "not yet sincerely in the work."

Sixth Line: *Lamenting and sighing....* This and the preceding line sometimes refer to our relationship with the Sage. In the preceding line we may be clinging to the *I Ching* or to the path because we think that thus we will achieve the gains we seek, rather than because it shows us the correct path. Restlessness and indecision in times of adversity imply that our trust is incomplete. We are not yet firm in our center. If we recognize this and "reach out for help," an alliance with the Sage becomes possible.

If this line refers to another person, we should be open-minded when he reaches toward us.

We "lament and sigh" because of how long it takes to make enduring progress. Our childish heart still carries some resistance to the way of the Sage. Desires and lamentations defeat the inner independence which insures progress. It is important to ask for help to attain the higher understanding that will enable us to become free of these emotions.

46.

Shêng / Pushing Upward

$$\frac{\text{K'un}}{\text{Sun}} \quad \begin{array}{c} == \\ == \\ == \end{array}$$

(Through sincerely following the way of the Sage we attain the help of the Cosmos.)

This hexagram has to do with the direct and immediate growth suggested by the image of pushing upward. When we grow, all those connected to us "by their roots" (see *Peace*, Hex. 11) also grow. By making a sincere effort to be resolute against our fears, by holding to the great-man potential in others, by remaining tolerant and alert, we retain our innocence, and push upward determinedly. We dismantle our barriers and defenses, our plans and ambitions. We carefully maintain our inner independence through each challenging situation. We yield to being led blindly by our teacher, the Sage. Strengthened by humility and conscientiousness, we engage the helpful powers of the Cosmos.

First Line: *Pushing upward that meets with confidence.* We maintain spiritual fitness through keeping aware of our inner feelings, and by keeping free of our ego. Such humility and sincerity invoke the help of the Higher Power.

Second Line: *If one is sincere, it furthers one to bring a small offering. No blame.* The strong element mentioned is ambition to achieve our goal. We desire to change entrenched habits or trends right away. This ambition interferes with our need to be patient and persevering. We have the goal in mind instead of the necessary steps at hand. We look too far ahead in anticipation of how things will be if we act, or fail to act. It is best to be purposeless. In spite of these defects, and because we are fundamentally sincere in attitude, we make progress. No great harm comes of the deficiency. A "small offering" means that sacrificing ambition would perfect our humility.

Ambition is also present when we desire to be recognized. We should not call attention to our good behavior in the hope of obligating others to do what is correct. Neither should we seek to be seen as good. We cannot create change by such means. We can rely on the power of truth to bring about change. We need not strive at all.

Third Line: *One pushes upward into an empty city.* The empty city means that we "push upward" without obstruction. Neither good nor bad fortune is promised, because we are not free of ego-pressures. We should not be discouraged, however, for further self-development will correct this defect.

Fourth Line: *The king offers him Mount Ch'i.* We are sincere and conscientious in our effort to correct ourself therefore we attain the help of the Higher Power.

This line also confirms that our work on ourselves has established our spiritual existence.

Fifth Line: *One pushes upward by steps.* Each step of progress is a separate entity, having its own beginning, middle, and end. Each step is small. The moment of influence opens, then closes. When it opens we are free to advance; when it closes we must disengage. We should take care not to press for progress beyond the potential of each moment. When we try to prolong or maximize this moment, striving begins. We should withdraw to renew ourself. We need to realize that each step of progress is minuscule and unobservable. We should not seek visible changes as a measure of success. We will have succeeded if we have stood firm and correct during the challenges.

Withdrawal does not mean that effort ceases. Returning to humility may open yet another opportunity to have an influence. Then we should try to be aware of when we will need to withdraw again.

Whenever we seek to rush another person's development, our ego is involved. People must have the space and time to digest knowledge at their own pace.

We also skip steps when, through reserve, we bring another person into a correct relationship, then drop our reserve to enjoy the moment. Only when the other person has completed the many steps of self-development needed to guarantee his continued progress can we re-enter a close fellowship with him. It is not enough that his improvement should occur only in response to our inner firmness (see *The Taming Power of the Small*, Hex. 9); his improvements must result from his having made a firm choice to follow the good through perceiving that it is the only path to take. Until then we must maintain reserve.

Sixth Line: *Pushing up blindly.* Each opportunity to relate to others in a creative way occurs only during brief moments of mutual humility and receptivity. If we keep tuned to our inner voice we will know when these moments open; if we remain alert we will also know when receptivity wanes. Precisely then we should disengage and renew our modesty before impatience, a sense of disappointment, righteous indignation, or alienation intrude. Indeed, jeopardizing ourself almost invariably leads to disappointment, then to injured pride, then to alienation.

Once our ego becomes involved we no longer are able to hear our inner voice. Ambition takes over and we push forward, throwing ourself away. Meanwhile, ambition arouses others' distrust and closes down the opportunity to have a good influence. In throwing ourself away, we give way to anger, wounded pride, and alienation. Thus, our personality "splits apart."

We also need to realize that once we achieve advances, steadfastness is hard to maintain. We easily shift from caution to enthusiastic self-confidence. Self-confidence quickly turns into arrogant self-assertion. We should be content, therefore, with small gains, retreating after advances. Otherwise, we will act when we ought to hold back, and speak when we ought to keep still.

47.

K'un / Oppression (Exhaustion)

$$\frac{\text{Tui}}{\text{K'an}} \quad \begin{array}{c}\equiv\!\equiv\\[-2pt]\equiv\!\equiv\end{array}$$

(We disbelieve that someone can, or will, ever change. We believe it is too late to rectify matters, or that we can have an impact on the situation.)

We receive this hexagram when our spirit is oppressed by certain fundamental untruths: when we believe the Higher Power does not exist; when we doubt its goodness because things have gone badly; when we suspect it will not, or cannot help us, or that the help will come too late; when we suspect that Fate is conspiring against us, that the situation is too difficult, and that we lack the means to deal with it.

The Higher Truth (Sage, Cosmos) is the source of all spiritual nourishment. This nourishment, or essential energy, is called *chi*. Chi flows first to our higher nature, and through it to our bodies. When we are true to ourselves, chi flows without resistance or blockage. When we are not true to ourselves the chi energy no longer flows properly. We know this because believing an untruth causes inner conflict and depression. If the disruption in the flow of this energy, or nourishment, continues, we experience what this hexagram calls "exhaustion." Exhaustion affects both the essential self, and the body.

Disruptions in the flow of chi occur when we harbor ideas which are foreign to the Higher Truth. This hexagram counsels us on ways to free ourself from the oppression of false ideas.

It is well known that major emotional shocks such as the loss of a parent can be followed by major illnesses. It is our tendency to react to shock by questioning our purpose in life, and to doubt our relationship with the Higher Power. This activity leads to doubt and despair, consequently a loss of the will to live. Similarly, over a period of years we may adopt false ideas that depress our health in a chronic way so that we are not well. To restore health we need to bring these ideas to the surface and free ourselves from their depressing effects.

All delusions are dangerous to our personality. Chief among deteriorating ideas is to see the Higher Power in a negative way, or to give up on the great-man-potential in others.

When we doubt that things will work, we are really doubting the creative power of the Cosmos. Such a doubt obstructs acceptance of the way things are going, and the corrective power of such acceptance. It prevents us from realizing that by following our path we do have an impact, even though it is not yet evident.

We need to realize that we cannot judge matters by their appearances, for the way of the Cosmos is zig-zag and subtle. It achieves change by remaining out of sight and beyond the interfering reach of our egoistic expectations and manipulations. It is able to benefit everyone and everything in the situation if we will but invoke its corrective action. We need only be patient and not shut the creative process down through doubting it. (To watch for results, for instance, is to doubt it.) We need to discern that, although all by ourselves we lack the means, the help of the Higher Power is not out of our reach.

Invoking the help of the Higher Power requires achievement of the correct attitude. It is not necessary to adopt a point of view, or "do" specific things; we need only cease doing that which blocks our natural relationship to the Higher Power. We need to rid ourselves of negation, free ourselves of distrust, and disperse all traces of doubt. We do not substitute belief for disbelief, or replace doubt with faith. We simply rid ourselves of disbelief so that we become open-minded. We cultivate a "willing suspension of disbelief." The resulting neutral, open mind is the very essence of trust. A neutral, open mind, through invoking the titanic creative powers of the Cosmos, is capable of "moving mountains," while holding onto a doubt "as small as a mustard seed" can prevent all progress.

First Line: *One strays into a gloomy valley.* So long as we are influenced by doubt or hope, we are blocked from seeing the solution to the problem. We must firmly resist hope, doubt, and hopelessness, to restore an open mind. The way out will show itself at the right time.

Second Line: *One is oppressed while at meat and drink. It furthers one to offer sacrifice.* An obstruction in our attitude prevents progress. We must sacrifice feelings of impatience and the inner demand that visible progress should result from our efforts. If we doubt that our goal can be attained, that matters can be rectified, or that a correct relationship with others is possible, the dark force operates, and the light force is blocked. Through sacrifice of self-comforting negative views we free ourself from the oppression that obstructs unity with the Sage.

Oppressed "at meat and drink" also refers to being depressed even though we are in need of nothing. Depression may occur if we have not yet realized our purpose in life, or if we have decided there is no purpose to life; depression occurs when we perceive that no progress is being made. Although help is at hand, we discount it; although progress has been made, we ignore it. Sometimes, because we have grown comfortable with the situation as it is, we are afraid that progress will be made.

Third Line: *Oppressed by stone*. We rely on effort rather than non-effort, and thus interfere with the beneficial forces that would remove the obstructions. We may not acquire this help so long as we persist in doubting the way.

Stone is oppressive because it is inert. When we decide that someone (or something) is hopeless, we kill them in our minds. It is oppressive to see them dead. To "lean on thorns and thistles" is to feel the prickling of untruth, especially the untruth of doubt, either about ourself, others, the Sage, our path, or the situation. When we give up our trust in the potential for good that others have, we are unable to "see" them. When we have declared them dead by ceasing to care, they are no longer there for us. All that remains is a depressed feeling.

Stone also refers to seeing situations as worse than they really are.

The statement that we are oppressed by things which "ought not to oppress" us, refers to becoming depressed because our path requires us to withdraw from a bad habit of mind, or to disengage from a person who is not receptive to us.

Fourth Line: *Oppressed in a golden carriage*. A golden carriage can symbolize any of the following: indulging in negative ideas, as if to whip ourselves (the ego seeks to undermine our will to go on); adopting a fixed negative idea about what is happening; imagining a bad outcome to the present train of events; thinking the worst about someone in order to harden ourselves against him. Fixed ideas are hedges against the Unknown. By nature they are oppressive; maintaining them is exhausting.

We lose our path when we have doubts about succeeding, or allow ourselves to be put off by the oppressiveness of other people's inferiors, or hesitate because we think we lack the stamina to persevere to the end. To indulge in this kind of bad nourishment is to associate with "powerful and wealthy acquaintances" in the form of ideas. This danger can be overcome if we renew our acceptance of our path and our determination to resist doubt within ourselves. It is important to ask the Sage for help.

Fifth Line: *His nose and feet are cut off.* To receive help we must return to acceptance and dependence on the Unknown; we relinquish inner resistance and silence the complaining, self-indulgent inferiors. Thus, modesty overcomes the obstructions.

Sixth Line: *Oppressed by creeping vines.* Creeping vines symbolize the way the slightest feelings of negation grow unnoticed to usurp our attitude and collapse our resoluteness. Then we begin to doubt that we can succeed. The inferior element always gives the impression that we are helpless against it, but if we are resolute, we will find that this is only an illusion. Resoluteness breaks the spell of helplessness that the ego casts over us.

If we doubt that another person can overcome his inferior self, our disbelief only makes his path more difficult. Such doubts are creeping vines that choke out the truth.

Creeping vines also refer to our failure to realize that we are being helped, and that progress is being made. To see this fact clearly is to overcome the creeping vines of doubt and their negative effects.

48.

Ching / The Well

K'an
———
Sun

(Don't remain locked in a conventional view of the way things work.)

The Well represents the *I Ching* as a source of universal truth and nourishment, and a way of gaining access through one's deeper nature, to Universal Truth.

Even after thousands of years, the *I Ching* is a good well, making inner truth accessible to all who draw from it.

Whether we are able to use and understand its counsel depends on our state of mind. If we come to confirm wrong ideas, we come to "shoot fish" rather than to drink the well's pure water. If we ask it frivolous things, we "drink the mud of the well." Sometimes our effort is half-hearted, or insincere, or infected with doubt; then it is said that the rope does not reach down far enough. When we distrust the *I Ching*'s counsel, the jug, our inner container for nourishment, is said to be cracked, and lets the water out. If we ignore its counsel, we fail to "drink the water," and so do not obtain its benefits. We sometimes receive this hexagram when we are not really interested in following the *I Ching*'s advice; our attitude towards it is indifferent, or insensitive.

The well also symbolizes our self-development and education in the fundamental truths of life. The *I Ching* guides us through the hidden world that parallels and mirrors our external life, a world which may be seen in meditation, and sometimes in dreams. Receiving the hexagram means that we should develop ourself through making a keener effort to understand the fundamentals of human behavior. Above all we must not remain locked in the conventional view of the way things work.

A person whose "well is being lined," has not yet come to a sufficient understanding of these fundamentals to relate to others in a constructive way, consequently, for now he can "do nothing for others."

Good character is here compared to a clean, dependable, well-built well, dispensing an abundant supply of pure water. The image of an old well that has been cleaned suggests that anyone, regardless of the degree of decadence to which he has succumbed, may still nourish others beneficially and thereby give meaning to his life, provided he will only develop himself to follow the good in an enduring way.

Just as water drawn from a good well is clear and pure, so must we hold to what is true and pure in our natures, and cultivate the water-like virtues of sincerity, simplicity, and serenity. In this regard we are counselled to hold to the essential and let go of the trivial, so that we may avoid becoming entangled in issues which do not concern us.

Receiving this hexagram often indicates that a hidden doubt inhibits our learning from the *I Ching*. While the *I Ching* provides a means to tap universal truth, we need to ask what we are hoping it will say. To benefit from its counsel we need to be free of personal, selfish motives, and preconceived ideas. We should search our inmost thoughts for self-indulgent, self-satisfied, or self-important feelings which would cause us to bypass true self-development or ruin the work we have achieved. We may think the *I Ching* path is the "same" as all other spiritual paths. In thinking we already know, we are unable to grasp what it is really saying. Through such thoughts our ego, in the form of pride, keeps us aloof from learning.

Another message implicit in *The Well* is that fundamental human nature is like the classic well. However culture, politics, and tradition alter through the ages, human nature, like the classic well, remains the same; it can always be counted on to respond to the power of inner truth. Moreover, drawing water from a well suggests the correct way to draw on the inherent goodness in human nature. Obviously, each person's 'well' will be in a different condition, depending on what he does with his opportunities for self-development. In spite of these differences, if we see in him only inferior things (fish), we will be unable to connect with his potential for good. If we are put off by externals (mud), we will be unable to reach the humanity that lies deep within him. There is always something good on which we can draw if we will only remain patient and open-minded. This does not mean that we should accept fellowship under incorrect conditions. It means that a creative attitude helps others free themselves from the dominance of their Inferior Man.

First Line: *One does not drink the mud of the well.* Mud symbolizes involvement with trivialities or externals, such as irritation at the way a person dresses or presents himself. It is a throw-away of self to dwell on another person's petty, negative qualities.

In a similar way we should not dwell on the unpleasant situation we have had to endure; it is past; we should let go and go on our way. To concentrate on negatives is to drink the mud of the well.

Second Line: *At the wellhole one shoots fishes. The jug is broken and leaks.* The jug refers to our inner container for nourishment, and to the quantity of good that can be achieved in a situation. If we doubt that we can achieve our goal through following the path, the jug is broken, and even though we draw good nourishment from the well, it leaks out and is useless. Doubt enters because we are irresolute or careless. In abandoning our path, the potential for good that could have been achieved is lost.

Fish symbolize inferior ideas. The presence of desire and pride prevent us from judging other people's mistakes moderately. We realize that they are potentially good, but we concentrate on their bad qualities (the fish).

Coming to the well to shoot fish also means that we come in search of wrong answers, or that we are asking wrong questions. (See *Conflict*, Hex. 6, for an explanation of questions of inner conflict.) Instead of looking to the essence of the matter we pay attention to peripherals.

This line also refers to times when we come to the well with a disgruntled attitude, suspecting that it might give us an incomprehensible or disagreeable answer, or we accept only the answers we want to hear. Truth is never disappointing; when we perceive it, it is accompanied by a sense of relief and joy.

Third Line: *The well is cleaned...but no one drinks from it.* In spite of understanding things correctly, we cling to traditional defenses. The king, our inner self, is not clear-minded enough to trust and draw on rich inner resources, such as asking for help, trusting the Unknown, and persevering in allowing ourself to be led docilely and receptively. The *I Ching* wisdom is trustworthy. No one will drink the water of our well if we ourselves do not drink it.

Fourth Line: *The well is being lined.* This line may refer to ourself, to another, or to a situation. It means the time is not ripe to achieve our goals. It is more important that we spend this time in self-development. If this line refers to another person, it indicates that we can really trust that he will succeed, since "his well is being lined" through his work on himself, and through his relationship to the Higher Power.

Fifth Line: *In the well there is a clear, cold spring.* It is not enough to draw the water of the well; for it to be of use we must drink it. If we have doubts about the *I Ching* and its way, it cannot work for us. We can only make knowledge ours by accepting the hazard of depending on it, and by putting it to the test of experience. It is important, therefore, not to get caught up in dreading the future, or in anticipating negative situations. We should keep our mind innocent and free, and allow ourself to be guided by the Unknown.

Sixth Line: *One draws from the well without hindrance. It is dependable.* The hindrances to understanding are overcome. Through understanding the truth of the matter, and correcting ourselves, we are able to bear with the mistakes of others. In knowing that their mistakes are like ours—caused by hidden fears and misconceptions—we are able to be compassionate.

49.

Ko / Revolution (Molting)

$$\frac{\text{Tui}}{\text{Li}}\ \ \begin{array}{l}\text{==}\\\text{==}\\\text{==}\end{array}$$

(Changes are now possible.)

On your own day you are believed. When our inner independence is such that we cannot be disturbed by events, however contrary, or however beneficial, we attain the confidence of others that is necessary to bring success to everything we do. When we are able to remain balanced through any buildup of tension or challenge, a "revolution" in our situation occurs, and "we are believed."

While receiving this hexagram may mean that such a revolution has occurred, it may also mean the time has come to revolutionize our attitude. No further progress can be made until this has been done. It is as if we have been practicing all the steps that lead to swimming, but we must now take our feet off the bottom. Every difficult step of progress stretches us to the limit of our capabilities. Each step forward is called a revolution. The word revolution is used because all such changes occur in an atmosphere of turmoil, challenge, and risk. Willingness to trust the Unknown takes courage. The reward is that we free ourself of one more of the fears which prevent us from putting our full personality together.

In the beginning of self-development our personality is like pieces of an engine waiting to be put together. Removing fears and doubts is like cleaning off rust and other obstructions which prevent the parts from fitting together. While this work is tedious and difficult, the time of revolution never comes prematurely. It comes only when we are ready to rid ourself of a particular doubt or fear.

Receiving this hexagram tells us that although preparing for revolution occurs on the unconscious plane, the actual revolution requires making a conscious step. For example, we consciously choose to let go of a habit which has its origin in fear; we choose to suspend our disbelief in the power of the Unknown, or we dispose of a fear, sacrifice pride, or disperse an invading doubt. In giving up old defenses against the Unknown, we risk trusting it to lead us past the difficulties in question. Instead of contriving a response, we take the risk of relating to the problem by keeping our inner attitude correct.

Receiving this hexagram also means that as a consequence of growing, a revolution occurs in our relationship with others. Through tolerance, withdrawal, and adherence to our path, we bring the process of revolution and growth to them. They will make the "next step" towards improvement if we continue on our path, allow ourself to be led, make sure our motives are correct, and require, in our inmost thoughts, only that which is universally just. Victory is assured through the power of inner truth. We need only wait.

First Line: *Wrapped in the hide of a yellow cow.* This means that we wrap ourself in an attitude of innocence and docility while we wait for the correct influences to approach. If just this line is received, the hexagram changes to *Influence* (Hex. 31), implying that we should keep our minds open and free.

Sometimes this line simply means that we are to wait patiently and keep our mind open until understanding, or the appropriate changes, occur. Meanwhile, no harm will come of our not having a prepared approach to the problem, nor will it be of consequence that others misunderstand our perseverance in non-action.

Second Line: *When one's own day comes....* When our firmness of character cannot be swayed (when we no longer lose our firmness, inner independence, and detachment), we attain the confidence of others. "To prepare for the condition that will inevitably come" means that we must be on guard against relaxing our requirements of what is right and essential, once the difficulties of the moment have passed.

Inner independence comes from maintaining a balanced alertness; like the tight-rope walker, we are neither stiffly watchful, through being fearful and agitated, nor carelessly enthusiastic and presumptuous once we succeed.

Third Line: *When talk of revolution has gone the round three times, one may commit himself.* "Three times" refers to having an effect after a long period of perseverance. It also refers to understanding what we must do to carry on.

Changes are difficult to make. If we expect great changes to be made right away, we are too hasty; if we do not put forth energy to persevere because we think the task will take too long, or if it seems too difficult, we are excessively conservative. We need strength to persevere through the minuscule steps of growth that lead to enduring change; strength comes only from seeing clearly that we must make the effort to wait through the changes with a detached and modest attitude.

Fourth Line: *Remorse disappears.* When revolution is founded on the authority of a correct inner attitude, there can be no remorse. If we would change others, we must be just and firm in our values, and detached and independent within ourself, always ready to withdraw and go on our way when others are not receptive to us or correct with us. Only when they clearly see that they must change will the revolution endure.

This line also warns us to be sure that what we require is universally correct, for capricious demands from our inferiors only have a bad effect and act to prevent true changes for the good.

Fifth Line: *The great man changes like a tiger.* The revolution occurs because we have related to the problem in the proper way (see Line 2). People (or we ourself) begin to understand, therefore they change. Understanding gives them strength to overcome the inferior power, and consequently the change is dramatic and swift.

Sixth Line: *The inferior man molts in the face.* The inferiors change only temporarily. Habit is strong and clarity short-lived. Permanent change occurs only through repeated experiences which force us to grow, and through repeated efforts at disciplining our inferiors. Giant steps lead to rebellion and back-sliding. Patience and perseverance are necessary.

It is important not to become attached to the progress achieved. The victory at hand is only a knoll on the mountain to be climbed.

We must remember that every step of progress, every revolution, emancipates us from a particular cloud of obstruction which up to now has imprisoned us.

Meanwhile, we need to remember that every large step of revolution requires the help of the Higher Power. We must seek this help through perseverance (not giving up one's goal), and willingness to keep correcting ourself.

50.

Ting / The Caldron

$$\frac{\text{Li}}{\text{Sun}} \quad \overline{\overline{\overline{}}}\overline{\overline{\overline{}}}$$

(Acceptance of one's fate, and of being guided.)

This hexagram is related to *The Well* (Hex. 48), in which water symbolizes effort. In that hexagram water nourishes wood, which symbolizes character. This suggests that it is through effort that we develop character. In this hexagram wood, symbolizing developed character, nourishes fire. This means that through developing the good and great potential within us, we shine as an example, lighting the way for others.

Ultimately, it is sacrifice which "lights" the wood. Through sacrifice of self-interest we offer nourishment to God. The Ting is a vessel for offering such sacrifice. Our inner thoughts at any given time are offerings in the Ting. When what we offer in the way of our thoughts is good, we provide good nourishment to the Higher Power, but when our inner thoughts are corrupted, the "prince's meal is spoiled," as it is put in the fourth line. It is important, therefore, that our inner thoughts be kept pure, and our attitude careful and conscientious (modest).

This hexagram calls for sacrificing that which is of the highest "earthly value"—the feeling that we are in command, and we have the ability and right to guide ourself. The fact is, we are *not* in command. Growing older, or being pinned down by an adverse fate, makes us aware of this. The idea of such power over self is only an illusion created by our ego. To sacrifice this illusion is also to sacrifice the ego. Simply by relinquishing this pretense we allow ourself to be guided (and protected) by the Higher Power. Nothing else is required, for the sacrifice of the ego automatically empowers the Creative (Higher Power) to act beneficially in our lives.

The ego (self-image) often manifests itself in disguises so that we are unaware of its presence. We often do not understand what needs to be sacrificed. For example, we may need to sacrifice the ego as an emotionally satisfying point of view. Our personal, emotional viewpoint isolates us from the Higher Power because in clinging to it we seem to say, "it is this view which makes me human, and therefore I cling to it." In clinging to our "human" faults and prejudices we maintain a residue of rebelliousness based on a distrust of God's will. By sacrificing inner resistance we attain true acceptance and humility.

We may also need to sacrifice our tendency to "feel good" when things go well, or to "feel badly" when times change for the worse. Instead, we should pursue our course straight ahead, independent of events, letting go of things. If we succeed, it is good, if not, we continue forward, working at self-correction, keeping to our path, and maintaining conscious innocence and inner independence.

When we receive this hexagram without lines, or as a second hexagram, it either means we should relinquish inappropriate thoughts, or it confirms that we have established a connection with the Higher Power through having made a true sacrifice of our ego.

First Line: *A ting with legs upturned.* This line counsels us to cleanse ourself of inferior elements such as pride, and to be open-minded about people even when their worst inferiors dominate. We tend to make a mental file of other people's transgressions to keep on guard against them. However, these negative ideas become a barrier to their correcting themselves, as well as a source of self-conflict to us. It is against our nature to take close care of evil memories. Bad memories are "stagnating stuff."

Other stagnating stuff is seeking to "be somebody"; we should seek only to do something worthwhile.

It is also stagnating stuff to want people to be factional toward us, tolerating our carelessness, bad habits, and mistakes.

Second Line: *My comrades are envious.* While inner worth, stability, and inner independence are elements which cause people to follow us with their inner eye and help them make changes in their lives, they are also qualities which arouse the envy and rebelliousness of their Inferior Man. Until their Inferior Man is firmly displaced by their emerging Superior Man, their Inferior Man will continue to test, probe, and challenge us. It does so in an attempt to prove to the inferiors that our virtue is weak or fake, and hence not worth following. If it can succeed in this effort, the inner conflict and discomfort at going along in the same old way will be dismissed, and no changes for the better will occur. For such reasons we need to stand firm in our way of life.

The envious testing of others leads to danger if we allow ourselves to be drawn into self-defense, or if we allow our pride to be engaged. We should refuse to be drawn off what we see as essential, and should never engage in slanderous exchanges. During such times we must be extremely careful to maintain our innocence.

Envy sometimes manifests itself as unreasoning anger. In such cases we must deal with it as if we were a bull-fighter, facing a bull. The bull is allowed to expend its anger harmlessly against the red flag while we allow it to think it engages us. We stay carefully detached. When we are confronted with unreasoning anger, we need not try to reply reasonably, since a reasonable reply is no better understood than a nonsensical one. It is better, in such instances, to reply nonsensically.

Another form of envy shows itself in servile attachment, or infatuation. To such people we seem to possess the image they would like to present to others. They study us in search of our "formula" for success in hopes that they can imitate it and achieve the same results. They distrust our independence, suspecting it is an act which easily can be emulated. They also seek ways to prove that, unmasked, we must be identical to their "Inferior Man." The correct response is to keep disengaged. In no way should we allow ourself to be caught up in flattery, or to become involved in any game plans they initiate. It is better that they totally misunderstand us and be allowed to go on their way, than that we should adopt some image they seem to need, or allow ourself to be used.

If our ego does interfere in their affairs, their ego will spring to their defense. This situation resembles challenging a snake in its den. If we are more adroit than the snake, we may avoid the hazards, but the snake is poisonous and good at self-defense; it is better not to enter its territory.

Third Line: *The handle of the ting is altered.* Our usefulness is impeded because we have yet to attain true spirituality. We still cling to doubt and embroil ourselves in inner conflict. We should stop looking at that which causes inner conflict and doubt. We need to truly let go, and sacrifice self-interest.

Modesty (the handle of the ting) is the foundation of all other virtues. The sense of injustice that comes in the face of evil must not become a power in itself, as in righteousness and pride. Resoluteness must not become rigidity of attitude, devoid of compassion. In spite of all things we must fall back on the larger truths which sustain a just and moderate view of mankind. Obstinacy and pride make our virtues ineffective. This larger sense of justice, when combined with humility, gives sublime power to the Sage. It is necessary to sacrifice both righteousness and self-defense if we are to acquire true spirituality. If we depend on the trustworthiness of the Sage, we will need no other defense.

Fourth Line: *The legs of the ting are broken.* We receive this line when we have become presumptuously wrapped up in ourselves, unobserving and out of touch with our inner voice. An opportunity to have an influence occurs, but we are so involved, either with enjoying ourselves, or with feeling put upon, that we fail to perceive it, and thus blunder through it. In so doing we set a bad example of our way of life and spoil matters for the Sage whom we serve. It is true modesty to remain careful and alert, keeping contact with our inner self so that what we do is mild and pure. We do not forget our path and abandon it through neglect.

Fifth Line: *The ting has yellow handles, golden carrying rings.* In spite of the pressures of the moment we should sacrifice pride and self-defense to remain modest and approachable. Through self-abnegation we nourish others correctly, serve that which is higher than ourself, and acquire the help we need to right the difficult situation. Self-abnegation means to keep strictly correct, neither luxuriating in carelessness, nor indulging wrongs in others by failing to retreat the instant evil shows itself.

Sixth Line: *The ting has rings of jade.* We counsel others as the Sage counsels us, by his example. This means that we maintain our will to persevere quietly past all obstacles. In spite of insults, injuries, and injustices, we hold to our path, remaining mild and pure. The Sage is as firm as jade, but always retains his soft lustre in the form of gentleness. This is a true example to follow.

51.

Chên/ The Arousing
(Shock, Thunder)

$$\frac{\text{Chên}}{\text{Chên}} \quad \begin{array}{c} \equiv\equiv \\ \equiv\equiv \end{array}$$

(Despite the rumblings of shock, we should keep our
attitude neutral and disengaged.)

Shock means thinking about, or being subjected to, unsettling
events. Receiving this hexagram refers to the way we react to those
events. Shock may occur when a person gets fired, loses his license
to drive, has a car accident, or wins the lottery. It occurs when we
encounter the prospect of long term changes in our life, such as a
divorce, the death of someone close, or the sudden perception of
growing old. We see that such changes have placed on us a new set
of limits which deprive or penalize us. The sense of being projected
by events into a drastically different set of circumstances is what this
hexagram calls "Fate."

The primary message of this hexagram is: *Shock is good!* Receiving it reminds us that if we keep our mind open, disturbing events can
be constructive of good. Instead of reacting blindly to shock, we
adjust our attitude to accepting, even greeting the challenge imposed
by the new circumstance. In all instances in which our attitude is
jolted (even in the slightest degree), we are here counseled to retain
our inner balance.

One purpose of shock is to force us to acknowledge that we are
meant to find a new, more correct way of dealing with circumstances. We are meant to find the answer that harmonizes with the
overall good. Finding this answer often requires that we undergo
spiritual development. If we disregard this imperative and continue
in the old ways of reacting, we are subjected to repeated shock.

Shock also has the helpful effect of discrediting (at least momentarily) the neat grid of logic by which we explain life and its
phenomena. While clinging to this grid of certainties makes us feel
less threatened, it is the chief barrier which prevents us from seeing
things from a new perspective. Shock and adversity are often the

only circumstances which make us re-examine the ideas in that grid.

Since the ego-self-image derives its power and sense of reality from this grid, having the grid momentary discredited deprives the ego of its basis for existence. During this brief time our true self (Superior Man) learns that it is able to get along without relying on the defenses and stratagems of the ego. Awakening to this fact, the true self gains strength. However, the ego, and the old ideas with which it is associated, have only momentarily lost credibility. Gradually, they re-insinuate themselves back into leadership of the personality through force of habit. The shock process must be repeated until the ego and the old ideas finally lose credibility. In this process the real self gains enough strength to keep the ego separated and in check.

Another purpose of shock is to make us aware that we are wanderers and strangers in the Universe, that there is a Cosmic structure to which we are meant to relate, that we are subject to higher Cosmic laws, and that we are meant to find our life's meaning in relation to this higher existence. Shock is meant to make us ask what are these laws, and how we may have been disregarding them. We are also meant to question whether our understanding of the Higher Power and our map of the Unknown correspond to the higher truth. We are meant to cease relying on commonly-held viewpoints, and search for the truth within ourself.

When the beginning student of the *I Ching* receives this hexagram, he is usually being subjected to shocking events. This happens because of our disbelief and doubt in any reality beyond the reality defined by the five senses. These doubts may be phrased as rigid belief systems, or even as stubborn disbelief. It takes the major rumblings of shock to overcome this rigidity. As we become more receptive and our doubts and hesitations regarding the Unknown lose power, the degree of shock needed to make us think lessens, until merely receiving the hexagram has the necessary salutary effect. Then, receiving it merely reminds us that we are in danger of falling back into old patterns of doubt, and to correct the situation promptly.

Shock for the most part occurs in the context of unpleasant events; at times, however, the hexagram warns us against being jarred off balance by a sudden release from tensions. With good times we tend to slide back into old luxurious attitudes. Depending on good things to continue, we become careless, assuming that the Sage will cover our mistakes. While we may "cling" to what is right, as one clings to a life preserver, and in this way create good luck for ourselves, if such clinging changes to "relying on," in the sense of expecting things to go well, our luck is sure to change for the worse.

Sometimes shock comes in the form of a challenge from those who secretly mistrust us. They challenge us because we are not yet firm in our path, and they sense our vulnerability. Until we become firm in our values and allow ourself to be led, we will be subjected to this sort of challenging. We should learn to recognize the challenges and their causes. Once we cease wavering or doubting our sense of inner truth, all challenges will end.

We may observe a pattern of reaction when we become infected with doubt. Once doubt enters, we rely on bravado; then we strive to solve the problem by wrestling with it. Having reacted badly, our inferiors mistakenly think we have jeopardized the situation; however, truth cannot be jeopardized. In removing our doubt of the truth we remove the problem and restore balance. We simply need to reaffirm that inner truth—what we have learned through our experiences with the *I Ching*— is reliable. It has in itself the power to shine without effort. We may cling with utter safety to inner truth, as we would to a life raft.

Shock, on the whole, is meant to make us recognize our natural limitations; until we do, the situation retains a vise-like quality. The Cosmic hammer pounds at our consciousness until we wake up to the inner realities. It is as if the obdurate external situation exists to make us develop ourself. When our awareness is such that we see the hand of the Higher Power in every situation, and its purpose as constructive, the repetitive shocks end. Allowing ourself to be led, we find the easy and safe route around every difficulty. The way of the *I Ching* is the easy way. *I* means the easy.

The ultimate development of character is expressed thus: when the thunder spreads terror "a hundred miles around," we remain so composed that the sacrificial rite is not interrupted.

First Line: *Shock comes—oh, oh!...ha, ha! Good fortune.* What seems to be a bad fate will eventually be seen as the only way we could have grown, and the only way that good things yet to come can happen.

Second Line: *A hundred thousand times you lose your treasures....* Thinking about losses, mistakes, or unpleasant events disturbs our tranquillity. In mulling over negative things we are tempted to resist Fate. We must retreat from these images and the dangers they bring. We will regain what we have lost in due time, through relating correctly. We need to redefine the situation, not as "bad," but as exactly what is needed for our learning process.

Third Line: *If shock spurs one to action.* The shock of encountering Fate, which seems unbearably harsh, causes emotional trauma. It is as if we are suddenly and irrevocably put into a predicament from which there are no options. This negativism, however, means that we are still under the effects of shock. If we can withdraw from all negative views, we will see that there are workable and correct ways out of the problem. We need to be openminded to allow the options to become visible. This requires that we keep still within: we steadfastly refuse to listen to our clamoring inferiors, or to look at the negative images they press on us.

Fourth Line: *Shock is mired.* Shock makes us feel that all is lost, or that there is no solution to the problem. We no longer see our progress as meaningful, and we are not open to the correct perspective. All effort seems to have been wasted. This reaction is simply the effect of shock, or the way our childish ego sees the situation. Since it cannot see without distortion, it over-reacts. As long as it rules, our ideas remain fixed in tradition, not yet liberated by the realizations to come. We can control our ego by keeping still (see Hex. 52). Talking about or regarding a situation as bad tends to keep it that way simply because we are locked into a negative point of view. We need to realize that each situation is exactly as it needs to be, either to help us, or to help someone else to grow. We need to accept the unpleasant situation as a signal that it is time to learn something new, if nothing more than to have a new perspective towards shock. We need to relinquish the childish heart and the way it perceives things, and to return to an unstructured, open mind.

Fifth Line: *Shock goes hither and thither...but nothing is lost.* Many events occur which seem unrelated and meaningless. We must stay disengaged and try to do what is right. What we need to know will be revealed. Everything is for the best.

Sixth Line: *Withdraw from the effects of shock.* We must not allow shocking events to cause us to vilify the Sage, Fate, God, or the people who have wronged us. Shock brings both an end to the old, and a beginning to the new. While these changes are occurring we must withdraw from the negative effects of shock which make us stop to look at what has happened. It is important to keep going forward.

If we wonder how to relate to bad or good events, the answer is: "Do not take hold of the problem or get involved in its particulars." To regain clarity and understand the shock, it is necessary to cease looking at the problem.

52.

Kên / Keeping Still, Mountain

$$\frac{\text{Kên}}{\text{Kên}} \quad \begin{array}{c} \equiv\!\equiv \\ \equiv\!\equiv \end{array}$$

(Keep one's inner thoughts quiet, and relinquish the childish heart.)

We receive this hexagram either when our thoughts are entangled with our emotions, or when the situation is such that we may become emotionally involved. Once our emotions are involved it becomes impossible to acquire clarity of mind; thus, we are counseled to "keep still."

Keeping still means quieting the "thinking" of the heart. In the *I Ching*, when our emotions are aroused the heart is said to think. The childish heart thinks in terms of its wants and needs, and of what it dislikes and wishes to avoid. It also thinks in defense of any pretensions we may have adopted; thus it is also the egotistical thinking of vanity, and pride. It constantly measures the direction and pace of events to see if its goals are being furthered. The object of 'keeping still' is to quiet this frenetic and focussed mental activity.

If we could detach long enough to see such thoughts objectively, we would realize that they arise from fears of the bodily self, some of which are conscious, some subconscious. The *I Ching* recognizes these thoughts as voices of 'the inferiors.' So long as they dominate our mental space, it is impossible to attain the neutrality and acceptance that leads to a correct and reasonable perspective.

There are several ways in which we may quiet the inferiors. We may explain to them the need to be quiet so that clarity will be possible. We may tell them that they must not become confused by the appearances of things, that change is the rule of life. We may reassure them that if they can be disciplined, we will draw the help of the Higher Power to make the impossible possible. We may explain the need for their obedience, as in *The Army* (Hex. 7), and that we must cling to the Unknown to show the way, as in *The Clinging* (Hex. 30). By encouraging them in such ways we may attain their cooperation and perseverance. This method of limiting inferiors is called "sweet limitation" in *Limitation* (Hex. 60).

To obtain these results it may be necessary to sit quietly in the meditative state. Very often, receiving this hexagram is a call to meditate, or at least to get in touch with the worries and fears of our inferiors. The inferiors need to be reassured that if we will only trust the Unknown, and allow the Creative to work through the vehicle of time, everything will work out correctly. Sometimes this work requires that we recognize our pretensions and pride—culprits which must be "killed" through firm perseverance.

Once we have come to a state of acceptance and docility, we attain the peacefulness described by the image in *The Joyous* (Hex. 58) as the "shining lake." The unruffled surface of the lake symbolizes the contentment of inner peace. The moment any emotion arises, a ripple is created on its surface.

Keeping still also symbolizes the *I Ching* way of meditating, which entails bringing oneself to a state of inner emptiness through systematically clearing out the clamoring voices of the inferiors. Keeping still as meditation requires sitting in a relaxed but alert position so that the nerves of the backbone become quiet. The spinal column is not only the route by which the brain conveys messages to the bodily self, it is also the pathway by which the bodily self conveys its complaints to the brain.

By sitting in a self-supporting position (we lean on nothing), we remain awake while our body relaxes. As our blood pressure and energies subside, the inferiors become quiet, as if asleep. At this point ego-separation occurs: the pretentious, defensive, assuming voice of the self-image separates from our consciousness so that we are able to hear its thoughts separately from ourself. Its voice is sometimes subtle and tempting, sometimes strained and harping, sometimes demanding and furious. Ego-separation gives us an opportunity to hear and understand the ego and its pretensions. Once we understand it, we can liberate ourself from its domination. Once we have heard it in meditation we can recognize its insinuations from the sideline during our everyday activities. Recognition enables us to resist its demands.

Once the ego has separated we may also see and hear the inferiors. In listening to their concerns and complaints we will notice that they are like children. Like children they focus on wanting, wondering, and worrying. Body cells, or organizations of cells, have both verbal and nonverbal ways of telling us we are hungry, tired, or afraid. During normal conscious activity we would think these thoughts to be integral to our makeup; in meditation, however, we hear and see them as separate from our central self. Through contacting them in meditation we find that they have been under the control of the ego; we also find that now we are able to enlist them in working towards the goals of the higher self. In this way our superior self, the Superior Man, gains the ability to command the inferiors. Once this happens, the personality resumes to its natural true order.

Listening to the needs of the inferiors, and putting their fears to rest, seems to reassure and pacify them, and our heart comes to rest. In a state of true quiet we sit, as it were, in a space of total neutrality and acceptance. We see or hear nothing. Sometimes it becomes possible to hear a new voice and to see new things. The new voice is the quiet, unobtrusive but firm voice of the Sage. We listen and watch, as if we were waiting for a movie to begin. We may also see images which demonstrate the lessons of universal truth. While we may participate in what happens, we do not control it.

Meditation is also the time in which we make the sacrifices called for in various hexagrams such as *Contemplation* (Hex. 20). Sacrifice means to turn over to the Higher Power questions of inner conflict, and emotions such as justifiable anger, the feeling of having rights, indignation due to injustice, impatience with evil, and our tendency to focus on the petty elements in others which tend to bring on the question, "Why are things this way?" We sacrifice these feelings and perceptions because they obstruct progress and inhibit the general good. Such sacrifices enlarge the spiritual being.

To the serious student of the *I Ching*, the daily practice of meditation is essential. Through meditation we perform the inner-cleansing that returns us to purity and innocence; freed of thoughts which generate restlessness and inner deafness, we return to the alertness and inner attentiveness that makes it possible for us to interact with others in a creative way. Freeing ourself from the pre-ponderating concerns of the inferiors has the effect of cleaning our inner house. Just as our external house becomes dirty through living in it, our inner mental space becomes cluttered with extraneous and unnecessary preoccupations. These may consist of belief systems, concerns, fantasies, and false ideas which make inner peace and harmony impossible to achieve. Inner cleansing implies that we let go of the world and its preponderating concerns, and we let go of all belief systems. We let go of old anger and hostility, and any attachment to injuries people have done us; we discard all philoso-phies of negation, and petty likes and dislikes. On cleaning our

"Ting" (see *The Ting*, Hex. 50) in this manner, we become freed of the enormous burden entailed by carrying such mental trash.

If, in trying to meditate, we seek to achieve inner quiet without first performing inner cleansing, clarity and communication with the Sage will not be possible. To bypass this step is to "force meditation," as the third line warns. To practice daily inner-cleansing is the "daily self-renewal" which enables the Superior Man to remain at the height of his powers (see *The Taming Power of the Great*, Hex. 26).

Through meditation the Sage allows us to glimpse our ego as an organized defense-system which we, through abdicating leadership of our personality, have allowed our inferiors to construct in defense against the Unknown. We are permitted to see, one at a time, the fears which give life and power to the ego; we see our fears both in the demonic disguises which enable them to terrorize us, and as the really harmless things they are. To unmask such fears in meditation is like discovering the Wizard of Oz in the act of manipulating his frightening machines from behind the curtain; never again are they able to wield power over us.

Since this sort of meditation seems indispensable to a serious study of the *I Ching* it is not surprising that Confucius said, "study without meditation is labor wasted; meditation, without study, is perilous."

First Line: *Keeping his toes still. No blame. Continued perseverance furthers.* Wanting a thing to happen will not make it happen. Until conditions are correct we should find peace in acceptance, and keep steadfast and detached. "Continued perseverance" means that it will take time to correct matters. Meanwhile, we must not depart from what we know is true.

Second Line: *Keeping his calves still.* It is important not to do anything now because we are still being pressured by our ego to act. If we doubt that the correct way will work, or if we are caught up in desiring something, we lose our inner independence. As long as fear, doubt, or desire pervade, any action will be wrongly motivated.

He cannot rescue him whom he follows. If our inner eye is fastened on what another does, we follow his path rather than our own. We can only rescue him if we follow our own path. When he sees that he is truly alone in doing the wrong thing, with no one to rescue him

237

but himself, he will cease to do the wrong thing.

This line indicates that we must disallow our emotional self. It is often difficult to see that desire has its roots in fear, or doubt. We desire only what we are unsure of getting. Perhaps we desire the equitable resolution of a situation, or the return of someone from whom we have become separated. Perhaps we wish to escape an adversity which we fear may continue indefinitely. Adversity, we should remember, lasts only for a time; meanwhile, it serves as the fire which clarifies, and renders off the fat—our impurities of character. Doubt of this eternal truth tends to lock us into negative patterns. If we can let go of fear, doubt, and distrust, progress will be made.

Third Line: *Keeping his hips still.* When we strive to trust, or be quiet, we force a state of mind on ourself. The way to composure is not to try to "be" something, but to work at freeing ourself from any elements which make us more or less than what we really are; usually, these elements are pride, or negative thoughts. We need not like people, for example, but it is important to disperse hostile feelings and come to a moderate and just view of them. This is to find the "middle way," and to come to an acceptance of life which is called "noblehearted keeping still."

Enforced quiet also means that we are still harboring worries and anxieties. We must let go of all pressing matters. Such resignation brings good luck, whereas dwelling on issues prevents it, because the dark force still operates.

When we make a great effort to find the negative element to be dispersed and still cannot find it, it will come through naturally if we keep our mind humble and free. To strive hard, even in trying to do the right thing, causes "splitting apart" (see *Splitting Apart*, Hex. 23).

Sometimes we think that to get rid of doubt we must "believe." This is yet another attempt to force tranquillity on ourselves. It is impossible to replace doubt with belief, for then we have not really dealt with doubt; we have only covered it up. Because doubt is still present, we are continuously forced to justify and defend the belief system which keeps it at bay. We also accept beliefs because they flatter us in some way and make us feel better. Sometimes we try to flatter the Unknown by creating a belief system which we think will please it, in the primitive fantasy that worshipful obeisance will placate it. This is similar to the practice, in primitive religions, of sacrificing animals to placate angry, or trickster, gods. Indeed, with this view the Higher Power leaves us alone to our own devices. The *I Ching* way is to let go of doubt and replace it with nothing. We humbly accept the Unknown, and offer no resistance to it. The trust needed is only an absence of distrust.

Fourth Line: *Keeping his trunk still.* The presence of fear, doubt, or desire causes unrest. Desire is a form of fear that we may not achieve our goal. We hardly ever desire what we are sure of having, and often desire what we think we cannot have. Thus, desire contains both doubt and envy. In letting go of these negative feelings we bring the heart to rest and attain a higher level of tranquillity.

Fifth Line: *Keeping jaws still.* When we have not attained inner tranquillity our words and actions are bound to reflect the presence of fears, doubts, desires, impatience, or other restless forces. For example, if we focus on others' failings, they sense our supervisory attitude and become more resistant to doing the right thing. Their increased resistance further unbalances us and makes it harder to persevere. Because of these and other bad effects of speaking or acting when we lack tranquillity, we should make a special effort to be reserved in speech.

Sixth Line: *Noblehearted keeping still.* It is noblehearted if, in spite of attacks by our inferiors who keep asking "why," we turn our backs on them and keep still. Such perseverance leads to detachment and peace of mind.

53.

Chien / Development
(Gradual Progress)

$$\frac{\text{Sun}}{\text{Kên}}$$

(Allow time and the giving of space to be the vehicle of progress. Time is not of the essence, time is the essence.)

Development refers to making progress in the difficult situations which comprise our fate. Gradual progress is the means by which the unfavorable trajectory of events caused by incorrect attitudes may be changed or reversed. It is the means by which both the great and small problems of life may be resolved.

Progress and change are necessarily slow because growth is an organic process. Organic processes require perseverance and fidelity because they are completed only by working in concert with natural forces.

The image of the wild goose, which remains faithful to its mate throughout its lifetime, symbolizes perseverance and fidelity. The goose's life is perfected when it attains the "cloud heights." The image counsels that despite challenges, we should remain true to our principles, and faithful to our duty to rescue those who comprise our sphere of responsibility.

The lines enumerate the changes, dangers, and misunderstandings which threaten our will to remain true to our path. Chief of these is the challenge presented by time. We are required to wait, it seems, interminably. This challenge can be overcome only through steadfastness. The situation is not unlike that experienced by Columbus during his first crossing of the ocean. He held to his vision when everyone doubted him. His steady point of reference was the North Star. In remembering and clinging to his knowledge that the North Star always stayed in its place, he remained sure of his vision and was able to carry out what was then deemed impossible.

Of the many attributes of character discussed throughout the *I Ching*, steadfastness is seen as overcoming all assaults by the negative forces. The hub of the wheel, being a stationary point

240

around which the spokes revolve, is given as example of something which is capable of moving heavy loads. Just as the stars stay in their places in the constellations, the Sage, through his constancy, attains the ultimate power. Constancy means that we do not allow ourself to be pulled or pushed off center balance, either by our ego, or by our inferiors. This also means that we do not react to what others do or fail to do. We are able to follow our task to correct our own sphere because we see that if everyone works at correcting his own sphere, there will be order and justice in life, and suffering will be eased; we do not, therefore, seek to be released from this task.

Effort to maintain consistency of character during his slow, organic growth, enables the developing person's character to become strongly rooted, like the tree. His stature and quiet dignity provide example for all those around him who are developing themselves. At first the seedling pushes upward through effort and adaptability. During this time it is susceptible to dangers, but when the tree is mature, it is well-adapted and balanced, in harmony with itself and its environment.

Receiving this hexagram reminds us to accept the time required to complete our task, and to free ourself from any resistance that may have entered our attitude. We receive this hexagram repeatedly if we are impatient, as a signal to analyze why we are in such a hurry, and to cleanse ourself of the ego-pressures which cause impatience. Being impatient indicates that we have not yet come to terms with Fate; we distrust where we think it leads, thinking we will be caught in a difficult and hopeless pit, and that there will be no remedy but to take matters in hand, and do things our way. Our ego (childish heart) would rather do anything than nothing at all. To be patient and accepting is in harmony with Fate.

First Line: *The wild goose gradually draws near the shore.* During the early part of self-development we are easy prey to doubt and fear. Doubt causes us to attach ourselves to solutions, or to success formulas which seem to promise quick progress. We should not resist the slow pace of progress by looking for such means. It is wise to detach and wait in an attitude of neutrality and acceptance.

Second Line: *Eating and drinking in peace and concord.* This refers to a lull in the dangers of making progress. While danger tends to make us careful to keep ourself correct, release from danger makes us forget to be careful. Receiving this line implies that we should be alert to keep our inner attitude correct. In thinking of others we should avoid wishing, wanting, worrying, or wondering—thoughts which give rise to doubt and despair, and which disturb our serenity. The *I Ching* regards our entertaining such thoughts as "bad nourishment."

Sharing our good luck with others means not to forget our duty to rescue them after we have attained a measure of security for ourselves. During times of peace we are tempted to give up on those who are troublesome.

Third Line:...*draws near the plateau.* This line warns against plunging too rashly into a struggle. On finding ourselves in an unsuitable situation we tend to judge it as hostile; then we feel pressured to do something about it. We should not interfere, but should allow matters to take their course. If we keep still within (disengage) and let time develop things, the way out will show itself. Every "bad" happening isn't necessarily bad. Each thing that happens to us during our development is necessary to reveal our defective attitudes so that they may be corrected. Both time and Fate are friends. We need not become anxious when things go around a difficult turn. It is only when we resist, or strive against the flow, that we come to harm.

Fourth Line:...*a flat branch.* The flat branch symbolizes yielding to what is happening rather than resisting Fate. The goose rests on what is available, even though it is difficult and unsuitable. Through nonresistance we will gradually find our way past the difficulty. Danger comes when we feel impatient, ambitious, desirous, or fearful, or when we sense an injustice, or look at the difficulties and despair.

Fifth Line:...*draws near the summit.* Periods of isolation are unavoidable in the process of self-development. People misunderstand our failure to act or react and we are not able to explain ourselves. We must wait through these times with patience and perseverance.

This line is also a statement that although for now we are misunderstood and there is little apparent progress, continuing to follow the path of the good and the true will lead to a great success.

Sixth Line: *The wild goose...draws near the cloud heights.* When we adhere to the strict formation required by duty, we energize the power of the Creative to correct the situation. When we stick to our path in spite of adversity, and remain sincere in attitude, we reach the cloud heights.

This line also means that on seeing people who wronged us in the past, we should keep strict discipline to maintain our inner independence. We neither dwell on what has happened, nor erect defenses; we maintain caution and reserve. In this way we avoid dangerous presumptions and remain free to respond to any real changes which have occurred.

54.

Kuei Mei / The Marrying Maiden

$$\frac{\text{Chên}}{\text{Tui}} \quad \begin{array}{c} \text{☳} \\ \text{☱} \end{array}$$

(Wanting empowers evil.)

The image of the "marrying maiden"—a woman who marries on the basis of desire—symbolizes one who, either through choice or circumstance, finds himself in a position of little influence. The persons with whom he must deal pay him too little regard and seem not to notice or care about him. There seems to be no adequate way to deal with the situation; he is tempted to give up.

Each time we face a problem of this sort three choices appear: allowing things to work out, forcing advance, or abandoning the problem altogether.

If we allow matters to work out, we learn to influence through the power of inner truth. We further strengthen our personality by maintaining our inner independence and self-esteem while under the pressures of adversity.

If we force matters we abandon the way of the Sage and compromise our self-esteem. Our victory is both hollow and temporary, for we achieve only conformity rather than the change of heart and willing adherence we really seek.

While it is not always wrong to abandon a problem, allowing the I Ching to guide us through it gives us an opportunity to gain rich new insights into human relationships, and into the way of the Sage.

The counsel given by this hexagram is contained chiefly in the lines which point out the problems that come from wanting.

Wanting causes us to lose our inner independence. Others immediately understand this on the inner level, and tend to exploit it much as one holds candy before a child to get it to behave as desired. If, however, we maintain our inner independence, we influence others without any loss of self, for people also intuitively recognize and respect those who have inner independence (i.e., firm inner principles, and no need for their recognition).

The first seeds of wanting arise when we doubt that we have any influence on the situation, or when we begin to fear that things, in themselves, will not work out correctly. We begin to strive to be understood, or to force events to proceed straight toward the goal.

Desire also operates when we want to be seen in a certain way, or to be understood. We are so intent on having an influence that we overlook whether the one we want to influence is correct in relating to us. Ambition thus causes us to lose not only our integrity, but our powers of observation.

Indeed, many of the social and work situations of our time are designed to unbalance us. A subtle king-of-the-heap game goes on causing others who are envious of our inner independence to challenge us. They may find some way to force us to fulfill an unreasonable demand, hoping to make us angry, and thereby question our values. Once doubt takes hold we will seek ways to improve the situation, and thus enter the king-of-the-heap game. The first device of control is to make us doubt ourself. If we begin to play "their game," either by attempting to combat the situation, or by accepting their way of manipulating, the evil is only multiplied. This need not happen if we learn to relate correctly to situations which threaten to unbalance us with desires, or which otherwise make us doubt ourself. The correct response is to remain neutral and persevering.

In addition to betraying our inner dignity, wanting leads to unreasonable assessments of what can be accomplished, so that we expose ourselves to failure. For example, wanting may lead us to fanciful risks in buying stocks, in playing the lottery, or in getting ahead.

Wanting too much from others always leads to unreasonable expectations, causing them to rebel. These failures arouse our pride, further complicating matters. Even being ambitious about self-development leads to disappointment. It is as if the ego, seeing that we are determined to correct ourself, joins the effort. Characteristically, it believes that an "all-out" effort (envisioning itself as a white knight in shining armor) will win the day; with each self-sacrifice it watches to see if gains are made. Its participation is always conditional, hesitant, and glory-seeking. Nothing of enduring value can be achieved by our ego.

Undertakings bring misfortune. Nothing that would further. The marriage discussed in the *Marrying Maiden* is that of the concubine. In *Influence* (Hex. 31), affection is aroused when we sense another's kindness, sincerity, and humility. In *The Family* (Hex. 37), chaste conduct is specified as the father's role, while the mother's is to nourish the family correctly. In *Duration* (IIcx 32), the goal is to create an adequate basis for relationships so that they will endure; this is possible when people are steadfast in their way of life, and in their individual loyalty to the truth. In *Development* (Hex. 53), marriage finds its full expression through continuous organic growth—the slow maturing and endurance of a single relationship as it passes through challenge and change.

The marriage of the concubine, while it is based on affection, is problematical because of desire. As a situation it implies (by drawing attention to the negative dynamics created by wanting) that we should allow relationships to develop to sufficient maturity before we commit ourselves to them, for if they are to endure and be harmonious, they must be founded on correct and enduring values. To proceed without having established the correct foundation is to put ourself in the position of a concubine. We "proceed" when we open ourself in confidence, give ourself freely, commit our loyalty and trust to another, or merely want to do so.

The above principles are demonstrated in the lines: In the first line the maiden becomes a concubine because she has not waited through the correct steps; she has rushed into the relationship. Seeking happiness as a thing in itself, without regard to the fundamentals which create it, she gives herself lightly and easily. As a consequence, she must accept having only the influence on her husband that kindliness secures. The third line pictures a woman who wants the joys of marriage so much that she accepts the position of concubine, and thus compromises her self-esteem. In the fourth line she is willing to wait past the customary time to obtain a proper marriage. Because she resists being controlled by her desires and holds to what is correct, she finds happiness, though belatedly.

If we draw others to us for the right reasons we will have no need to suffer. Only when we are strict in maintaining our values and inner independence will others take the care to relate to us correctly. In assessing our relationships with others it is essential to ask, "Are they open and sensitive to us, or guarded and closed?" We should also ask whether we are likewise open-minded, whether we imprison them in doubt, or retain hurdles they must surmount to assuage our pride.

This hexagram indicates the correct procedure, whether we are looking for a job, or a mate, beginning a business relationship, or buying or selling something. The person who controls his desires, and puts the fundamental considerations of just and correct conduct above all else, will not end in being a slave to anyone or anything. His relationships will be free of the troubles and annoyances that plague easy relationships.

The hexagram also indicates the correct behavior to follow once we find ourselves in a secondary position. The image presented is that of being a friend to a powerful person. Although we have no real power, we are able to have an influence through tact and kindliness. Above all, we should chivalrously endure those who do not follow our values.

First Line: *The marrying maiden as a concubine.* We are in a position of limited influence, and lack any direct power to change the unfavorable situation. We are hampered (lame) when we are emotionally affected through not being able to deal with the difficulties of a situation. Even though we have little influence, we must not compete with whoever or whatever has more influence, but accept the fact that kindliness is the only constructive way of relating at the moment.

We must not, as second wives, compete with or supplant the first wife. If, because of wounded pride, we structure how they must change, we put a negative pressure on the situation, whereas if we require only what is essential and correct, and if we let go and trust the Unknown, help will come.

The situation is like being tied to someone who has an addiction. We must not attempt to deal with the addiction directly, or compete with it for influence, but concentrate on keeping our attitude correct.

Second Line: *One-eyed man is able to see.* Although there is nothing on the surface which tells us of greatness, and although there is no quality of trustworthiness on which we can rely, if with our inner eye we can faithfully hold to the image of what another person can be, and to his potential to rescue those qualities within himself which would make him reliable and faithful, then we will have a creative effect. This is what it means to be "one-eyed, yet able to see."

The "great man" may be an image of him when he's humble. We cling to this image by remembering that he has it within himself to be humble, even though all that is externally visible is to the contrary. Beyond clinging to this we abandon the inferiors which control him, and persevere in loneliness.

The *I Ching* mentions love only in *The Family* (see Hex. 37) in relation to the father who "does nothing to make himself feared...love governs their intercourse." Love, thus defined, means faithfully clinging to what is right, though in this case it be at the cost of being lonely and misunderstood. Our sacrifice of self-interest and self-importance supports the great man in others.

Being faithful also refers to clinging to the inner truth of the matter, regardless of the outward appearances of things.

Third Line: *The marrying maiden as a slave.* If we follow desire or comfort, wanting something that is not yet worth having, accepting unity at the expense of principle, who can we blame for having lost our self-esteem? We cannot short-cut the true path to take happiness before the time is right. Fate endows him who waits and wrestles with him who takes.

The question is that of being enslaved to our own ego (self-image), with its demands to be recognized, or seen in a certain way, and its insistence on occupying the central place of influence. So long as we continue wishing to return to "the way things were," to the luxury of old, self-indulgent relationships in which, through unstated contracts, we flatter someone else's ego in exchange for their flattering ours, the ego continues to rule, and we remain blind to the disastrous loss of self-esteem thus incurred.

If we find that in any such manner we have compromised ourself, we should accept the mistake and go on. We compound the difficulty if we give way to pride and humiliation by adopting a hard or vindictive attitude. Rescuing ourself does not mean that we cast others into oblivion because we deem them hopeless.

Fourth Line: *The marrying maiden draws out the allotted time.* By waiting past what would seem to be a reasonable time for difficult situations to clear up, we avoid throwing ourself away and thus retain inner peace and self-respect. One day the situation will clear up. Meanwhile, we should avoid wanting what is not ready, just as we would not want to eat green apples. When we do find ourselves engaged in wanting, we should ask why we want something that is not worth having. We need to recognize the spoiled baby within who would jeopardize self-esteem to obtain a cheap facsimile of joy, the hidden price of which is suffering.

Fifth Line: *The embroidered garments...were not as gorgeous as those of the servingmaid.* Although the princess marries beneath her station she accepts the situation with grace. Each of us is on the same spiritual path, some ahead, some behind. In occupying a position of advantage we should be free of vanity and arrogance. (We should not attempt to say things as "brilliantly" as the servingmaid.) In occupying a secondary position we should be free of envy. If we are misunderstood, we should not strive to let people know our inner thoughts; we should simply adapt to the unfavorable situation with grace. If the way ahead is still unclear, we should search our heart and mind for elements of vanity, self-importance, pride, condescension, or obstinacy that may yet block the path, or influence the way we react to the situation.

Another meaning of this line is that we do not choose our ultimate mates, or the time in which estrangements will end; nor are we able to consciously choose the winning combinations, or solve our fundamental problems; the Sage, here referred to as the Emperor, does. He takes the initiative and we only need to wait and not throw ourself away; the time will mature all the faster if we are patient.

Sixth Line: *Nothing that acts to further.* Outwardly we do the right things, but inwardly we still desire to indulge comfort, vindictiveness, or anger at having to wait the allotted time. We resist the way the Cosmos works.

We cannot return to the old ways of self-indulgence, nor even long nostalgically for the past. Success will begin when we are ready to leave behind, once and for all, desire as the basis for relationships. This is the meaning of the true sacrifice required by this line.

Regardless of the extent to which we correct our childish self, if we still look forward to a goal in which we return to "lost comforts," it is as if we observe all the forms of correctness but do not correct the heart of the matter. We need to relinquish the childish heart, with its desires.

Rescue means that whether we gain or lose what our inner child wants, we manage to cling to another's potential to be humble and high-minded. This is what the Sage does for us. It is true love which gives space, which waits patiently, which perseveres without regard to self and reward, and which has nothing to do with surface manifestations, displays of affection, statements of love, or possession. Selfless love invisibly sustains another and pulls him toward the good within himself. It is a love whose only reward is privately to oneself; in maintaining it, we are at peace.

54. The Marrying Maiden

A real sacrifice occurs when, at the heights of difficulties, we remain resolute and determined to go on with the work of purifying ourselves. Without this determination and humility "nothing acts to further."

55.

Fêng / Abundance (Fullness)

$$\frac{\text{Chên}}{\text{Li}} \quad \begin{array}{c} \equiv\equiv \\ \equiv\equiv \end{array}$$

(There is an eclipse. Clinging to the power of truth will
cause it to pass.)

Thunder and lightning symbolize a brief period in which we are able
to have an influence on others. When this influence wanes we must
withdraw without delay and no longer focus interest on the situation.

Times of abundance refers to times when people are receptive to
us. It is said that the Sage is never sad because he knows that to hold
to the power of the truth is to overcome all darkening trends. He also
knows that only slow progress endures, therefore he is able to control
his ambition. Because he knows that all learning must be committed
to experience, he is able to let go when the moment of influence
wanes, giving others the space they need to find themselves. The
Sage trusts the power of truth to prove itself. Being free of doubt, he
is also "free of sorrow and care," thus, he continuously produces
times of abundance.

The power of truth is engaged by an accepting, modest, and
independent attitude. We can safely hold to this attitude, for it is
capable of producing the beneficial changes we seek.

The individual lines of the hexagram illustrate the principles of
abundance, and emphasize the momentary and cyclical nature of
close and open communications between people (including our relationship with the Sage). In the first line, a short period of friendly
receptivity and freedom from distrust exists—a time of abundance.
The second line notes that this receptivity has been undermined by
distrust so that everything we say is regarded with suspicion; the
light power is eclipsed. The third line indicates that the eclipse has
become total, but that we can counter it by holding inwardly to the
power of truth. The fourth line indicates that the eclipse is ending;
Receptivity reawakens because we have related properly, but we
should remain on guard against egotistical enthusiasm and arrogant
self-confidence. Such attitudes would return all to darkness. The

fifth line indicates that by retaining an open mind, we receive the help we need to rectify the situation. Once again we develop an influence for the good. The top line warns that if we use our renewed influence to gain personal power and recognition, the situation will return to stagnation and we will lose what we have gained.

First Line: *When a man meets his destined ruler, they can be together ten days.* "Ten days" symbolizes a complete cycle of influence, although the actual time period may be for as little as fifteen minutes. During the time of influence others are receptive to us and we are in tune with the inner truth of the situation. We are able to proceed so long as we retain a hesitating caution and maintain connection with our inner voice. If the other person's receptivity wanes, we disengage. We neither try to prolong the moment, nor exceed the opening they have granted. If we presume, or self-confidently press beyond these limits, not only will we invalidate the good already accomplished, but we will also throw ourself away and suffer a loss of self-esteem. It is important to preserve one's personality.

It is important to recognize the cyclical and momentary nature of influence. People grant us only limited and conditional openings. Beyond the time they have allotted—a time we can only know if we keep assiduously attuned to their moods—our influence goes through a progressive and swift eclipse. Any reaction other than patient acceptance and withdrawal into emotional neutrality only increases the power and duration of their resistance to us. If, however, we persevere through such periods of darkness by holding to the power of truth, our influence will be renewed and the eclipse will quickly pass. This would not be true, of course, if we seek only to exert our personal will, or to use the power of truth for personal ends. Influence for the good arises only from a steady will to serve the good.

Receiving this line can also indicate that there is a potential opening for having an influence, but that we should take care to keep attuned to the openings and the closings.

Second Line:...*the polestars can be seen at noon.* This line often refers to times when our influence for the good is blocked for one reason or another. Whatever the reason, the remedy is to cling to the power of truth. Such an attitude engages the help of the Creative to disperse the inferior power.

This line can also refer to times when our attitude creates an eclipse which isolates us from the helpful influence of the Sage. For example, we may distrust the Sage's counsel, or suspect that Fate is hostile or that the way of the Cosmos is evil. In the face of such thoughts the Sage retreats until we undergo a change of heart.

Third Line: *He breaks his right arm. No blame.* Influence is always a momentary thing, whether we are being influenced by the Sage, or whether we are having an influence on others. Misunderstandings are bound to occur in which pride is aroused, along with the ego defense system which accompanies it. The eclipse swiftly becomes total so that it is as if the one seeking to help has a broken right arm. During such times it is not our fault if we are unable to help others, nor is it the Sage's fault if he cannot help us when we are resistant. During such times we must let go and wait. This attitude will cause the eclipse to pass.

Fourth Line: *He meets his ruler who is of like kind.* Because we relate to the problem correctly, resistance and obstruction begin to give way. When tension gives way, however, our childish self emerges to search for rewards, or to luxuriate in the improved situation, or to indulge in self-assertion. This self can take over if we drop our careful, hesitating caution and reserve. It is important, therefore, not to stop and revel in the good news, but to carry on as before. Just as bad events test our steadiness and inner independence, so do good events.

Fifth Line: *Lines are coming.* At the critical juncture the right thing to say or do comes of itself. As it is said in *Grace* (Hex. 22), "a white horse comes as if on wings." When we are harmonious within, what we say harmonizes with the Creative, and we win the assent of others.

Sixth Line: *His house is in a state of abundance.* If after being helped we selfishly seek only to luxuriate in the situation, or to dominate, then we lose all the benefits of having acted correctly. To make progress we must remain selfless.

What kind of inner house do we grant those we seek to rescue? Is it cramped or roomy? Have we allowed them enough space, or do we think they are not fit to live in a roomy, beautiful house? How do they fit into our lives? Can we include them with our friends and family? If not, how much does our vanity have to do with the problem? If we require them to conform to a list of capricious demands, or to jump over a number of prideful hurdles before we will grant our approval, our "house is in a state of abundance." So long as vanity plays even a minor role in our effort, we will be unable to rescue others. We must disallow all self-flattering considerations, and require of others only what is universally just, essential, and correct.

We also seek to be master when we stubbornly refuse to relinquish pride and alienation; by abandoning as hopeless those we are meant to rescue, we "execute" them. By heeding the call of our Inferior Man to pursue self-interest, we cast aside our Cosmic responsibility and depart from our path.

56.

Lü / The Wanderer

$$\frac{\text{Li}}{\text{Kên}} \quad \begin{array}{c} \rule{1em}{0.5pt}\ \rule{1em}{0.5pt} \\ \rule{1em}{0.5pt}\ \rule{1em}{0.5pt} \\ \rule{1em}{0.5pt}\ \rule{1em}{0.5pt} \end{array}$$

(We are uneasy about trusting the Unknown.)

In the inner universe we are ever wanderers and strangers. Although we can observe and catalog the causes of events in the outer world, that which governs their coming and going—the great Tao—is unknowable. Even though we have worked hard to serve the good, we cannot assume that our position is secure, or that we can attain an independence of the Higher Power. We never attain rights and privileges; therefore, we should take the greatest care to remain modest and unassuming.

We receive this hexagram when we look to anything but the Higher Power for our security. If we look to the Sage for help and guidance, the right way will show itself and we will receive all the help and support we need. If we look to others to support us, we might or might not receive what we need, for the Sage steps back and no longer participates in our fate. The inner independence of the spiritually developed person is not, as it might appear, the result of his graduation into self-sufficiency, but the result of a confirmed and steady awareness of his dependence on the Higher Power to show the way through events.

Everything we do in the outer world is subject to the absolute standard of equality and justice of the inner world, where favoritism and factionalism do not exist. When we take part in such practices we lose our home and friends in the inner world, and find ourselves subject to Cosmic punishment. This punishment is referred to in the third and sixth lines as "the inn burns down" and the "bird's nest burns up." Everything we do, every thought we think, every false comfort which we indulge, every presumption we make is observed, is heard, and is felt in the inner world. Even though a faulty attitude may escape notice in the outer world, it does not escape notice in the inner world. We cannot escape the burden we create through

255

carelessly selfish actions. A great part of the work of self-develop-ment is to remove this burden, to regain our lost self-esteem, and to re-establish our Cosmic credibility. Wanderers and strangers, we are required to prove ourselves before this credibility is returned.

Every time we come into or depart from harmony with universal justice and truth in our inmost thoughts, we create our fate; we either engage the help of the Creative, or shut ourselves off from it. When we are in harmony, the Creative promotes and aids us. When we are out of harmony, we are out of relationship. What happens to us then depends on chance.

The mode of action of the Creative is to spring from justice and universal truth. The light is always there; we need only be open to see it, and to receive its benefits. When we are not open we are in the dark, abandoned to our own devices, and subject to the vagaries of chance. If we incur a bad fate, it is not so much that the Cosmos punishes us; it is rather that we lose its protection through playing with the edge, and through approaching life too arrogantly. Because of the impersonal quality of justice, Lao Tzu said, "The Sage regards all men as straw-dogs." This means that the Sage does not care about our petty attachment to who we are, or from whence we come; he is interested only in what is great and good.

When a person begins to serve the good and the true, he finds himself accompanied by the spiritually nourishing force; wherever he is, he is not alone. The force is felt as a presence and friend, filling the empty spaces and lighting the inner path. If we then take this presence for granted, we lose it. We also lose it when we turn over to others our responsibility to direct our lives, and our affairs. We lose the friendly presence when we begin to use our inner independ-ence to be hard on others, and when we stop to enjoy the moment at the expense of correctness. After making these mistakes we gradu-ally become aware that the light is gone and we are alone. Our self-esteem and inner independence, which depend on our relationship with the Higher Power, dwindle. We are never so secure in our inner home that we can safely forget this dependence.

The hexagram also discusses Cosmic punishments and imprison-ments. Having incurred an evil fate, or a bad momentary situation, we may not easily regain the protection and help of the Sage. Isolation from the Higher Power is its way of punishing us. But, as the hexagram tells us, prisons are meant only to be temporary abodes, not "dwelling places." A hostile fate will last only until we undertake the work of self-correction. The Sage uses adversity fruitfully to teach. While working our way out of adversity, we may find excessive the set of limits under which we labor. This, of course, is a perception of our ego, which sees all punishment as excessive, and finds all limitation intolerable. The degree of punishment (or length of time the adversity lasts) is the amount needed to overcome the power of resistance. Fate is like the little boy who wrestles the other little boy down and then says, "Do you give up?" and then again, while twisting his arm a little harder, "Do you really give up?" Our ego must unequivocably give up.

Not all isolation from the Higher Power is punishment; sometimes isolation serves as a test of our virtue, or as a means of encouraging self-reliance in following our path. When we receive this hexagram, however, punishment is the usual meaning.

The superior man is clear-minded and cautious in imposing penalties, and protracts no lawsuits. These words have to do with punishing others, and warn against punishing them excessively, thereby creating "lawsuits." It also warns against putting people into permanent imprisonment by deciding that they are hopeless.

A lawsuit is an ongoing inner conflict between people (families, nations, etc.). One sues and the other counter-sues, one ambushes and the other seeks to pay him back; one accuses or insults and the other replies with an even greater accusation or insult. Such lawsuits are difficult to end; once distrust becomes established, it is hard to eradicate. One party is always suspicious that the other might start a new hostile action. Each secretly waits for the old issues ("spoiled game," as it is called in *Biting Through*, (Hex. 21)) to be brought up. To be "clear-minded" either means to recognize that a lawsuit exists, or that we should avoid causing or continuing them.

We create lawsuits when our ego seeks to punish other people's egos, and when we feel vindictive pleasure at seeing someone get his comeuppance; lawsuits occur when we give others up as hopeless, or dismiss them as worthless because of class, race, or other facetious considerations. If we would avoid feuds, with their endless reprisals and hatred, we should take care not to lose our modesty before the Higher Power which created everything.

Lawsuits of a lesser nature occur when we mentally fix people as "problems." Even though they heavily tax our patience and good will, we increase their opposition if we mentally fix them in a negative way. To end such lawsuits, we should let go of mental fixes and reopen our minds. Then, the opposition will gradually decrease.

First Line: *The wanderer busies himself with trivial things.* We must not disgrace ourself by indulging in gossip, or thinking gossipy thoughts about people.

"Trivial" refers to issues on which we can have little (if any) impact. Our job is always directly before us in the way we relate to the people around us.

Trivial also refers to concerning ourselves with nonessentials, such as physical considerations—whether or not a person is physically attractive, or whether he has correct manners, or shows off well in comparison to others. Such trivialities are often excuses made by our ego (as vanity) for indulging in feelings of alienation.

Busying ourself with trivial things can also refer to our having lightly turned over our real responsibilities to others in order to free ourselves for less important matters.

Second Line: *He wins the steadfastness of a young servant.* If we do not concentrate on a person's evil side, we can win the allegiance of his good side. Through our inner thoughts we are able, so to speak, to travel through the domain of people's spirits. We have the ability, if we will, to connect with what is good in them, and thereby to help liberate them from their ego's domination, and from their fears.

This line also means that if we don't concentrate on reaping some personal reward from each stage of progress, we will not arouse the envy and distrust which threaten our work. In being strict, both with ourselves and with others, we win their adherence to what is good. By remaining conscientious we win help from the inner world to complete our work.

Third Line: *The wanderer's inn burns down.* Truculence, as in a menacing or bullying attitude, to intimidate other people's inferiors, does not succeed. Neither does an aloof or arrogant attitude. If we disdain our inner world obligation by giving up on the situation, we act in a high-handed manner towards the Sage, and thus lose his help and protection. Our inner world "resting place" refers to times when we feel free and independent. This resting place "burns down" if we self-confidently abandon our task to rescue those for whom we are responsible. A half-hearted, or almost negative acceptance of this task indicates that our ego has intruded to collapse our will. We may overcome this assault by the evil power if we realize that being half-hearted comes from misunderstanding the wonderful way things work when we allow them to.

This line also refers to times when we seek answers from the Sage to questions of inner conflict. Since these questions spring from an emotional drive to be released from doubt, rather than from a quest for truth, no rational answer will satisfy them. To make progress, we must cease the inner conflict which causes us to distrust the Creative. We must cease asking this kind of question, let go, and return to the path of humility and acceptance.

Fourth Line: *My heart is not glad.* Even though we conceal our desires, their pressures still operate and we must defend ourself against their bad effects.

Desire encroaches when we are unsure that through "following" (see *Following*, Hex. 17) we will attain our goal. When we distrust the direction of events we tend to interfere in the work, or we adopt a careless attitude, as if what we say or do carelessly will not matter. The Sage cannot help under such conditions. Since we are strangers in a strange land we should pay careful attention to the contents of our inner attitude.

Fifth Line: *He shoots a pheasant.* A "pheasant" is an egotism, a delicious pleasantry to which we are particularly attached, such as a glamorous self-image. On encountering every new problem we must free ourself of pretenses—"shoot down" our self-image to acquire humility, and give up decadent habits or ideas. We especially need to discard any presumption of having rights and privileges, or any ideas which cause us to lose our reticence and humility. All such deviations bring progress to a halt.

Sixth Line: *The bird's nest burns up.* The wanderer symbolizes making our way through the hidden world; the "nest" refers to the degree of protection we have acquired through following the good, and through being faithful to our task to rescue those to whom we are bound by inner ties. Should we become careless by disdaining this obligation, or give way to encroaching desires, we would lose this protection. If we sacrifice our inner sense of truth to desire, or to a careless, luxurious attitude, we will lose both the influence we have acquired, and the progress we have gained through our hard work. Thus, our "nest" (inner world home) "burns up."

57.

Sun / The Gentle
(The Penetrating, Wind)

$$\frac{\text{Sun}}{\text{Sun}} \quad \equiv\!\equiv$$

(Only consistently firm, yet gentle, inner thoughts penetrate
to others with good effect.)

The Gentle, Penetrating refers to the way the Sage's thought penetrates to us, and to the way our thoughts penetrate to others. It describes an influence on others which is unconscious and automatic.
This influence occurs through maintaining a ceaselessly correct
inner attitude in which we are balanced, detached, innocent, and
independent through all the changing events.

Sun, the trigram of the second daughter, represents wind which
penetrates cracks in buildings, and wood as roots which penetrate
soil. Through their ceaseless but gentle energy the wind and roots
penetrate the most obdurate objects. Just as roots penetrate the
cracks of boulders and break them apart, the influence of the Sage
penetrates our subconscious until one day, in a flash of insight, we
understand with amazing clarity. This is the step-by-step enlightenment by which spiritual mysteries are penetrated as we progress
along our path.

Receiving this hexagram indicates (1) that the truth we perceive
has been penetrating to us over a long period of time, and (2) that our
dependence on the truth must be consistently maintained if it is to
penetrate to others with dynamic effect. Striving to improve the
situation through argument or persuasion may produce some
momentary gain, but such efforts violate others' spiritual space.
Enduring results, which are achieved through penetration and enlightenment, depend on our consistency of character. When we
waver in following our path, we produce hesitation and doubt in
those who follow us with their inner eye.

Receiving this hexagram often means that elements in our attitude
prevent good influences from penetrating to others. To have the
correct influence we need to penetrate (understand) the root of the

problem. Through sincere introspection, and through asking for help, the Sage's message penetrates through, and we understand.

Because this hexagram is concerned with self-correction, we often receive it together with *Work on What Has Been Spoiled* (Hex. 18). The self-correction most often needed is to cease striving to influence. Because striving is based on inner doubt, it negates any influence we might have. Our doubt further inhibits others' ability to find their way, and prevents the Higher Power from intervening in the situation. To empower truth and engage the Creative force, we need to keep firm in what we perceive as correct, and turn the matter over to the Cosmos. Then we disengage from it, and allow to happen what will happen.

In penetrating to the root of the problem we need to ask why we contrive, or defend ourselves. Why do we revert to old habits of worrying and trying to make things happen? In examining the situation we often find that someone or something has threatened our inner independence. In perceiving our vulnerability they (subconsciously) engage us in a king-of-the-heap game. When we realize that we have been thus engaged, we are able to return to an inner independence and detachment which resolves the matter.

Sometimes, on perceiving how events are marching toward an appropriate conclusion, we develop an enthusiasm to hurry things along. We do this because of desire and fear, which create a pressure to intervene. We should keep desire and fear, and the ambition they generate, at bay. We should remain disengaged, content to observe events without hurrying or resisting them, keeping in mind that once we turn the matter over to the Sage, he has means which are beyond our understanding.

We should also cease reacting to shock. We need to bend like the bamboo, without becoming bent or broken through rigid resistance to the situation. Through nonresistance the wind passes and we return to the upright. We need to ask why we keep reacting after the shock has passed. Do we like clinging to negative possibilities? Do we find solace in distrusting the Cosmos? Are we tired of persevering and being tested, or impatient to enjoy the rewards of our discipline? Who is the one demanding the reward? Who seeks the comfort imagined at the end of the journey? Who hates our helpless dependence on the Unknown? The root of impatience may be the fear that those we seek to influence will not find their way to the truth. We do not want to give them the time or space they need because that means we must wait. Our ego may also insinuate that, in the end, our efforts will come to nothing and we will be cheated of happiness, because history, or literature, or experience has proven time and again that "the course of true love never did run smooth," or "life is meant to be nothing but suffering," or is a paradox, or only a dream and doesn't exist at all, or some other idea that supports our negative mood. We sometimes listen to these ideas in a fit of pique and selfishness, forgetting the myriad miracles we have experienced regarding the power of truth. Just as a modest, humble acceptance of being helpless leads to the inner independence which correctly influences others, a negative resistance to Fate, in which we close our minds regarding others, has a destructive effect on our situation. We need to remember that when we insist on what is correct during times of challenge, and wait for others to go through the learning experience, giving them the space they need to find themselves, the boulders of entrenched evil and hardness will be broken by the penetrating power of truth. We also need to reassure our anxious inferiors that in the end everything will work out better than we could have expected.

First Line: *The perseverance of the warrior furthers.* This means we must be resolute against the encroaching inferior element. Usually this element is mistrust. Mistrust causes us to erect defensive barriers against what others might or might not do. We should withdraw from any frontal assault aimed at resolving our problems, or any defense of self. When others approach aggressively we should keep disengaged, retreating from any impulse to join in conflict.

Second Line: *Penetration under the bed.* This means we should search our heart and mind for hidden enemies such as self-pity, pride, a structured view of what "should" happen, or any inner complaint that might be causing resistance in others. The presence of hard, arrogant, soft, self-indulgent, self-pitying or complaining feelings obstructs progress and endangers perseverance. "Priests" and "magicians" refer to the almost magical help that comes when we sincerely seek to find and free ourself from these elements. Sometimes we need only ask the Sage for help.

Third Line: *Repeated penetration. Humiliation.* On discovering the harmful element we are counseled to be resolute against it. The

262

harmful element may be an inner conflict. For example, we may have settled into an involved inner quarrel about why things work the way they do, why we are put through difficulties, whether life is real, or a bad joke perpetrated by a hostile Cosmos. Through inner conflict we relapse into negativism. We allow our ego to take over through its flattery that the only reality is ourself, and therefore it is up to us to make everything happen. In wrestling with events, we attempt to overturn them; in the end, however, we only throw ourself away.

The moment we consciously touch on the inner problem, we may be unwilling to recognize it as meaningful because it seems to be so minute a defect. However, we must not underestimate its importance since it keeps us unbalanced and in a state of conflict, and it harms our good work.

Fourth Line: *During the hunt three kinds of game are caught.* In finding and being resolute against evil in ourself we also solve all the problems facing us at the moment. It is part of the economy by which the Sage teaches to show us how one fear can produce seemingly unrelated problems, here described as three kinds of game.

Fifth Line: *No beginning, but an end.* Before the new can begin, the old must come to an end. If relationships are to be mended, they must first be freed of the destructive and decadent elements to which we cling. Having perceived these elements, we can now let them go, but we must remain on guard against their return. Such a return is probable simply because the attitudes are well-established. We must keep alert to their resurgence until we are truly rid of them. A new beginning occurs when we have ended a particular bad habit of mind.

Sixth Line: *Penetration under the bed.* Sometimes a diligent search for the hidden enemy reveals nothing specific. In receiving this line we should let go of the search, for in sincerely seeking, our attitude has been corrected of the defect of careless over-confidence.

We should be aware that careless self-confidence is not the same thing as neutral inner independence. Self-confidence returns us to old habits of mind, as when we dismissed the help of the Sage as nothing, and intervened in matters as if the effect of time and the power of good did not exist. To be self-confident is to shift trust in the Unknown (in the form of a willing suspension of disbelief) back to a belief in the power of the ego self-image in the guise of being our self. For this reason we need to return to humility, realizing that "under the bed" refers to the place we hide old habits of mind.

58.

Tui / The Joyous

$$\frac{\text{Tui}}{\text{Tui}} \quad \overline{\underline{\overline{}}}\ \overline{\underline{\overline{}}}$$

(Through wanting, we waver.)

This hexagram refers to the difference between true freedom in detachment, and apparent freedom in the bravado of careless indifference, self-importance, and arrogant self-confidence.

The image of the placid, unruffled surface of the lake symbolizes true joy as serenity which arises from the sublime source. Even the slightest wrinkle of the brow, like the ripple on the lake, indicates the presence of an emotion which, if it is allowed to continue, will cause the turmoil in which true joy disappears.

The crucial moment which leads away from serenity and inner independence is the moment of wavering—when we begin to listen to seductive fantasies put forward by our ego. These seductive images cause us to want, wonder, or worry, and thus lose the leadership of our superior self.

The first moment of wavering is often only a vague, discontented mood. Next, we hear our whining inferiors saying such things as, "Nothing works!" Wavering is already progressing unchecked towards the next stage of discontent in which the leadership of the ego is re-established. Under its leadership we are no longer sensitive to our inner voice. Next, we start to be indifferent to our path as we proceed to an active disbelief. Disbelief, in turn, conjures up alternate courses of action so that we begin to pursue pleasure, comfort, and self-aggrandizement. Doing this creates self-conflict, then doubt, which we feel as a gnawing hole in the chest or abdomen.

The chief sign of one who feels hopeless is his striving to force happiness or success. Because this leads only to disappointment, he attempts by conniving to steal it; this failing, he ceases to care and pursues pleasure in a contrived indifference. Contrived indifference becomes vengeful indifference if or when he seeks to punish those he blames for his disappointment.

Neither true joy nor true pleasure can be found by pursuing joy, pleasure, or success as things in themselves. The hexagram counsels us to pay attention to times when we become seduced by the notion that the pursuit of these things will lead to happiness. It also counsels us not to adopt contrived attitudes simply because they worked before. All contrived approaches or attitudes are based on small but powerful doubts put forward by our ego—doubts which enable it to retain command. The *I Ching* always counsels us to keep open, neutral, and unstructured in attitude.

The basis for true joy is inner independence—a stability created through accepting life as it is, and through accepting each new moment without inner resistance. Acceptance is achieved through imposing discipline on our whining inferiors, and through encouraging them to be patient. We need to remain unstructured, willing to be led. If we entertain doubt, argue with Fate, or think of ways to evade this discipline, we lose our inner equilibrium and direction by the true self. If we allow our ego to long for the soft and comfortable path, it will then begin to seek ways to short-cut the necessary steps that lead to our goals. This takeover by the ego creates self-conflict— the quietness of the shining lake is disturbed. In all these activities the ego secretly insinuates doubts into our inner ear. By keeping aware that it is behind these activities, we deprive it of its power. When we see that we are wavering or wanting, we should return to acceptance. In freeing ourself from wanting we return to harmony with the Cosmos.

Two people attain true joy only when both are sincere in trying to keep correct within themselves. Their independent searches for the truth within themselves serve as inexhaustible wellsprings, supporting each other and nourishing everyone around them.

First Line: *Contented joyousness.* Contented joyousness means arriving at inner harmony through being free of desire. Even though everything around us now seems difficult, stubborn, and decadent, if we empty our heart of desire, and sacrifice wanting, we will attain the emptiness which leads to the insights needed to proceed correctly. No longer being jostled by the appearance of things, we are able to have a good effect on those around us.

We should also realize that it is one thing to require others to be correct with us, and another to want it. Wanting implies doubt. If we are being treated unjustly we should not relinquish our requirements that we be treated correctly, but keep detached, open-minded, and free of wanting. With this attitude we can win the assent of others to do what is right. Both time and the power of the Cosmos will come to our aid to rectify the matter.

Sometimes we receive this line at the moment that we begin to doubt the creative impact of following the true and the good. Receiving it reassures us that we do have an impact, even though it may not be apparent.

Second Line: *Sincere joyousness.* We are tempted to adopt fixed ideas of ourself, or of our situation, as a means of self-comfort, and as rationalization for giving way to the pressures of the situation. Such images may be positive, as in "I am special, I don't have to put up with people's bad behavior," or negative, as in "Life is meant to be a bad experience," or, "I need someone to help me." We lean on such images in an attempt to evade acceptance of the Unknown, dependence on the Cosmos. All self-defensive images come from the ego, or baby part of ourselves, and must be firmly resisted.

Sincere joyousness may also mean that we look for the wrong solution to our problems. For example, we may be wishing for unity between ourself and another when this would be at the expense of principle. The remedy is to refuse decisively to consider the idea further.

Another temptation is to adopt special attitudes which we think will speed things along, or which we think once helped us solve similar problems. We should remain unstructured and not lean on any special devices to make progress. Our ego is at work, suggesting these ideas.

Third Line: *Coming joyousness.* It is important not to spend time lamenting our mistakes, but to accept the situation and move on. Otherwise, we will begin wanting to see visible progress, or wanting things to be more secure, less ambiguous, and more relaxed and comfortable. Such emotions give rise to self-pity, useless recriminations, doubt, and despair. Wanting always initiates successively larger attacks of these feelings. Fear, restlessness, desire, pride, jealousy, or anger are similar strong elements which quickly take over and cause movement which is not self-governed. In this manner wanting (coming joyousness) causes us to lose our direction.

Coming joyousness also refers to times when we place importance on being recognized, as opposed to being content with whether we are recognized or not. It is important not to be pulled in by the world and its lures. We should remain free of envy, of dependence on others, of desire for position, and of the lure to be recognized and understood. It is important not to value things which are not intrinsically valuable. True joy springs from guarding the sanctity of our inner being, and from retaining our inner freedom.

Fourth Line: *Joyousness that is weighed.* We weigh whether or not to sacrifice some of our values in order to gain unity with others. For example, we consider tolerating a certain amount of indifference and unjust treatment; or, we begin to consider new involvements because we doubt that our current situation will ever be resolved; or, we are tempted to do something that might jeopardize our inner dignity because we think it will improve the situation or hasten progress.

This line states implicitly that the pursuit of pleasure inevitably brings suffering. While this mainly refers to the pursuit of physical pleasure, it also refers to indulging self-importance through a display of bravado, power, correctness, helpfulness, wit, intelligence, skill, sharpness, or independence. Self-importance (reawakened by suggestions put forward by our ego) is contrary to our inner nature and creates self-conflict. We show off when old fears of not being equal to others are reawakened by our ego; these are fears which cause us to compare ourselves with others, and to envy them. Such comparisons are always harmful.

Also, we should not allow ourselves to indulge such thoughts as, "I would be happy if only this were so."

Fifth Line: *Sincerity towards disintegrating influences....* This means we are sincere in listening to self-flattering fantasies and seductions that tempt us to pursue self-advantage. For example, we think of doing something to improve the situation, or to rush things along. Or, we listen to feelings of self-pity, hopelessness, doubt, impatience, or fear, or to thoughts about our "rights" and the demands created by such rights. We may be wanting to be recognized for one reason or another, or we may feel we have earned independence and no longer need the Sage's help.

Another seduction is to think of doing something because we imagine a tempting consequence. Seduction is always a wrong motive.

Sometimes we are sincere in listening to what we want to hear; or, we are too sincere to someone who is insensitive. We need to let such a person go on his way.

Sixth Line: *Seductive joyousness.* Because of the seeming intransigence of the situation we are tempted to "do" something. If we are irresolute, the seductive fantasies put forward by our ego will cause us to stray from our path. Some of these seductions occur as feelings of self-importance, self-pity, impatience, anger, or alienation. Others occur as feelings of negation, restlessness, or desire. If these feelings are not firmly resisted, they will destroy our will to persevere.

Of all evils, vanity in the form of self-importance is the most seductive, and therefore the most dangerous. The ego, as vanity, constantly watches to see how others see us. Even during self-development the ego intrudes when it tries to draw attention to how well we serve the good.

59.

Huan / Dispersion (Dissolution)

$$\frac{\text{Sun}}{\text{K'an}} \quad \equiv\!\equiv$$

(Dissolve all hardening feelings.)

Dispersion refers to dissolving feelings and thoughts which lead to a rigid viewpoint, such as "I'll never do this again," or "I'll never again buy that." Such thoughts lead to giving people up as hopeless and incapable of changing.

We experience such hardening thoughts when we have opened ourselves to others, only to find that they are less receptive than we anticipated. It is important to disperse or dissolve doubt, hurt feelings, or anger, to return to an unstructured, innocent, and independent attitude. Once our inner independence is restored, others will relate to us more sincerely.

As an image, dispersion describes a technique of freeing ourselves from the grip of emotions. This technique entails letting go of feelings by allowing them to drift off on the wind (*Sun*), or to be washed clean by water (*K'an*), the active, working water which is associated with effort. Through effort of will we summon the strength to let go of all negative feelings and thoughts.

Sun is also associated with gentleness—as in the gentle breezes. We disperse egotism through gentleness rather than through brusqueness. We are gentle with ourselves, in spite of our errors, and we are gentle with others who suffer from the pressures of pride, alienation, and feelings of inferiority. (The more guilty people feel, the more rigid and sensitive their pride-system becomes.) Gentle perseverance dissolves the hardness and defensive rigidity that these pressures create.

We also need to disperse feelings of hopelessness which would lead to breaking our ties to others. It is important to disperse the inferior element, whether it be doubt, fear of continuing to follow our path, anger, inner conflict such as "Why are things this way," or the temptation to lapse into indifference. This includes all emotional reactions and frustrations about the deficiencies of ourselves or

270

others.

This line also refers to rigid feelings that we must do something. When we feel pressured it means we are emotionally entangled. We need to step back, detach, and allow a new perception to break through.

On realizing that we have made such mistakes, rather than lapsing into despair or self-flagellation, we should hold firmly to what is correct and wait. With this attitude, the harm will be corrected and the tension will dissolve, leaving no after-effects.

Dispersion also refers to dispersing our attachment to points of argument, and to childish resistance to the way things work. We resist only because we misunderstand, or only partly understand. By giving up resistance we make it possible for a full understanding to emerge. Meanwhile, it helps if we take the attitude that the Sage knows how to make everything work, both the impossible and the unlikely. Once we accept this possibility, the Sage is free to bring about the "impossible" and the "unlikely." Acceptance also enables the emergence of a larger insight into the problem.

First Line: *He brings help with the strength of a horse.* This line counsels us to disperse and dissolve feelings of alienation. It also reminds us that the reason for alienation is misunderstanding. We should not overlook the possibility that we may be misunderstanding the Sage, or Fate, such as when we think Fate is hostile, or when we think people are impossible. In the process of self-development we must go through difficulties that we later realize are absolutely necessary for growth.

Second Line: *At the dissolution he hurries to that which supports him.* When other people do seemingly unforgivable things we must try to discover, in an unobstructed way, how they have come to their point of view. If our final opinion is resentment, our understanding is still inadequate. That which supports us is a *moderate and just judgment of men, linked with goodwill.* We need to remember that people cling to false ideas as crutches, thinking they are unable to proceed without them. We must be patient and tolerant with such people.

One of the great false ideas is hopelessness, a bad situation cannot work out, or human unity is impossible. Hopelessness is so foreign to our natures that we switch back to the hope that some last efforts will work; we seek to persuade others of our point of view; this failing, we fall back on a contrived indifference. When this has no effect we attempt to force a solution; this failing, we engage in pleasure-seeking and diversions. Soon we make other forceful attempts. Each time we throw ourself away more until the loss of self becomes dangerous.

Each phase of hopelessness is built one on the other. At each stage we damage our self-esteem and further increase the ego's power. To compensate we build defenses through feelings of retribution and hardened pride. The more we have humiliated ourselves, the more our wounded pride can turn to hatred and violence, either in a suppressed form against ourselves, or against those we see as having humiliated us. In such ways people barricade themselves with pacts and defensive walls, and become isolated from any meaningful relationship with each other.

We must keep in mind that the beginning of this vortex of the dark force has its roots in a negative assessment of people, the first ploy of our ego. To doubt, or to decide negatively about people, is simply against our nature. The extent to which this vortex is carried out depends on the strength and persistence of our ego.

A humble or moderate person will not regard difficult situations as impossible. Nor will he take reversals as assaults to his pride. He will be able to accept it when mistakes have been made. He does not put himself in the place of God to decide the future, but he accepts the present. He allows others to go their way without giving them up as hopeless.

In recognizing that a person has become stuck—not able to make progress in his self-development—we must not give up on him, but leave him to see things for himself. Meanwhile, we carry on with our lives.

Third Line: *He dissolves his self.* This line counsels us to relinquish the accumulated feelings that comprise our perception of our self. These feelings are mainly defensive. It is as if we always have our guard up. Or, we stand on a knoll looking down at others, presuming we alone know what is right. In defending ourselves we may have condemned as hopeless those we are meant to rescue. We need to dissolve these barriers and the negative feelings that support them, such as ill will, resentment, and alienation.

We may also need to dissolve all ideas of how we want things to happen, and allow the Sage to do the job his way. We may need to realize that others are able to obtain the help of the Sage, and that in and of themselves they are able to find the truth, without our intervention. Only when we have dissolved the constructed self are we able to 'come to meet' others halfway.

Fourth Line: *He dissolves his bond with his group.* We should not follow what our group does (what is customary, or what our friends or family think we ought to do), but what is conscientiously correct.

Holding to "our group" also refers to times when we sacrifice the long term good to obtain short-term gains.

Sometimes "group" refers to an abstract group of white knights in shining armour with which we identify ourselves. Our "good" group invariably opposes the "bad" group. We should avoid casting people into "them" as opposed to "us," for such groups do not really exist. The rescue of one inevitably creates the rescue of another. To retreat from reacting to evil in others pulls them away from evil-doing. To be clean and clear in ourself is to create cleanliness and clarity in others.

Another meaning of this line has to do with lessening our standards to accomodate those around us who are not behaving as they should. In this case we should dissolve our bond with our group by reaffirming our own standards.

Fifth Line: *Loud cries as dissolving as sweat.* Misunderstanding is swept away when we realize how well our goals are achieved through dispersion—allowing negative thoughts to dissipate. One such negative thought is to decide we are in a "bad situation."

It is a great and liberating idea to realize that it is not our responsibility to correct or "save" others through taking charge of situations, manipulating people, or making other such efforts. Instead, we should disengage, let go, and leave matters to the Sage and Fate to correct. When we see this clearly, it is a great relief from an enormous burden we were never meant to assume.

A man in a ruling position refers to an idea so obviously true that anyone can follow it. To realize that through energetically correcting our ideas we can correct and change our lives, this is a great and liberating idea.

Sixth Line: *He dissolves his blood.* This means to resist thinking about, or bringing up, subjects which invoke wounds or anger. It is important not to stir up the mud, or the blood, of bad thoughts. If we think about things which arouse feelings of alienation, or doubt about a situation, we cannot relate to the situation correctly. We also endanger perseverance if we indulge in such thoughts. In dispersing these thoughts we keep them at a distance and become free of the doubt and alienation that fuel them.

We should also stop reminding ourself that someone is incapable of changing, or that we have no way of bringing about changes. All people are capable of responding to what is high and good within themselves, and we can help them achieve these changes. We may realize how this is possible if we think of how a flock of pigeons flies. Such a flock may seem to whirl and turn synchronously, making it difficult to determine which is the lead pigeon. Considering that each pigeon beats its wings synchronously with the rest, and all of them speed up, dive, climb, or soar at exactly the same time, it would seem that the leader transmits his will to the whole by simply feeling a thing. Being responsive, the others follow. The *I Ching* teaches that human beings, on the inner level, relate in the same way. The more a person's attitude is in harmony with the Cosmos, the more his will and perception subconsciously penetrate to others, effecting changes. For this reason it is said in *Breakthrough (Resoluteness)* (Hex. 43) that it takes only one persevering person to make great improvements in the world.

60.

Chieh / Limitation

$$\frac{\text{K'an}}{\text{Tui}} \quad \begin{array}{c} \equiv\!\equiv \\ \equiv\!\equiv \\ \equiv\!\equiv \end{array}$$

(Acceptance of limits.)

This hexagram has to do with placing on ourselves the limits which comprise correct behavior. Because we have absorbed ideas from our culture which the *I Ching* regards as decadent, this hexagram counsels that limits are essential to achieve our goals. Very often the thing that is decadent is our customary view of what comprises correct moral limits.

Limitation also has to do with accepting that it is our Fate to learn how to respond correctly to challenges and adversities. Acceptance means that we cast out any element within ourselves of resistance to having to go through the necessary learning process. We may be willing, spiritually, but logic resists; we may have gained assent from logic, but body rebels; we need to gain the willing assent from all parts of ourselves—an assent which is not conditioned and hedging. While there is still a remnant of resistance, we need to impose a discipline which the resisting element may view as "galling."

The limits we observe have to do with being a wanderer in a strange land; we may not proceed presumptuously, as we like, or arrogantly. Changes may be achieved only through gaining insight into the nature of the problem, attaining the help of the Sage, and depending on the penetrating power of inner truth. This way of achieving change at first seems feeble and restrictive, but when we later see that truth is empowered, and that the changes meet with universal approval, we realize how limitation gives meaning to life and power for good.

First, it is necessary to come to an understanding of what is the inner truth of each situation. Then we must trust it to indicate the vehicle of change. This vehicle often remains unknown to us until the instant we can make use of it. In some cases the problem may be entirely resolved; other, long-standing problems may only be solved through small increments of progress achieved over a long period of time.

In interpreting the lines of this hexagram, we should remember that each line has to do with limitation. To "go out of the door," means that whether we advance or retreat, we must exercise the appropriate self-limitation, and not do as we please.

Finally, the *I Ching* means of action—to produce results through force of character—cannot be attained without long practice at self-limitation. Such practice requires us to be patient and gentle with ourselves. We should not attempt too much self-improvement too soon, or focus ambitiously on the goal. We should likewise avoid being excessively ascetic, or flagellating ourselves for mistakes, or taking vows, or making pacts. All such ambition and asceticism comes from the wrong source. It seems that once we realize that limitation and self-development are necessary, the ego tries to force advance through sweeping effort; this effort often entails adopting fetishes, unusual practices, obsessive behavior, or any procedure which we fantasize would enable us to skip steps. The presence of the ego spells defeat, for we may not achieve our goals through its means. Only gradual, gentle, modest, and persevering effort enables us to make progress without arousing the power of the ego.

Throughout the work of self-limitation we are dealing with troublesome body-inferiors which are accustomed to having their way. We are able to limit ourselves better if we explain to them that we need their cooperation. We can achieve their cooperation best if we explain that we are learning new ways of dealing with problems, ways that are far more effective and safer than those to which they have been accustomed. This procedure is a little like telling a twelve-year-old who is frantic to eat that he should not allow his stomach to rule his mind. The effect can be surprising. Our inferiors need to see that our ego is a snail-sized blot of fear which throws an immense shadow. Shall we allow such a blot to rule us?

First Line: *Not going out of the door and courtyard is without blame.* This means not going beyond the limits defined in *The Wanderer* (Hex. 56)—the limits naturally imposed on one who is a stranger in a strange land. Shorn of old defenses, we must now rely on inner dignity as a defense. Accordingly, we must be cautious, reserved, and obliging to others, on guard not to lose touch with our inner being. We avoid meddling in others' affairs, or being aloof and arrogant.

Receiving this line tells us that we should limit our action to saying what *we* are willing to do or not do in managing our own life; we may not tell others what to do or not do in regard to their affairs. We may defend ourselves against attack, but we must be extremely prudent in initiating attacks. If we do not forget that we are wanderers and strangers, help and protection will come from the Cosmos and we will be able to approach others to do the right thing; if this help has not yet come, we can only spend our time at keeping ourself correct, and avoid being pressured by fear or desire. In dealing with others we need to keep attuned, in order to advance when people are open to us, and to retreat when they are closed. We also retreat when we are no longer objective and disengaged.

We frequently receive this line in preparation for upcoming situations. We are meant to rehearse our limitations and review the discipline we will need to exercise on our inferiors. Then, in the heat of the moment, we will be able to keep free and spontaneous, impelled to action only by "real influences." (The reference to "real influences" means that if we have properly detached from our idea of what to say or do, becoming neutral in attitude, we will be able to see, at the right time, the real nature of the problem, and react to it properly.)

Second Line: *Not going out of the gate and courtyard brings misfortune.* Our custom is to take matters in hand to force a conclusion, therefore, the action indicated here is to make a constructive retreat—a step-by-step disengagement from the other person's ego. Anxiously hesitating to retreat and disengage is disastrous.

Third Line: *He who knows no limitation will have cause to lament. No blame.* Among the pleasures and extravagances indicated are those of self-assertion and self-indulgence, as when we play the role of the wise Sage and faithful follower of the truth—the one with the know-how. Another form of self-assertion occurs when we indulge in temper tantrums and rebukes. Self-importance and self-indulgence make us forget our job and miss our opportunities. Ambition to prove points, or to gain something from each moment of contact, makes us unable to hear. However, seeing and correcting our mistakes removes all cause for blame.

Fourth Line: *Contented limitation. Success.* If time is the limiting factor, we should work with time, rather than try to force success. Instead of struggling vainly with people who cause problems, we should keep attuned to the openings and closings in each situation, and not allow ourself to go beyond the peak moments of opportunity. This is to work with the situation and to observe the principle of water flowing downhill as the path of least resistance.

Fifth Line: *Sweet limitation brings good fortune.* Justice requires that if we would limit others, we must first set the correct example of self-limitation by remaining disengaged.

Sweet limitation is also a way of acquiring the willing cooperation of our inferiors by explaining to them in a friendly manner, as one might to a child, that we need them to remain disciplined and disengaged, and that the success they want will be achieved if they do not interfere in events, or give way to doubt. They need to be reminded that the true power for good always accompanies our acquiring inner independence, and that so long as they remain entangled with doubt and fear, inner independence cannot be attained. If they will turn all matters over to the Cosmos, inner independence will become possible. Freedom from fear and doubt engages the help of the Cosmos, by which all things are made possible.

Sixth Line: *Galling limitation.* At times we must severely limit our inferiors in order to save the situation. Receiving this line means we may not tell others what to do, or engage in conflict, or try to change a situation through contriving, striving, or self-assertion, no matter how important it may seem that we do so. To restrain ourselves under such conditions may seem especially galling, but when through such restraint we reach our goal, all cause for remorse at so much self-denial is removed.

This line also mentions that we should not engage in limits which are "too galling." This refers to obligations we have taken on which are not correct. For example, we are never obligated by Fate or others to participate in morally inappropriate activities. We may be required to forebear while inappropriate situations go on around us, but we are always free not to participate in them. If those involved in the wrong thing are open to why we do not participate or approve, we may or may not explain it, but we should carefully monitor our feelings so that we avoid being drawn into conflict through self-righteous pride, or by the another's testing to see if we can be drawn into defending our point of view.

We are also warned by this line that we should not attempt, by applying galling limits to ourselves, to achieve giant-steps of progress. Even small steps of improvement require all of the limitation and sacrifice we are capable of sustaining. We should therefore be kind and sympathetic to our inferiors while we undergo limitation and change. It helps if we express sympathy for the heavy burdens we must necessarily place on them.

61.

Chung Fu / Inner Truth

$$\frac{Sun}{Tui}$$ ☴ ☱

(You know what the problem is.)

Pigs and fishes. Good fortune. Inner truth refers to what we inwardly know to be true. Often this hexagram seems to say, "You know what the problem is, and you understand the truth of the matter." At other times the hexagram is about dealing with evil in others through the power of inner truth. The image of "pigs and fishes" refers to the stubborn qualities of a person's ego. The buildup of inner power, through clinging to what is right, must be very great to penetrate through to them.

Two types of inner truth are discussed, one an effect that emanates outward from our inner thoughts (correct or incorrect), having a force either for good or evil, and the second as the Cosmic aspect of the situation...inner truth as the heart of the matter, with its own power to correct all wrongs ("visible effects of the invisible manifest themselves").

Before the inner truth of our thoughts can have power for good we need to apprehend the inner, or Cosmic, truth of the situation in question. To attain this truth, we must first become receptive, suspending all previous judgments. We keep our minds open about people. This means we do not "execute" them by classifying them in a negative way, or by considering them to be hopeless, or assuming that they are dishonest, ungrateful, or whatever. We also free ourself of any ideas that a thing cannot work. We allow that the unlikely and the impossible can and do happen. Then we turn the matter over to the Cosmos. The inner truth of the matter will become apparent at the right time.

Clinging to this process (which in some ways is to proceed blindly) empowers truth. The more we can rest content to be led blindly, allowing the power of truth to act as it will, the more powerful truth becomes.

Dependence on the Cosmos to be guided results in total inner independence. The power of truth and inner independence are interrelated and interdependent. The power is maintained so long as we do not waver, but if we lose our inner independence, the power of inner truth becomes blocked.

The power of inner truth accumulates as we gain knowledge of the Cosmic laws. For example, we soon learn through our studies with the *I Ching* that it is incorrect to try to produce results through conflict, and that anger, while often justified, blocks the correct solution, and that there is a Cosmic law against being vindictive. We acquire this knowledge only gradually under the tutelage of the Sage, and through the slow, step-by-step work of self-correction. It is something we can depend on to guide us in all sorts of situations, for it concerns the fundamentals of how to proceed, the way a technique in singing, playing the piano, or tennis enables the participant to do well.

When we are firm in clinging to this body of inner truth, our firmness imparts great power to what we know so that it can be felt and understood thousands of miles away. It penetrates through even to "pigs and fishes." If, however, our ego interjects doubt, the power quickly disappears.

Inner truth also refers to the higher truth we do not yet know. We may rely on this form of truth by keeping open, for keeping open enables it to solve any given situation, even when we are not able to understand what is happening. If we need to know it, this truth will show itself at the right time.

Inner truth cannot be used for our private purposes. It is not something we may mentally master, memorize, or hold to slavishly. We must first grasp it intuitively, then confirm it experientially. In this way the insight becomes "knowledge of the heart." We cannot even grasp it until we become in tune with our deeper, true self, and to the feelings and vibrations that emanate from things. Once we attune ourselves to the inner truth, we can draw on it as an infinite resource, and rely on it completely to point the right way through all kinds of difficulties.

Inner truth can also be reached through meditation once we become receptive and open, and once we have dispersed all prejudice and structured explanations. If we vacillate about holding our minds open, the door to the truth and the light will remain shut. Worrying and wanting will keep the door shut. When the inner truth of a situation emerges, its clarity is such that everyone is brought into agreement with it.

First Line: *If there are secret designs, it is disquieting.* This line implies that there is a danger that we might form a secret relationship, or a secret reservation of attitude. This means that in our inmost heart we allow a wall to develop between ourself and the Sage. It happens when we ally ourself with our ego and allow it to lead, or when we hedge in our commitment to the good, saying, "I will follow the path of the good only so long, and only so far; then, if I don't get what I think is due me, I'll abandon it." In such situations we form a faction with our ego. This also occurs when we join in factions with others, or when we do things we intuitively know to be wrong.

Receiving this line indicates that we should search our innermost thoughts for any form of hedging, factionalism, pacts, secret promises, or secret barriers which would isolate us from unity with the truth, or with the Sage, and sacrifice them on our inner alter.

Our first commitment should be to serve the truth, and in this service to maintain forever our inner independence. This is a commitment to marry oneself, for only then can we marry, or extend a selfless loyalty to, another. If, in uniting with someone (or an idea, or a plan), this first loyalty becomes displaced, we lose our inner balance, our self-esteem, and our connection with the Sage who helps us.

Unity with another is tripartite: it always includes the hidden Higher Power, or Sage. If we put another, or something else, over the Higher Power in our hierarchy of commitments, we effectually exclude the Higher Power. In doing so, we undermine the foundation for enduring unity.

Another form of secret relationship occurs when we hedge against being truly dependent on the Cosmos by making a "little room" for desire. Or, we hold to pretensions of being better than others, or to having the right to advance ourselves at their expense, through pointing out their mistakes and our better judgment. When such thoughts exist, in spite of what we have learned about the inner world and the Creative, it means we still harbor doubts at a deep level. These doubts insure failure; the negative power is not quiescent, it is an actively destructive force.

Other examples of secret reservations of attitude: we meet someone under the pretense of innocence, but really plan to bring up, in a sort of ambush, a controversial subject; we cultivate friendship in order to gain some benefit; we take a dim view of someone in order not to feel disappointed should he not measure up to what we expect or wish; we ignore the Cosmic equality of all beings by assuming rights and privileges as parents over children, teachers over students, or any other title of elevation or proprietorship over a 'lower being.' Behavior which exceeds the mean violates Cosmic law. Anyone in a position of power over other beings must be even more careful to be correct, rather than less so. In receiving this line we should check ourselves for presumptuous and culturally decadent attitudes. Conscious innocence and humble dependence on the Cosmos underlie the power of inner truth.

Second Line: *A crane calling in the shade.* This image shows the fact that firmness or weakness in our values, and emotional dependence or independence is communicated to others on the inner level. Our inner attitude is what people feel and know about us, the way astute politicians know what their constituencies will accept or reject. If we forget our first loyalty to the truth, others will know we are separated from our source of strength, and will test us. It is no use pretending we are strong if we are weak.

Self-development is the only way to attain the power of inner truth. When our values are firmly in place, and when we nourish ourselves with correct thoughts, a good influence on others cannot be prevented.

Third Line: *Now he sobs, now he sings.* This line underscores the importance of maintaining our center of gravity (inner independence). The power of inner truth depends on it. This means we must keep free of worrying and wanting.

Inner independence means just that: we do not emotionally depend on anyone. We become dependent on others when we say to them, "Here, I give you myself. Henceforth my happiness and self-esteem depend on you, and how you regard me. I belong to you." This, of course, is the work of our ego-self-image, which cannot exist unless it sees itself reflected in others' eyes. It will make any kind of bargain on the hope of being affirmed. If we have allowed such a thing to happen to us, we must take back whatever we have given. We don't have the right to give ourselves to anyone, and while it may flatter the other person, he can only despise us for it, for he does not want that responsibility. Once he tires of the flattery, or the convenience of our servitude, he will abandon us. The only correct relationship we may have with another is one in which both people independently follow the path of the true and the good.

Even if we have not gone so far as to give ourself away, we should avoid 'emotional leaning.' This happens when we 'look sideways.' This means we define the meaning of our lives or measure our progress by the effect we may be having on others, and on what others do and think. It is impossible to take the care necessary to walk our own path if our inner gaze is always fixed on them. The only way to self-sufficiency and inner strength—qualities inseparably linked to the power of inner truth—is to pursue our path independently of all others, and even of the train of events.

When people are incorrect in relating to us, we lose our inner independence if simply to get along with them we "forgive and forget." We should not feed their egos by giving them the impression that no matter what they do, everything is all right. With this attitude it is only a matter of time before they will become tyrants over us. On the other hand we must not allow ourselves to dwell on their behavior; we become infected with the inferior thing, and again lose our direction. We must recognize the incorrect situation for what it is and carefully keep disengaged from it. This is to judge it without allowing our attitude to become judgmental. In such situations we need help from the Higher Power. Awareness of this need enables us to keep balanced "on the high wire," as it were, for that is what is required.

Fourth Line: *The moon nearly at the full.* The power of inner truth results from depending on the Sage, Fate, and time to work things out. This dependence is the heart and soul of our inner independence and strength, and is what arouses the power of the Creative. Once this power has been generated and things begin to improve, we must not forget its source by flattering ourselves that "we did it." When we immodestly forget that our dependence on the Sage is the source of our power, the power begins to wane, just as the light of the moon, which is dependent on the light of the sun, begins to wane once it becomes full. When we measure our progress in the mirror of self-approval, the ego has entered to claim success; if we fail to reject the ego's flattery, we form a faction with it which excludes the Sage. We may never presume that we possess the power of inner truth; it always comes from relating correctly to the Higher Power as its source.

Fifth Line: *He possesses truth, which links together.* The power of inner truth, which comes from clinging steadfastly to our principles and maintaining our inner independence, develops adamantine strength, subduing the inferior element in others.

There is such a thing as truth (here, "the Sage" and truth are interchangeable). We all know what it is on the deepest level of consciousness even though we may hold it in doubt on the conscious level. When we cling to this inner body of truth, it has the power to unify people, even though it may appear to others that our actions lead away from unity. However, when we are led by our ego, by its worrying and wanting, by its eagerness to push things to conclusion and to mastermind things, we no longer follow truth, and we lose its power to help.

People who are morally correct and strict with themselves automatically draw others' respect, but if they then seek to be credited for their virtue, their influence diminishes. When a person becomes free of all vanity, the power of his personality is restored. Once more the distrust and suspicion which block his influence dissipate. In this way the power of truth unites.

Sixth Line: *Cockcrow penetrating to heaven.* While we can help people who are open and receptive, we should realize that there are limitations to what we can achieve purely through verbal explanations. People must perceive the truth within themselves. Because progress is the result of many small steps built one on another, we should not try to rush others' development, or skip steps by saying things for which they are inadequately prepared. People can relate only to what they are ready to perceive. Any idea not ready to be accepted cannot be accepted. From mental stimulation a person can achieve great clarity, but such clarity is short-lived. Lasting improvements occur when a person commits himself to learning, and then to putting his knowledge to the test of experience. Through his commitment and perseverance, he will gradually re-educate and reorient his attitudes and habits of mind. Meanwhile, we can only give him an introduction, a summary view, and point the way.

This line also counsels us to take our words seriously, to be conscientious and sincere in speech. We should not think that what we say, even idly, does not matter. If we are not modest, our words may do harm.

62.

Hsiao Kuo / *Preponderance of the Small*

$$\frac{\text{Chên}}{\text{Kên}} \quad \begin{array}{c} \equiv\!\equiv \\ \equiv\!\equiv \end{array}$$

(Thinking of taking action in distrust of Fate.)

This hexagram deals with our own, or other people's, rigid attitudes. Strong elements such as fear, envy, anger, desire, vindictiveness or obstinacy preponderate, and consequently we feel pressured to act. From the perspective of our ego non-action seems ineffective and unnatural; nevertheless, receiving this hexagram indicates that non-action is required.

We should resist pressures which make us distrust the creative power of the Unknown. We should also beware of attaching ourselves enthusiastically to "solutions" simply because of this pressure, and we should avoid seeking comprehensive answers.

The answer we need now will be found if we allow ourself to be led through the small door of the improbable, which will open only at the precise moment of need. It helps if we remember that there is always a hidden solution to the problem at hand. Meanwhile we should keep ourselves open and unstructured, remaining calmly in the 'ambiguous spot.' This is possible only if we modestly keep our eyes turned away from the problem.

It is not necessary to venture so far as to trust the Unknown, but it is essential to disperse our distrust of it. Fear causes us to exaggerate the importance of succeeding. We know that the situation is important, and therefore we distrust ourself and Fate to carry us through. We should resist this fear before it turns into desire and ambition to do something.

First Line: *The bird meets with misfortune through flying*. Being fledged means being free of pressure to act. Flying before we are fledged means acting before it is correct to do so. We follow a plan or strategy because we distrust the Creative to show us the way as we go. We should flow with the course of events, responding spontaneously to each situation as it occurs, without defining its meaning or importance. We should also remain loose and open, clinging to the Creative for help, even though we must remain in an emotionally uncomfortable situation. Resistance blocks aid when we most need aid.

Second Line: *He does not reach his prince. No blame.* Not "reaching his prince" means we have not yet received a clear or comprehensive idea of how to proceed; it also means that the situation has not yet developed to the extent that success is possible. We should not be discouraged. We should keep our mind open and unstructured, allowing the way to show itself. Meanwhile, it is an expression of modesty to cease looking anxiously or disappointedly at the situation. We need only do our best, and meet the result with acceptance.

Third Line: *If one is not extremely careful...misfortune.* When we decide for or against someone, we hasten to resolve the ambiguous moment. Such self-confidence will backfire. We abandon the path by choosing to follow our impatient and childish ego, rather than allowing the Creative to work.

In close proximity to evil, our inferiors try to crystallize themselves into a knight in shining armor in order to jump into battle with the evil thing. This ploy, however well-intentioned, fails, because we go too far. Instead of recognizing evil for what it is, and asking the Higher Power for help, instead of keeping detached and allowing the evil thing to die of its own accord, we fight it tooth and nail. The white knight is our vainglorious ego involving itself in the situation. Much damage is done because of the fallout.

Fourth Line: *Do not act. Be constantly persevering.* Because we have persevered and our goals have not yet been achieved, we begin to feel that Fate is hostile, or we doubt the beneficial nature of the Cosmos, or we distrust the Sage's guidance. In bearing with difficulties, an element of hardness has crept into our character. We need to yield modestly to Fate. We are like an overloaded mule, poised on the edge of the canyon, ready to buck. The mule distrusts the master's guidance, but rebelling would endanger its life. Things seem impossible to bear, but if we endure through this situation, all will be well. We should not act simply to get rid of our load. Here, "Do not act" means do not give up.

Fifth Line: *Dense clouds....* To distrust our path is to distrust the Sage who guides us. We cannot make our way in the hidden world alone; we need the Sage's help, which can only be obtained through a modest acceptance of our fate.

Even if we were born to set the world in order, we could achieve this goal only by the small means of self-correction; self-correction, in turn, cannot be accomplished without the Sage, whose help we may obtain only by seeking it modestly.

Sixth Line: *The flying bird leaves him. Misfortune.* If through fear and doubt we restlessly turn our backs on the Sage and on our path, we will energize hostile forces. Such obstinacy leads to misfortune. As the mother said whose intuition warned her against sailing on the Titanic, "For its owners to say the ship was unsinkable was to 'fly in the face of God.'" To adopt an "I don't care" mood is to leave caution and modesty behind.

63.

Chi Chi / After Completion

$$\frac{\text{K'an}}{\text{Li}} \quad \begin{matrix} \equiv\!\equiv \\ \equiv\!\equiv \end{matrix}$$

(On reconsidering, and other unbalancing thoughts.)

At the beginning good fortune, at the end disorder. We have been firm in following our path, but now that the situation has improved, we reconsider: "Isn't there an easier way to proceed with life?" "Haven't we been too hard in withdrawing from someone, too firm in requiring him to be right with us, or too soft in following the path of non-action?" "If I stick to my principles won't it turn others away?" Such wondering is the first seed of decay that follows a period of patient perseverance; through wondering the ego regains leadership. We must recognize and resist its resurgence.

If we wonder whether we have been too hard, then we must realize that we do not have the right to help people avoid the hard learning process. Such wondering implies that we have assumed a magnificent attitude in which we put ourself in the place of God to decide others' fates. We should avoid wondering whether we have been too hard, or too soft, or whether we should do something, either to relax back into old habits of comfortable dependency, or to act in a hostile way in order to re-establish the correct distance. We should not adopt any special attitudes because they once seemed to influence others to change, nor should we be afraid that people will misunderstand us. We need only relate sincerely to each moment as it approaches and leave matters to Fate.

Comfortable dependency means that we relax our inner discipline by indulging small, seemingly insignificant thoughts which we know are on the border of being incorrect. For example, we indulge in a "little intervention," a "little curiosity," a "little involvement," or a "little nostalgia." Indulgence is also to relax into comfort; we cease to be alert, and we forget to keep a proper balance with others. Either we want to feel good about another person before he has corrected himself, or we find comfort in alienation and indifference. Such a relaxation of inner discipline usually occurs "after completion," when we feel free of pressure, and self-confidence returns. With relaxation we allow wondering to begin, permitting seemingly small desires to re-emerge with great strength. Because of these tendencies, "after completion" is the time when we should remain disciplined and alert to intercept the "seeds" of wondering and wanting, and thereby ward off their consequences. If we fail to resist these unbalancing thoughts, we will make mistakes. Over and over the *I Ching* emphasizes that peace can be maintained only if, during the times we feel secure, we remember the possibility of danger. We must be as firm towards others when they are behaving well as we are when they are behaving badly.

After completion we also tend to forget that it was the invisible Sage's help that pulled us through the difficult time. We begin to think everything was only a bad dream, with no particular causes, and only chance remedies. We even think we created the improvements all by ourselves. In thus losing our modesty we lose our protection, and our ability to make progress against evil.

After completion is also a time when we may experience uncertainty. Uncertainty, in turn, may bring to the surface residual doubts we have about ourself. Receiving this hexagram tells us that this uncertainty is the problem. We should abandon uncertainty, not for certainty, but simply to return to neutrality. It is important to avoid any kind of unbalancing thoughts which disturb our inner dignity and independence.

First Line: *He gets his tail in the water. No blame.* At the height of pressure we fail to accept the situation. The ego reasserts itself forcefully, and accuses the Higher Power of being too harsh and unfeeling, and of perhaps being a trickster. Being impatient, we press forward, presuming that matters are righted when they are not, or that the bad times are over. By presumption we attempt to make things better, but this does not work.

Development must proceed slowly, in steps. Meanwhile, we must retain our reserve and inner independence, neither giving up nor forcing things forward. By presumption we should not commit ourself to a relationship or open our inner thoughts to another before the fundamentals of equality and justice are firmly in place.

He brakes his wheels means we have been going in the right direction but we suddenly slow to reconsider whether we have been too strict. Such wavering causes problems, but there is no real blame,

290

because we have not abandoned the path.

The image of a fox that crosses thawing ice has to do with our attitude to the tensions we face. The cracks in the ice are "sore points" better left alone. To nearly cross the danger and then lose our sense of caution will surely cause trouble (causing the fox to get his tail in the water). Also, a premature sense of confidence may cause us to lapse back into an older, structured view, and so, cause progress to collapse. In recognizing and correcting such errors, there is no blame.

Second Line: *The woman loses the curtain of her carriage. Do not run after it. On the seventh day you will get it.* In presuming things to be better than they are, or by allowing ourself to be flattered, or by slipping back into a dependence on another's regard for us, we have slipped from a safe place into a pool of slime. The only thing to do is to accept the situation modestly and return to working on the rescue. It is of no use to bemoan the situation or feel like quitting, as if inner kicking and screaming will engage the sympathy of the Sage, who will then miraculously produce the progress we seek. Such progress can be achieved only if we continue with patient, honest work. Acceptance and conscientiousness to start over from a decreased position is the piety referred to in the fifth line. It contrasts with *magnificence*, shown when we fail to accept the reverses encountered on our journey. By accepting reverses we acquire help in solving our problems.

This line also refers to times when our incorrect attitude has been perceived by others, so that we lose our influence with them. We do not need to strive to recapture our good name, however, for by correcting ourself our influence will return, and our error will soon be forgotten.

Third Line: *Inferior people must not be employed.* If we become lax after having corrected and set limits around the spoiled child in ourself or others, this spoiled child will then begin to reassert itself to test its boundaries. When this happens we must recover our emotional independence and firmness. This effort is arduous, but it is only when we abandon the inferior element, either in others or in ourself, that it loses its strength and becomes subjugated. If we revitalize our attitude, the mistake will correct itself. The same thing happens if we begin to reconsider the doubts we have just conquered. We cannot afford to appease our subjugated inferior element.

The "urge to expand" refers to the luxury of wishing to capitalize on our gains in order to achieve something luxurious and personal.

Fourth Line: *The finest clothes turn to rags. Be careful all day long.* Laxity, such as wanting to luxuriate in desire, allowing ambition to return, or stopping to enjoy the progress made at a time when we should remain strict and reserved, will certainly ruin what we have achieved.

On the other hand it is also dangerous to think that we may have gone too far in our strictness, so that we begin to feel sympathetic to the other person for being cut off. We must not dwell nostalgically on good times we have had, and thereby allow weakness to enter by seduction.

This line may also warn us that the person we presume to be correct has not yet become trustworthy, and we should therefore remain cautious and reserved.

If we stop in the middle of crossing the great water to bemoan our situation, we are easily overwhelmed. It is essential to get past the danger by going forward, accepting the situation as it is. Similarly, we must not dwell on past injustices, or debts of gratitude owed us and unpaid. We should go on with life and leave the resolution of these matters to Fate.

Fifth Line: *The neighbor in the east slaughters an ox.* When we stop to think that we have been so hard that now we might indulge a more comfortable relationship, we play God. It is egotistical magnificence to overlook a person's incorrect behavior and favor him at a time when we should, through reserve and inner strictness, require him to do his best. We have no right to coddle anybody's ego.

Magnificence is also failure to accept reverses, or the time required to change bad conditions. Spiritual acceptance generally has nothing to do with the amount of time society might regard as reasonable. Spiritual acceptance is unconditional.

Sixth Line: *He gets his head in the water. Danger.* We "look back" when we presume the struggle to be over, and now we can relax and enjoy the situation. Now that we have obtained a little progress we must tip-toe around the person, or everything will come undone. We must not lose our dignity and inner independence in this way. (See *Approach*, Hex. 19, Line 3.) We must be firm and go forward, or the work will be undone.

We also look back when we are not sure that we have done the right thing. It is important to go forward; if we are sincere in attitude, even making a wrong move will not prove injurious, for some way will occur to rectify the mistake. It is important not to stand in the crossroads, wondering.

64.

Wei Chi / Before Completion

$$\frac{\text{Li}}{\text{K'an}}$$

(We need to gain a correct perspective of the problem.)

Crossing the great water means getting past a period that is dangerous to our perseverance. When situations threaten our emotional balance, we must be like an old fox walking across thin ice. This hexagram says that our affairs are in a new regenerative phase of growth. We should be aware that during times of regeneration, the pressures on our inner independence and balance become intense, and therefore we must be cautious, circumspect, and persevering. For example, we may find our thoughts drifting toward others primarily because theirs may be fastened on us, for when we have established inner independence, we automatically draw others with whom we have inner connections. It is particularly important, therefore, to keep our childish heart from wanting, wondering, or worrying—activities which lead to a loss of inner independence.

In this hexagram, fire (clarity) is above water (effort), and hence out of relationship. Clarity must be the foundation of effort, as in *After Completion* (Hex. 63), where fire is below water and can bring it to a boil, producing energy. This symbolism indicates that we must put ourself in the proper position to the matter at hand before we can attain clarity, for clarity must precede effort.

Receiving this hexagram indicates that we have not achieved true inner quiet; therefore, we are poised to act. We have come to a conclusion without first attaining the correct perspective—a dangerous situation. We must seek the correct viewpoint—one which is not tainted by a single emotion.

Clarity gives us the strength needed to overcome the dangers threatening perseverance, and is the "vehicle of crossing" mentioned in the second line. Before we can attain clarity it is necessary to attain true inner quiet; only then can we become attuned to our inner voice; only then can the correct view show itself.

Possibly we may only need to realize that what is required is that we hold firmly to our path, that this alone enables us safely to bypass the danger. This means that we continue forward without looking back. We do not allow ourselves to become involved in the pressures of the moment. Holding to our path means that we maintain our inner independence—a willingness to carry on alone when the situation warrants it. We accept our fate and sacrifice our ego (the clamoring and complaining of the childish heart) without reproach to anyone.

Cracks in the ice refer to sore points of contention. These sore points must be dealt with indirectly; to bring them into the open is to "step on the cracks." Bringing them into the open violates the principle of taking great care. It is as if the other person is always waiting for us to bring them up. The best way to deal with problematical areas is to hold to the power of inner truth.

First Line: *He gets his tail in the water. Humiliating.* Premature effort to achieve tangible progress occurs when we have not taken the trouble and care to attain clarity. Clarity is to gain insight into the uselessness of striving, and to understand that by firmly clinging to conscious innocence and noblehearted acceptance we engage the power of inner truth to resolve the situation, or to get us past the danger points (cross the great water).

Second Line: *He brakes his wheels.* Idle waiting means that we allow ourselves to indulge in fantasies, vanities, nostalgic memories, and diversions which cause us to lose contact with our inner voice. Such activities diminish our will and cause us to become diverted from our path, and to forget our overall goal to rescue others. Only steadiness of purpose is capable of overcoming the standstill. What we need is back-burner steadiness. In turning energy to our work we must not assault the goal, but attend to keeping our innocence, steadfastness, and attunement to our inner voice.

Third Line: *Attack brings misfortune.* Our will to stand firm and alone, and to keep still, is undermined. We would rather fall back into a carefree and easy approach, or drop the matter, giving up perseverance. Perseverance is important, particularly now. We must be firm and "bite through" the obstacles through perseverance in non-action. We must overcome all temptation to take matters into our hands, or to assume anything from the situation. We must allow ourself to be led.

Fourth Line: *Shock, thus to discipline the Devil's country.* The struggle mentioned is that of keeping our inner equilibrium and detachment, for this alone "disciplines the Devil's country." This means that we resist the luxury of taking the lead, demonstrating our personality, or indulging our wants. It also means that we go forward without wavering in our values. We neither reconsider whether we are on the right path, nor wonder whether we have been too strict in requiring what is correct. By keeping firmly on our path we discipline those whom we are meant to rescue.

Fifth Line: *The light of the superior man is true.* We remain persevering despite inner conflict and temptation to leave the path. Such acceptance and steadfastness provide new insights and help from the Sage.

Sixth Line: *If one wets his head, he loses it.* With every change for the better, however slight, we are tempted to think the goal has been reached and now we may relax. Our ego, kept at bay, has been waiting for the opportunity provided by inner carelessness to return and involve us in its wanting and desiring. Wanting and desiring take over. We must keep strict inner discipline, wanting nothing, striving for nothing. This kind of modesty ensures continued progress.

This line also refers to drinking alcoholic beverages at times when we most need to be self-possessed and alert. It also suggests that alcohol and other drugs inhibit our ability to perceive the lessons of the Sage.

The line also refers to spiritual drunkenness, in which we are wishy-washy about what is right and wrong. We abandon what we know as inner truth in favor of a more liberal, sophisticated view, or we adopt a love-everyone-unconditionally attitude just when correctness requires that we be strict and reserved. In these circumstances we are "under the influence" of a wrong idea.

Glossary

The Sage is he (she, or it) who speaks through the *I Ching*.

Fate is the trajectory of events caused, to a degree, by our attitudes. Of the paired phenomena, the Sage and Fate bring things to completion.

The Superior Man is the true self within. It listens, looks, and decides.

The Inferior Man is our ego-self-image. The ego, here defined, is the composite of all the self-images we have ever adopted or would be tempted, through fantasy, to adopt. Once created, this composite self takes on a life of its own, and surrounds itself with a defensive and prideful barricade. It is as if we climb into a particular set of clothing because we like the way it looks, only to find that it dances off with us in it, out of control. It usurps leadership of the true self, and because it manifests itself as a pride system, it resists being displaced.

The Inferiors are bodily and emotional impulses which are often manifested as inner voices. They may be led either by our Superior Man or by the Inferior Man. When they are led by the Inferior Man (ego) they are in opposition to our true self.

Individual Tao. That which is consistent with our inner nature and the natural direction of the superior self.

Great Tao. The underlying direction(s) in which life proceeds; it is only partly knowable.

Inner (or Hidden) World. Everything that now exists in the "real world" first exists in the image, or inner world. Everything that is now becoming, pre-exists as a Cosmic image. The two, it would seem, are paired, with one being a shadow of the other—the "real world" being a shadow of the image world. Our inner-world existence is paired with our outer-world existence. Although our subconscious inhabits the inner world, its progress there is dependent on our conscious life here. To avoid pitfalls there the *I Ching* is given us as a lantern, and the Sage as a guide to make our way. How we fare there depends on whether in this world we are true to our individual tao.

Helpers. Support and help we receive from the hidden world. It is also the help we receive when we bring out others' superior natures.

Trust. A willing suspension of disbelief.

Evil. Being less than true to our superior nature.

Keeping Still. A method of meditating to achieve inner quiet and clarity. This method leads to disengaging from our ego.

Success. Adhering to our path in spite of challenges, thereby making progress.

Crossing the Great Water. Persevering through doubt and difficulty.

Press Forward. Failure to disengage. Allowing ambition, pride, annoyance, or other emotions to take over.

Obstinacy. To stubbornly hold to inferior impulses.

Disperse. To allow inferior impulses to dissolve, or float away. Through mental images such as "dispersing" we are able to undermine the power of recalcitrant or insistent impulses to do the wrong thing.

Penetration. The gradual dawning of the liberating perception.

Dark Principle. Fear, doubt, vanity, the ego-self-image.

Light Principle. Enlightenment, understanding, a liberating perspective.

Arrogance. Self-importance, confidence in the self; exuberant enthusiasm; carelessness, assumption of rights; taking up other people's space; disbelieving in the Unknown; deciding what the Unknown is.

Resort to arms: Taking action against the Inferior Man within us and against our obstinate inferiors, our pride system, or old patterns of reaction.

Sacrifice. Voluntarily relinquishing inferior impulses such as anger, for the good of all.

Powerful in the cheekbones. Telling people what is wrong with them.

Conscious innocence. Contrasted with the innocence of youth, which is that of inexperience, this is a conscious return to purity of mind. Through practicing inner cleansing and self-awareness, we rid ourself of conscious purpose. Our "work" is to be on guard against the interjections of our ego and to keep ourself free of its desires and demands, its hopes and fears, its beliefs and doubts, its pacts, vows, old areas of inner burnout, and habitual responses.

On Being Led

Throughout the *I Ching* there is mention of following, being led, and clinging. There are also warnings against the misuse of power, and of acting on our own. The impression we get from this advice is that the *I Ching* presents a passive approach to life. " This is not true.

When we are faced with a situation in which the *I Ching* calls for retreat, holding fast, and not acting, it refers to all these things in a moving time frame. We are meant to stop at the moment, retreat momentarily, hold fast and not act, until the right moment arrives to move ahead. It is not a static, permanent counsel to quit.

When does the right moment arrive to move ahead? When we have become emotionally detached, when we have perceived the inner truth of the situation with clarity, and when we have become independent in our inner attitude, yet firm in recognizing what is correct. Then we are able to seize the opportunities presented by the moment and move ahead appropriately.

If we are able to keep our attitude modest and sincere when we act, we will achieve maximum progress. We need, however, to be able to retreat the moment the opening begins to close. If we fail to disengage in time, our good effect will be diminished.

Acting from inner independence is different from acting from egotistical enthusiasm. The ego would dazzle us with "comprehensive" solutions. It is good at insinuating itself into the role of savior with clever, airtight remedies, and it is good at acting detached. That is why the *I Ching* counsels "hesitating caution." Caution keeps the ego at a distance.

If we move ahead without having put ourselves into a correct relationship, we fall victim to arrogance.

In order to be led we need to be open and alert. Even though we develop a firm knowledge of *I Ching* principles, we should avoid taking inflexible positions. A situation may be full of ambiguity. Without abandoning our principles, we wait through the ambiguity until we see how to resolve the matter without compromising ourself.

When we do not yet understand a new lesson, we should allow ourself to be led without resistance through the developing situation. We keep asking what we need to do to relate correctly to the moment. Often we need only wait in a neutral but alert frame of mind, like an actor in the wings awaiting his cue. He listens within, he feels the action going on, and when his moment arrives, he fulfills his role.

When we read the *I Ching* it is essential that our understanding be lifted above the level of blindly following words. This requires help from the Sage, and earnestness in contemplating what the *I Ching* is saying.

I Ching Meditation

I learned to meditate through suggestions given in my daily *I Ching* consultations. Since most of the insights I have gained into the *I Ching* have come by way of this form of meditating, I have included this section for those who may want to hear more about *I Ching* meditation.

The sort of meditation I learned differs from other, well-known meditation styles in that it leads to meditation experiences. These consist of images and voices which produce insights. For example, there was the scene in which I saw myself life-guarding someone who insisted on swimming with sharks; I realized that he felt safe because I was watching. The meditation told me that the only remedy was to leave the scene, that he would rescue himself only when he perceived that no one else would be there to save him. From this I realized that when we have inner ties to someone, focussing on what he does makes him feel no need to be responsible for himself. It confers on him a feeling of invincibility; no matter what he does, we will come to the rescue.

My meditation experiences varied greatly. Sometimes, when my eyes were closed, they began as small, seemingly insignificant specks on my field of vision. When I focussed on them, they became full-sized images. Sometimes they began as images, and I entered a scene already there. Sometimes images flashed across my view with such speed that had I not been attentive I would have missed them. Writing about them later required two or three pages to describe all I had noticed. Sometimes the images had a still-life quality so that I was led to observe minute details. Some meditations consisted only of sounds, followed by a brief explanation of their meaning. Sometimes a meditation consisted of a series of seemingly unrelated scenes which would provoke the question, "What could this mean?" After a few moments of waiting, a verbal explanation, or a mental understanding would follow. In some meditations I saw myself reacting to something in a characteristically emotional way, while I observed dispassionately. Often I sat and nothing happened. Sometimes I waited a long time, only to feel suddenly that it was time to get up and go about my daily life. Once in a while meditation experiences began the minute I sat down and closed my eyes. I could never anticipate what form my meditations might take.

Certain qualities were common to all my meditations. For instance, I always had the feeling that someone else was presenting the scene, drawing my attention to what was relevant. Also, the messages illuminated the hexagrams and lines I had recently drawn. Invariably, they answered a question in the back of my mind. Invariably, they came when I needed to know something. Often, but not always, they came when I wanted to know something.

Eventually, it became clear that certain attitudes are necessary for achieving the meditation state. These are the same attitudes mentioned in *Youthful Folly* (Hex. 4) as necessary to establish the relationship between the student and Sage of the *I Ching:*
  — a willing suspension of disbelief;
  — a sincere effort;
  — perseverance.
When I first began to meditate I had only a vague idea of meditation. I remembered my voice teacher telling me that when she had once overworked, her daughter had taught her the Transcendental Meditation technique. After that she "could handle anything that came."

I imagined that meditation required sitting like a yogi, and that deep breathing was necessary. I also decided to do light physical exercises to become more relaxed. All these things, I later realized, were important to meditating, for achieving deep inner quiet requires cooperation between the body and mind.

My hesitations about meditating concerned self-hypnosis. I did not want to hypnotize myself inadvertently. Years before, I had hypnotized a fellow college student and was unable to wake her up. Luckily, she woke up when I retraced all the steps of the mental journey I had led her through, telling her in advance that when we got back to a certain place, she would wake up. After that I would not repeat mantras, stare at lights, or do anything that might suggest hypnosis. The meditation technique I learned has nothing to do with hypnosis. It is similar to the concentration involved in reading a book. We look at the inner world and become absorbed by what we see there, but we can return our attention to the outer world at will. Because our attention will be disturbed by anyone entering the room, it is best to meditate in a quiet place.

Although I began my meditation efforts at night, I would find that on awakening, my mind would soon be swamped with the worries of the night before. Then I got the first line of *The Clinging* (Hex. 30), which mentions that the best time of day to meditate is during the

302

first moments after waking, when inferior impulses are only in "seed form." Then we are able to intercept them before they have become empowered to rule the mind. This was the beginning of much more effective meditation.

Before we begin to meditate it is good to do a few light exercises that loosen up the back. These help to counteract the effects of stress on the body. Stiffness is often the body's way of expressing fear.

It is also helpful to sit in an erect, yet relaxed position. A simpler version of that used in yoga is sufficient. Meditation experiences rarely occur while we sit in other positions. Being too relaxed seems to inhibit meditation.

Keeping Still notes that the first task in meditating is to quiet the thinking of the heart. The heartbeat, one will notice, quickens with stress and agitation, but it can also be slowed down through deep breathing. We need only breathe in and out deeply and slowly about six times when we first sit down to meditate.

To limit the heart's thinking we are counselled in the second line of *Keeping Still* that "the Superior Man does not permit his thoughts to go beyond his situation." Although these words might make us think that we are to suppress thought, the third line notes that quiet must "develop naturally, out of a state of inner composure"; it warns against trying "to induce calm by means of artificial rigidity." We are meant, in short, to deal with the thoughts that occupy our attention.

The first technique in dealing with our thoughts is that of letting them go. We need to imagine visually letting them go.

Sometimes we have the idea that if we keep our eye focussed on a situation we can somehow keep control of it. For this reason we fear letting go. This, of course, is the work of the ego. Watching a situation in no way imparts control. Recognizing this fact helps free us from the fear of letting go of our concerns.

When we first sit down to meditate, our minds may wander. The thinking of the heart concerns three things: worrying, wanting, and wondering. It is the thinking of the child-like body inferiors. This wandering is useful in that it leads us to hidden concerns, worries, and fears that need to be recognized and addressed. Sincerity of purpose allows us to look at them without getting caught up in them.

It helps if we take the attitude of a hunter. When he first enters the woods, all the hustle and bustle of animal life comes to a halt. Everything freezes to keep from being seen. It is the same with our inferiors, and particularly the Inferior Man (ego-self-image). If we,

303

like the hunter, will be content to go into the inner environment, sit down and wait in an attitude of neutrality, the activity we have interrupted will resume, and we will be able to observe it.

In this way we will both discover and calm the inferiors. We find that these are body cells, or systems of cells which seem to have a limited intelligence. This intelligence surfaces in our mind in such thoughts as "I am tired," or "I am hungry," or as other needs and wants. Like children, they usually respond willingly to suggestions, as when dentists or doctors give warning that "this will hurt only for a moment." If only we give them a bit of advance preparation, they will cooperate willingly. Quick changes, for which they have little preparation, make them freeze with fear. Thus, when one small muscle in the back is strained, the surrounding cells freeze, as if in fear they might be hurt next.

When we first attempt to meditate, the inferiors seem to occupy all our mental space with their needs, wants, and complaints. Often during our adult lives we simply repress them, living in our bodies as strangers. We may do any variety of things which stress them to their limits, such as going too many hours without sleep, failing to eat nutritious food, overworking, or drinking too much. Upon first hearing them in meditation we need to listen to what they are saying, apologize for having abused them, comfort those among them who are sick or tired, and ask for their cooperation. Then we explain to them that we need them to leave us alone, temporarily, in our inner space, so that we may do what is best for them. Through kindness we acquire their cooperation.

The next part of meditation involves bringing the nerves of the backbone to a standstill. This causes the ego to disappear, and we attain a clarity of view that enables us to bring ourselves into harmony with the universe. We are not meant, according to *Keeping Still*, always to be on the go. There is a time for activity, it says, and a time for being quiet. Achieving quiet requires that we allow activity—the inner static of restlessness— to subside. Once this has occurred we become detached from bodily concerns. Then we acquire a point of view that is in harmony with all the energies of the Cosmos.

The Clinging (Hex. 30), states that an attitude of docility, dependence, and acceptance leads to clarity. Docility implies allowing ourselves to be led. Who but the Higher Power can guide us through the meditative world? For this we need its help. To benefit from this help we need to be free of inner resistance to anything that happens in meditation. We maintain a willing suspension of disbelief. We cannot enter meditation if we hold a suspicious or fearful attitude. Meditation is a little like swimming; we must at last take our foot off the bottom.

The idea of dependence is contained in the image of fire clinging to wood. Fire, signifying light and clarity, is dependent on something else to burn. Dependence on something higher than oneself leads to clarity. Quite simply, the key to success lies in asking the Higher Power for help in understanding what we need to know.

The idea of acceptance has to do with humility towards that which is higher than ourselves. Resistance to our fate, or to the "way things work," obstructs meditating, for through resistance we put a wall between ourselves and the Higher Power. Acceptance not only refers to the present; we accept everything in the past as well. It helps if we realize that only through adversities do we bother to grow. The problems of everyday life should be viewed as Cosmic puzzles, which in Zen are called "koans." Their solution will lead us to understand the higher truths of life, and to achieving harmony with the Cosmos. It also helps if we recognize that life is made up of cycles of change. Neither good nor bad times last forever. Simply by correcting our attitudes, we have the ability to change the trajectories and patterns which operate in our lives. Indeed, the stagnation referred to in *Standstill* (Hex. 12) is the result of having adopted attitudes which put us out of harmony with ourselves and with the Cosmos. Progress will resume only when we understand and correct them.

The image of the shining lake is the image of perfect inner harmony(see *The Joyous* Hex. 58). All forms of restlessness—wanting, wondering, and worrying—disturb the lake, creating ripples and waves. It is helpful to see our inner self as such a lake, and to feel when emotions begin to disturb its mirrored surface.

Meditating is also like going to a well and drawing up water. If we approach meditating with doubt that anything can come of it, it is as if we go to a well with a cracked jug. Listening for what we want to hear, or suspecting that there will be only bad answers, is like drawing up the mud of the well. Many people fear meditation, having a superstitious fear that they may fall into madness, or be captured by an evil spirit that dwells in some secret place in the mind. Our attitude towards meditation should be cleansed of all such defects.

In consulting the *I Ching* we approach the Sage without thought of his name or his face, and thus we come to meet him halfway. In meditating we approach the Higher Power. To meet it halfway we need to free ourselves of all preconceived ideas about what, or who it is. In this way we truly open our mind and suspend our disbelief.

One may not enter meditation in the company of the ego. It must be left behind. As it is put in *Decrease* (Hex. 41), when three travel together, one must go. Some writers have said that in all Yang there is a small bit of Yin, and that in all Yin there is a small bit of Yang, giving rise to the image of the Yin/Yang symbol's having small circles of the opposite in each. My experience in meditation has been to the contrary: the light force will not or cannot enter while a bit of the dark force remains. To reach our spiritual nature, and to be permitted to see in the inner world, the inferiors must exit from our inner space. (Thus the line from *Keeping Still*, "He goes into his chamber and does not see his ministers.")

Keeping Still suggests a technique to defeat the ego in the image of bringing the nerves of the backbone to quiet. When these nerves slow to a standstill, the ego "disappears." This ego is the self-image—all the ideas we have adopted about ourself which shore up our sense of well-being. These props dictate the "look" we project to the world, and determine the clothes, hair-do, or occupation we consider appropriate.

Understandably, our ego resists meditation. It realizes that any time we perceive it as being separate from ourself, it will begin to lose control over our personality. It tries any number of arguments to discourage our efforts.

The line from *Keeping Still* , "Keeping his back still so that he no longer feels his body," suggests another technique to disperse the ego. Since the ego is unable to withstand a determined, persevering attitude, by persevering in keeping still we undermine its power. If, however, it has been in the habit of intimidating the self, the ego stays awake longer, and tries a variety of techniques to intimidate and discourage. The ego's power, we need to realize, is always based on the illusion it casts of being all-powerful. Determination on our part destroys the illusion.

Once we have contained and excluded the ego we find ourselves in an empty space. Achieving this may require meditating every day for two weeks. During this time we will have worked through a mass of residual restlessness. Residual restlessness is like the collected dust of the galaxy. It is as if we have lived in our inner house for many years without ever having cleaned it or brought it to order. Our first task is to clear up this inner dirt. Keeping our "inner house" clean is one of the ongoing tasks of meditation.

Reaching the clean empty space is our first milestone of recognizable progress. For a time we must be content to work without having any great illuminating experiences. Although we may feel that we are achieving nothing, we are making progress, and the necessary preliminaries are taking place. It is the way of the *I Ching*, and the way of the Sage, that we become accustomed to working in the dark, with no knowledge of whether we are making progress. Even though our goal is to reach the deep inner quiet state of meditation, we are not allowed to become goal-oriented and obsessively focussed. We have to be content to try without thought of reward.

Through the frustrations of learning to meditate we learn many important lessons of self-development: we learn to work for good simply because it is good; we learn the meaning of modesty; we learn that we are not allowed to make bargains with the Higher Power in which we say, "Because I am trying, you should do your part." We learn perseverance—to hold out against the pressures and resistances put up by the ego to deflect us from our purpose. Through perceiving the tactics used by the ego to maintain power, we diminish its power and add stature, strength, and leadership qualities to the true self.

Sometimes, just before achieving deep inner quiet, we experience grief from having let go of the props of identity. We experience the feeling that we are nobody at all. We find ourselves crying, yet we do not feel sad. We simply allow our bodies to cry as they give up feelings of attachment to the old props. Now they seem to stand naked and defenseless before the mighty Cosmos. Then this passes and we feel relief. We are in harmony with the Cosmos. A great weight is lifted off. Nothing now stands between us and the unbounded love that issues from the Cosmos. We emerge from the shadows into the light.

Meditation experiences are insightful, instructive, and liberating. We find that the empty space is prelude to great learning experiences.

At this point our inner eye is opened for us. We cannot do this for ourselves. It happens because we have persevered, and have come to meet the Creative halfway.

Even though we intercept our fears and frustrations during the morning meditations, they will tend to return later in the day, through force of habit. To counteract them we need only follow a three-minute rule. The ego returns in a succession of waves. The first wave gives the illusion of being irresistible. This is only an illusion. If we retain our resolve, the wave passes. The second wave comes shortly, but it is only half the strength of the first one; the third wave is only a ripple by comparison. This process occurs over a period of three minutes. The person who holds firm against his fears for three minutes, defeats their power.

By meditating every day, in conjunction with consulting the *I Ching*, we gradually shrink the ego's size and strength. Gradually, we react less and less impulsively to the ups and downs of life, and to shocking events. We become more and more steady in our way of life.

Although the images seen in meditation are often strong and seemingly unforgettable, they have the dream-like quality of quickly disappearing from consciousness. Clarity is invariably short-lived. The pull of the outer world is exceedingly strong. It is wise, therefore, to develop the habit of writing down meditation experiences. This enables us to reflect on their messages and to allow their imprints to become part of our conscious life.

Many times we have meditation experiences without realizing it. Dreams of a particular quality are meditation dreams whose message becomes clear after a little reflection. Flashes of insight occur when we are seeking solutions to problems. We may later realize that we were in a particular frame of mind (usually doing something mundane and unrelated) when they occurred. In my view, every experience of this kind is a gift from the Higher Power. The surest way to continue to receive these gifts is to continue to recognize their source. When we forget their source, when we allow our ego to appropriate glory by thinking we did it, we shut ourselves off from the constant stream of light that emanates from the Cosmos. We leave the sunshine and return to the shadows.

On Interpreting the I Ching

When I first began consulting the *I Ching* I had no specific way of doing it. Sometimes I consulted it many times a day, sometimes none. Gradually I concluded that consulting it too many times a day only confused me. The *I Ching* refused to skip about from one subject to another. It stayed on one question until I had understood it completely, which often took a week. Most of the time it answered the most important question in the back of my mind. Almost never did it answer questions of curiosity. It addressed questions of immediate need. If I were about to face a difficult situation, it gave me timely warning. Once the situation ended, it gave me a follow-up on what had happened. For this reason I also ceased asking direct questions.

Once I became its student, the events of my life seemed to present the questions I needed to answer, in a meaningful sequence. Thus, I was able to peel off layers of self-images, fears, and doubts.

Gradually, I developed the habit of throwing a sequence of six sets of hexagrams. To me this seems to be a complete "conversation." Each person, however, should develop the sequence that is suitable for him. There are times when people may be limited in their ability to take in spiritual nourishment. An occasional hexagram may be all they can absorb. The Chinese say the *I Ching* is not for everybody. I would say that it is not for everybody at the same time, but it is certainly for anyone who is open and receptive to it.

Many times the *I Ching* replies seem ambiguous. For instance, we may receive all six changing lines, some of which contradict each other. When this happens I see them as presenting a range of possibilities. For example, if we were to receive all the changing lines in *Preponderance of the Great* (Hex. 26), I would take it that I am about to be in a situation in which my inferiors (desire, or anger, perhaps) will be engaged, therefore, I should not act; if I am forced to act, I should be reticent and careful to keep emotionally disengaged. Having received the top line, which seems to indicate that all danger is past, I would take it that if I succeed in controlling my emotions, the pressure of the adversity will soon pass, and I will have had the correct effect, simply by holding firm within myself. The last line reassures me that I can surmount the situation if I will carefully adhere to my limits.

Confusion also may occur when the original hexagram seems to be the opposite of the changing hexagram. For example, we may receive *Splitting Apart* (Hex. 23) as the original hexagram and *Deliverance* (Hex. 40) as the changing hexagram. This combination means that although our personality has "split apart" through reacting to fear, relinquishing the fear will cause the splitting apart to end. Receiving this combination can be reflective in nature, meant to show us what has already happened. Also, it may forewarn us that something is about to happen which may cause us to split apart.

Sometimes these dangers occur purely on the mental plane, without our having engaged in an overt situation. Splitting apart can occur simply by allowing ambition, envy, fear, or desire to inhabit our thoughts.

Receiving a hexagram without any changing lines can sometimes be confusing. In such cases I think that we are simply meant to reflect on the hexagram as a whole.

Receiving the same hexagram two or three times in a row usually means, "Consider this again. You have not yet got the message." We may be meant to consider and reconsider the hexagram, taking all the lines into account. In actively searching out what the Sage is trying to tell us, we enable the message to break through.

How often should we consult the *I Ching*? Tradition has it that one question suffices, and that to ask more is to impose. This has not been my experience. Fortunately, I did not know of these traditions. Even though I did abuse and overuse it at first, it was tolerant. Many times I received rebuffs, but these, too, were helpful. When I insisted on doing things my way, ignoring its advice, I paid a price, but through paying, I learned.

Someone once asked me if I did not worry about being too dependent on the *I Ching*. On consulting it, it replied, "If you had a good friend who knew the secrets of the kingdom, and was able to help you in your work, wouldn't it be a shame not to make use of that friend?" I have never since then been worried about being dependent on it.

Through my *I Ching* group I was to learn that some people have only a limited ability to receive *I Ching* nourishment. The question arose between myself and a fellow meditator about a marijuana-dependent *I Ching* student who attended our group. I felt that while he was physically present, he was mentally somewhere else. I mentioned this to my meditating friend. Not long afterward she said she saw this person in a meditation. In it he was bandaged all around his head as if he had been a burn victim; there was only a tiny opening at the mouth from which issued a straw. She could see that he was

310

able, only barely, to sip tiny amounts of nourishment. Even small amounts of nourishment, however, may make a great difference. When I saw this person again several years later, he had broken entirely free of drugs and had entered a new phase of self-development.

At times our consultations are obscure. We are meant to accept these times. Even if the meaning is not clear now the message will gradually "penetrate" into our conscious mind.

The *I Ching* replies may concern the recent past, the present, or the near future. Often they help us reflect on the lessons of the recent past. Rarely do they concern some far future time. Only a few lines, such as the fifth line of Fellowship with Men (Hex. 13), reassure us that at some point in the future our goals will be reached. Most lines concern the now, and whether our state of mind leads to progress, to standstill, or to regression.

The *I Ching* gives us only pieces of the puzzle. Only our ego wants the luxury of knowing in advance, of feeling secure, and of having comprehensive answers. The object is to go with the flow, to be content not to know. We are not meant to live life as if it were a script already written.

How to Consult the I Ching

1. Shake three pennies and drop them in random fashion.

2. Count the head side of the coin as three and the tail side as two.
   Add the three coins up and write down the resulting number. For
   example, if three heads are thrown, the resulting number is nine.

3. Repeat this procedure six times, then place the numbers in an order
   from the bottom upwards, as shown below. Opposite all odd numbers, draw a straight line. Opposite all even numbers, draw a
   divided line. The resulting figure is called a "hexagram."

6th line (2 tails, one head)	7	———
5th line (3 heads)	9	———
4th line (3 tails)	6	— —
3rd line (3 tails)	6	— —
2nd line (2 heads, one tail)	8	— —
1st line (3 heads)	9	———

4. The bottom three lines of a hexagram are called the "lower
   trigram," the top three the "upper trigram." Using the key on the
   inside back cover, find the trigram that looks like your "upper
   trigram" on the horizontal row of trigrams. Then find the trigram
   that looks like your "lower trigram" on the vertical column of
   trigrams. The number where the two columns intersect represents
   the number of the hexagram you have drawn. Look it up in the *I
   Ching*. Hexagram 42 is the one shown in the above example.

5. Having found the correct hexagram in the *I Ching*, read it, up to
   the section that begins with "First Line." The "Lines,"called
   "changing lines," are read only if we have drawn sixes or nines.
   In the example above, in addition to the beginning section, we are
   meant to read, "First Line," "Third Line," "Fourth Line," and
   "Fifth Line."

6. A second hexagram is now constructed in which one changes the
   changing lines to their opposite forms. This means that we change
   the divided lines formed by the sixes to straight lines; then we
   change the straight lines formed by the nines, to divided lines. We

leave the lines formed by the sevens and eights unchanged. Now we are meant to read the new hexagram thus created, only to the beginning of the changing lines. This hexagram is meant to throw further light on the meaning of the first hexagram we have received. In the above example, the second hexagram would be Hexagram 56.

TRIGRAMS UPPER ▶ LOWER ▼	Ch'ien	Chen	K'an	Ken	K'un	Sun	Li	Tui
Ch'ien	1	34	5	26	11	9	14	43
Chen	25	51	3	27	24	42	21	17
K'an	6	40	29	4	7	59	64	47
Ken	33	62	39	52	15	53	56	31
K'un	12	16	8	23	2	20	35	45
Sun	44	32	48	18	46	57	50	28
Li	13	55	63	22	36	37	30	49
Tui	10	54	60	41	19	61	38	58

Key for Identifying the Hexagrams

Permission to reprint the above key from *The I Ching or Book of Changes*, the Richard Wilhelm translation rendered into English by Cary F. Baynes, has been granted by the Princeton University Press, Princeton, New Jersey.

314